A History of
PSYCHOANALYSIS IN AMERICA

by
C. P. OBERNDORF, M.D.

HARPER TORCHBOOKS ♦
THE ACADEMY LIBRARY
Harper & Row, Publishers
New York, Evanston, and London

To B. E. S.,
in appreciation of her
encouragement and help

HARPER TORCHBOOKS ▼ THE ACADEMY LIBRARY
*Advisory Editor in the Humanities and the
Social Sciences: Benjamin Nelson*

A HISTORY OF PSYCHOANALYSIS IN AMERICA

Copyright 1953 by Grune & Stratton, Inc., New York City.

Printed in the United States of America.

This book was originally published in 1953 by Grune & Stratton, Inc., New York, and is here reprinted by arrangement.

First HARPER TORCHBOOK edition published 1964 by
Harper & Row, Publishers, Incorporated
49 East 33rd Street
New York, N.Y. 10016

CONTENTS

	INTRODUCTION	1
1.	EARLY NINETEENTH CENTURY PRECURSORS OF FREUD'S THINKING	6
2.	ANTICIPATIONS OF FREUD'S THINKING BY NOVELISTS AND OTHERS IN NEW ENGLAND . .	23
3.	PSYCHOANALYTIC THEORY CRYSTALLIZES AND REACHES AMERICA	40
4.	A PERSONAL ACCOUNT OF PSYCHIATRY IN MEDICINE AT THE TURN OF THE CENTURY . .	61
5.	PSYCHOANALYTIC PSYCHIATRY TAKES ROOT AT MANHATTAN STATE HOSPITAL	80
6.	CLINICAL PRACTICE AND ORGANIZATION OF PSYCHOANALYSIS EXPAND, 1910–1920 . . .	109
7.	THE IMPACT OF PSYCHOANALYSIS ON MEDICAL EDUCATION AND THE PUBLIC, 1910–1920 .	122
8.	RECOLLECTIONS OF PSYCHOANALYSIS IN VIENNA, 1921–1922	138
9.	STATUS OF PSYCHOANALYSIS AT THE BEGINNING OF THE THIRD DECADE	152
10.	STORMY YEARS IN PSYCHOANALYSIS UNDER NEW YORK LEADERSHIP, 1920–1930	163
11.	FORMAL INSTRUCTION IN PSYCHOANALYSIS DEVELOPS, 1930–1940	186
12.	POST-WORLD WAR II DEVIATIONS IN PSYCHOANALYTIC CONCEPTIONS	208
13.	COMMENTS ON CURRENT TENDENCIES . . .	230
	APPENDIX	251
	INDEX	268

Psychological Conference, Clark University, Worcester, Massachusetts, September, 1909. (*Courtesy*, American Psychiatric Association, Dr. Jacob Shatzky, Librarian.)

1. Franz Boas. 2. E. B. Titchener. 3. William James.* 4 William Stern. 5. Leo Burgerstein. 6. G. Stanley Hall.* 7. Sigmund Freud.* 8. Carl G. Jung.* 9. Adolf Meyer.* 10. H. S. Jennings. 11. C. E. Seashore. 12. Joseph Jastrow. 13. J. McK. Cattell. 14. E. F. Buchner. 15. E. Katzenellenbogen. 16. Ernest Jones.* 17. A. A. Brill.* 18. W. H. Burnham. 19. A. F. Chamberlain. 20. Albert Schinz. 21. J. A. Magni. 22. B. T. Baldwin. 23. Lyman Wells.* 24. G. M. Forbes. 25. E. A. Kirkpatrick. 26. Sandor Ferenczi.* 27. E. C. Sanford. 28. J. P. Porter. 29. Sakyo Kando. 30. Hikoso Kakise. 31. G. E. Dawson. 32. S. P. Hayes. 33. E. B. Holt.* 34. C. S. Berry. 35. G. M. Whipple. 36. Frank Drew. 37. J. W. A. Young. 38. L. N. Wilson. 39. K. J. Karlson. 40. H. H. Goddard. 41. H. L. Klopp. 42. S. C. Fuller.

* Those names followed by an asterisk are of men who subsequently continued their interest in psychoanalysis.

Introduction

The writing of this description of the beginnings and development of psychoanalysis in America has been encouraged by my colleagues, especially those of the second and now of the third generation of analysts. A few even seemed to regard it as something of an obligation because I have been fortunate enough to participate in the growth of psychoanalysis from its first serious clinical application in this country at Manhattan State Hospital in 1909. This was shortly after Freud, in 1905, had published the *Three Contributions to the Sexual Theory* and Bleuler had openly approved the worth of dream interpretation and the value of psychodynamics for the understanding of dementia praecox. The obvious advantage of noting and interpreting the effects of now familiar mechanisms, such as repression and displacement and overcompensation and sublimation, and of tracing the individual's progress from the period of autoerotic impulses to heterosexual maturity led to a revolutionary psychiatry which has been expanded and modified in this country during the nearly fifty years which have followed.

In the course of checking certain dates and other data which must be included in a historical review, it has been necessary to refer to the proceedings of meetings recorded in the official journals. How far indeed such dry factual publications are from the vital interplay of personalities and opinions which resulted in these formal statements!

This book has not attempted to trace the revisions in psychoanalytic theory which were made by Freud himself and others during the past half century. This task has been ably done by others who are better qualified—because of their personal predilections to expound the original precepts, their current deviations, and their correlation with Freud's own revisions. For, from medical school and intern days, first and always, I have been a clinician using theory as it seemed available to alleviate the suffering of the individual, even harboring an aversion for abstractions, verbal solutions, and convenient reconstructions of theories which are sometimes devised to appease disturbing doubts of the doctor. Generally, psychoanalysts in America have turned in their practice and scientific discussions to the concrete and the utilitarian.

Charles A. Beard, the distinguished American historian, has observed that in writing history "the moment you select you begin to interpret." In some measure this applies to this account of the development of psychoanalytic psychiatry and practice in America, since it is written from a personal background. The latter encompasses the active participation as a clinician in psychiatry at general and mental hospitals; the direction of a psychiatric program in an institution which attempts to remedy the emotional and intellectual disabilities of children who have come from homes which are both impoverished and disturbed; and also work in outpatient clinics where the poor and generally less well-educated come for relief.

These have not been the only positions from which I have been privileged to view the psychiatric scene. In addition, for some thirty years in the editor's easy chair I have been called to pass upon manuscripts and books, reflecting very diverse opinions, which sought to clarify psychoanalytic theory or to improve psychoanalytic therapy. And, as a teacher I am still confronted with the challenging questions of the eager young minds who will carry psychiatry forward in the years to come. At the annual psychiatric meetings I gravitate to the spots where there are greetings and eatings and listen to the persiflage and history-making gossip which flits with its embellishments from ear to ear. In the lobby nooks and around tables over a slowly sipped highball one is most apt to learn how theory is used in practice, to what degree a man's practice agrees with opinions which he expounds from the speaker's platform—those details which eventually combine as facts for history. For even a longer time, as a practicing doctor from a chair behind a desk or beside a couch, I have been attempting to relieve the woes and ailments of unhappy people whose worldly wealth and favorable social position have not afforded a solution for their agonizing conflicts.

For whatever aid I may have contributed to the alleviation of the complicated and often gloomy situations that come to the notice of the psychiatrist, I am indebted first and foremost to the knowledge gleaned from the work of Freud. At the age of twenty-seven I learned from Freud's writings the new and ingenious understanding of the unconscious motivations which force people compulsively in perverse and disastrous directions. Because of the instrument put at our disposal by Freud, no day has since passed in my professional life without my resorting to it for an illumination of some obscure thought, action, or symptom. And to the writings of Freud one must revert for the essence of dynamic psychiatry. When I return to read his pages, especially in the original, I am still thrilled by the clarity, conciseness, boldness, and penetration of his simplest clinical discussions. To Freud's discoveries I owe whatever effectiveness I possess as a psychiatrist.

Among other teachers to whose skill and wisdom I am indebted are Walter Wilcox, Professor of Economics at Cornell University, and Doctors Adolf Meyer, A. A. Brill, and Smith Ely Jelliffe. Two other instructors have especially affected my philosophy or method of approach. One is Dr. George Smith, a teacher of English at the Morris High School in New York City, who in my adolescent years taught me that even more important than the facts is what we think about them. He insisted that Burke's classical "Speech on Conciliation with America," then required reading for college entrance, was to be studied not only as an argument but also in the light of how the argument appeared to you individually as you thought it over and over again. This applied to all other books, such as George Eliot's *Silas Marner*, through which a majority of high school students of that era were for the first time openly introduced to the problem of illegitimacy and sex. This may be an unconscious reason that this really undistinguished novel of the Victorian era has been retained in the high school curriculum for nearly fifty years. The second teacher is the distinguished neurologist and scholar, whom I subsequently mention quite often, Dr. C. L. Dana, perhaps a cherished father imago. His humility, kindliness, and patience have, I hope, guided my association with the mentally sick throughout the years.

It may seem odd that one whose theory of therapy places such strong emphasis on very early childhood memories should choose as determining influences in his thinking and philosophy men who entered his life relatively so late. Most likely each can be linked readily with earlier personal concerns—Freud with the mysteries of sex in childhood; Dana with a strong need for consideration and reward; and Smith with an authorization to express one's self independently from the controlled thinking of the household. But these are not contradictory, for the changes wrought through psychoanalysis probably rest ultimately upon authorized revaluation of precedent familial standards. The spirit of psychoanalysis definitely implies that something can be done to reappraise through a purposive procedure what has happened in the past, even though it is not unlikely that, as Freud wrote shortly before his death in *Analysis Terminable and Interminable*, "Sometimes we are inclined to doubt whether dragons of primeval times are really extinct."

Thus, although this book is offered as a narration of events, inevitably a philosophy of psychoanalytic psychiatry has crept in. Because of my leaning toward clinical medicine, it has been impossible for me to avoid an excessive interest in the therapeutic efficacy of that accumulation of psychological knowledge called psychoanalysis; for after all psychoanalysis has been an absorbing lifework and a livelihood as well.

In the preparation of this book I am indebted for valuable criticism and suggestion to Dr. Robert Bookhammer of Philadelphia and Dr. Paul Goolker of New York; for editorial assistance to my efficient and loyal secretary, Miss Frances Spiegel, and to Miss Anne Cooper, Miss Valerie Reich, and Mr. Edmund Brill.

C.P.O.

New York City
May, 1953

1. Early Nineteenth Century Precursors of Freud's Thinking

Histories are written to be read and studied, and an account such as this, of a scientific theory and medical method, psychoanalysis, is told in the hope that those who live and read in the present and the near future may gather the best from what has proven good in the past. In studying the procedures of the past, we may hope to avoid those errors so easily made when any undertaking is developing and to revalue our earlier findings for guidance on similar issues, with greater faith and surety, in the future. Before discussing the development of psychoanalysis specifically in America let us trace briefly its earlier beginnings.

The following anecdote will illustrate my comment about the value of history, especially as it concerns psychiatry. One day in 1925, I gave a lecture on psychiatry to a class of young nurses in training at a large general hospital. In the course of the talk I mentioned Joan of Arc's visions and auditory hallucinations and also the almost incredible episode of witchcraft in Massachusetts at the end of the seventeenth century. I explained that many unhappy people who were persecuted and hanged as witches on Gallows Hill in Salem would today probably be called hysterical or schizophrenic. Few of the nurses remembered having read of witchcraft in Massachusetts. As I was driving to my office after the lecture, three high school boys aged about sixteen thumbed a ride, and as we rode along I questioned them about that period in our colonial history. Two of them shook their heads blankly, but the third answered that he had studied about witchcraft in American history back in grammar school: "It was the time when they ducked witches in cold water and made them stand on red hot coals." When I asked him why their neighbors had done this, he said: "Because they were foolish." Then I asked: "And why do teachers of history make you learn about it today if it was so foolish?" To this the boy answered simply but wisely: "To make us know how foolish they were."

The story of psychiatry and also of psychoanalysis, which began to revolutionize psychiatry fifty years ago, is that of a slow, checkered process that changed the concept of mental disorder from wickedness and wantonness to one of uncontrollable deviation of thought and action from standards considered normal and healthful. It gradually became apparent that such a lapse from the norm into a state of mental aberration may be a fate to which almost any person might succumb under sufficient emotional provocation or actual changes in the brain tissue.

The progress in the understanding of the nature of mental illness is coupled with certain names that have become emblematic of their time. These include, first, the humanitarians who improved the housing conditions and attempted to abolish punishment and torture of the incarcerated insane. Outstanding among these are Philippe Pinel in France, the Tukes in England, and somewhat later, Dorothea Dix in America in the nineteenth century. Then there are the descriptive psychiatrists, Esquirol in France, and Griesinger and Kraepelin in Germany, the latter the first great modern psychiatrist, and Hack Tuke in England. They recorded with infinite detail what they noted of mental illness as it showed itself to keen, objective clinicians. In the twentieth century they were succeeded by the interpretative psychiatrists, most of whom, at least in America, utilize Sigmund Freud's theories to some extent. The psychiatrist of the present day seeks not so much to describe and classify a patient's disorder but to discover the meaning to the patient of what he, as the analyst, observes. He seeks to understand and interpret the situation from the patient's point of view, to help him solve those deep-seated problems that have produced his individual symptoms and the mental condition as a whole, and to help him make the best use of his potentialities.

Psychoanalysis is singularly the contribution of one individual, Sigmund Freud, who developed both the theory and method and opened a new era in the science of the mind, and whose name has become a synonym for psychoanalysis. The term psychoanalysis is used in three senses: (1) a system of psychology based on the knowledge gained through investigation of the unconscious processes of the mind; (2) the technique by which these processes are investigated, notably through the free association of ideas and the interpretation of dreams; and (3) a method of treatment intended to cure or alleviate abnormal emotional conditions which affect the functioning of the mind or body and usually both.

This multiple use of the term psychoanalysis has often been responsible for a lack of clarity in numerous instances where it appears in medical writing, literature, and conversation. Psychoanalysis, used originally in the treatment of neuroses, especially hysteria, which manifested itself in many physical forms, in later years has been extended to the cure of many other types of mental illness and to character distortions, such as unusual brutality, stubbornness, stinginess, or shyness, which may be obstacles to the individual's social adjustment.

Just when psychoanalysis may be applied to designate the treatment the patient is receiving has since its inception been the subject of much controversy, because many analysts have departed in one particular or another from the original procedures of Freud. These divergences, which have become increasingly wide and strong, will be discussed in later chapters.

An historical survey of psychiatry and psychoanalysis, which in America has become a part of it, reveals not only the contributions that medical science and biology have made to the understanding of mental disorder, but also the light shed upon psychoanalytic problems from other sources, such as literature, poetry, the arts, anthropology, pedagogy, sociology, and biography. The reverse process is also true. Many of the conceptions that Freud incorporated into his system as mechanisms were previously well understood, such as projection (the pot calling the kettle black), displacement (a wife might yell to her husband after a quarrel: "and don't slam that door when you go out"), appersonation (love me love my dog), and others. Likewise many of his theories, such as the enormous force and power of unconscious thinking, the influence of the mind over the body, the function of the dream, had already appeared in the literature of fiction, in the fantasies of the poets, and in the speculation of philosophers.

What Freud demonstrated and organized scientifically through his investigations, which lasted for a period of more than fifty years, was the importance of these isolated, precursory observations. He united his scattered discoveries and formed them into a workable theory for the understanding of human conduct. He then proceeded carefully, through clinical experimentation, not only on patients but on himself as well, to develop a method for the treatment of obscure abnormalities of thought and conduct which up to that time had been practically inaccessible by any systematic approach. To attain a clearer view of the current status of psychiatry, and more particularly psychoanalytical psychiatry, in America let us inspect some of the sources from which it emerged.

It has not been long—only about three hundred years, a very short time in recorded history—since the mentally ill were neglected, cruelly abused, and imprisoned in dark, vermin-ridden cells because their condition was thought to involve an association with supernatural evil powers. Sometimes, although not too often, the feebleminded or the harmless insane were regarded as being under the special protection of some benevolent deity.

The first change in attitude toward the mentally ill, that of the humanitarians of the late eighteenth and early nineteenth centuries, developed synchronously with the moral upheaval and the surge for recognition of the natural rights of man which culminated in the French Revolution. Therefore, it is not surprising that it should have been in France that some of the first great advances in the care of the insane were instituted under Pinel (1745–1826) about 1790. The tempest of rebellion that swept through France in 1789 was inspired, in part at least, by the spirit of searching inquiry of Descartes and Voltaire, by the exaltation of the virtue of the common man by the soul-racked Rousseau, and by the dissemination of democratic ideals by Diderot and his prerevolutionary encyclopedists. An irrepressible protest against the oppression, injustice, and cruelty of the vestiges of the feudal system suffered by the great mass of the population had occurred; Pinel epitomized this spirit of liberation, which was in the air, and transposed the new attitude into the realm of psychiatry. Moreover, there is good evidence that Pinel was essentially a product of his time and the prevalent medical concepts of illness. These reflected a period when the medical nature of mental disease and the interdependence of mind and body had already begun to be extensively noted.

Although Pinel's name has become identified with reform in mental hospitals, he, like many great innovators, had precursors who lived too early to receive their due. A thesis, "Tentamen Therapeuticum de Anίmi Perturbationibus" (An Attempt to Treat Mental Disorder), written in Latin but with numerous notes in French, by a student, Franciscus Naudeau, for his doctorate in medicine at the University of Montpellier in 1783, proves how much of that which is today considered modern was not novel before Pinel's time.[1]

Young Dr. Naudeau, like any candidate for a doctorate de-

---

[1] Oberndorf, C. P.: *Treatment of Mental Disease in France at the End of the Eighteenth Century.* Bull. of the New York Academy of Medicine, Vol. XVI, No. 11, 1940.

gree today, begins his dissertation with a summary of what was taught him as the best in the current thinking on mental disease. When he had exhausted these sources he floundered, and the brief study ends with irrelevant and poorly observed cases. Nevertheless his presentation indicates how the moot problems that confront the psychiatrist and psychoanalyst today were interesting the doctors of France almost two hundred years ago, with analogous controversies about psychical and physical causes.

Naudeau gives a definition of insanity that is terse and valid: "By diseases of the mind or mental perturbations we mean certain more vehement and disordered mental operations which depend neither on reason nor even on will power." Calling attention to the interdependence of mind and body, he continues: "It is evident from countless case reports down through the ages, how easily mental diseases can produce various diseases, even serious and stubborn ones, while in certain other cases they cure them," and "tempests raging in the human economy are not so constantly harmful that they do not sometimes benefit health to the greatest degree."

The use of shock induced electrically or pharmacologically through insulin, metrazol, or other drugs to effect a change in stubborn and stationary mental conditions of the schizophrenic group is a procedure that is in great vogue just now. This eighteenth century writer states: "Shocks which are very moderate or are induced at the right time are often very useful, and they may occasion certain reactions, certain changes which help to restore a person's nature, to improve his functions." Naudeau does not indicate how long the benefits lasted—like many of the reports of improvement in the patient's condition following present-day electric shock therapy. The tendency in psychiatry, and psychoanalysis as well, to evade a follow-up on results has not become outmoded.

To illustrate more vividly the operation of psychological shock, Naudeau reprints a detailed account of a case reported by Kaau Boerhaave, a nephew of Hermann Boerhaave, the famous Dutch clinician of the eighteenth century, of an epidemic of a convulsive disorder in a children's ward in the Charity Hospital in Haarlem. The disease had attacked one child after another and the hospital authorities were unable to check it. Then Kaau Boerhaave, a man of impressive appearance and voice, was called in. He had hooks of a certain shape heated until red hot in a stove of live coals and threatened to apply the iron to a particular spot on the arm of the first child who should have an attack of the convulsive disease. The shock of the threat of this painful remedy had a pronounced deterrent effect on these children, but one of the weakest of them, "excessively struck by this operation to which they were going to be subjected, died on the spot, and all the others were cured." The whole picture of this epidemic mass hysteria is reminiscent of the hysterical reactions which break out from time to time among girls in boarding schools, which Freud so brilliantly explained on the basis of identification.[2]

The drastic procedure of Boerhaave is strongly suggestive of the Paquelin cautery, a treatment once widely used (up to 1930) by some neurologists and psychiatrists to cure hysterical physical symptoms by counterirritation. The Paquelin cautery was a square platinum point heated to a glow, with which the doctor lightly and quickly stroked the part of the patient's body, the arm, the leg, or the back, where the functional disability lay. As I witnessed the vigor with which it was at times applied by visiting physicians at Bellevue and later at Mount Sinai Hospital, it seemed to me that the use of the cautery was not only to effect an alleviation of the patient's stubborn complaints but also the physician's irritation because the patient's illness had baffled him in his attempts to attain a cure by other means. Could it be that the current wide use of shock treatment at times carries a similar unconscious connotation for the

[2] Freud, Sigmund: *Massenpsychologie und Ich Analyse*. Internationale Psychoanalytische Verlag, Wien, 1921.

psychiatrist in the therapeutic impasses which still so often confront him today?

Psychoanalysis offers a theoretical explanation for the origin of such physical symptoms and a method that often successfully removes them. What is equally important, it proposes an interpretation of the emotional interplay between doctor and patient and of the role that the doctor plays, which may sometimes be a combination of shock and psychological threat.

The eighteenth century medical novice, Naudeau, had also gathered from the literature of his day a formulation of the protective value of anxiety, not too dissimilar to Freud's concept of anxiety as a warning signal against danger. "Anxiety (anxietas) sometimes eradicates, to the highest degree, the most inveterate mental defects, in curable types of insanity. It does so because the mind, with a very serious struggle on every side, agitated and stricken in its sanctum sanctorum [which we would in psychoanalytic terminology designate as the conscience or superego] undergoes an internal change and thus gains a new quality." Such a realignment of defenses of one's self (the ego) to diminish anxiety and bring about a change in the structure of the personality is considered one of the essential aims of psychoanalytic therapy. We know today that anxiety may have a defensive, protective function per se in mental disorder.

The reflections of this young student on the use of drugs in mental disorder, also, of course, borrowed from contemporary ideas of good practice, would receive the endorsement of many psychiatrists and especially psychoanalysts today, for he says:

We must not seek to employ a host of drugs to repair the bodily disorders which may be wrought by mental disorders. Moral support is the only remedy to be tried, and the only one that offers hope of curing diseases referable to behavior. While nature fails to function properly, while disorder affects her movements and functions, she cannot efficaciously direct the effects of remedies, which then only in vain cause loss of strength, increase the trouble, and aggravate the disease. This does not mean that care of the body is to be abandoned altogether; the body always presents sympathetic reactions, and often suffers even seriously when the mind is affected.

The close interrelationship between mind and body is further stressed in Naudeau's thesis in a footnote quotation from *Tristram Shandy* (1760). In this novel, which had attained great popularity, The Rev. Laurence Sterne comments: "The body and the mind are as a jerkin and its lining—rumple the one, and you rumple the other." In the same work Sterne has indicated the symbolism of the nose and the penis in a droll description of the argument of Tristram's great-grandmother in demanding more money from his great-grandfather, "because you have little or no nose, Sir." Indeed it was just the use of such symbolic interpretations which aroused the greatest ridicule from critics, professional and lay, when psychoanalysis first began to show the value of such symbols for diagnosis and treatment.

Perhaps the most surprising aspect of the old Montpellier University study is that, aside from shock, a psychological approach to the therapy of a "mind diseased" is the only one that Naudeau acquired from his preceptors. He summarizes this in interesting technical suggestions:

It requires above all that the physician be fully acquainted with all the resources which he may find necessary, and possess the sublime and difficult art of using these resources. He must know how to deserve the full confidence of the patient, for this ability works cures in the hands of certain physicians, cures sought by others in vain. The physician must, through the dominating affection and defect, seek to discover what things might impress the patient's mind and divert his attention in the opposite direction. Hence the physician must know how to employ all kinds of distractions to the right degree, amusements in the country and in society, music, dancing, the theatre, games, etc.

This last sentence, phrased slightly differently and embellished by pleasing photographs of patients in posed groups doing finger painting, creative art, or dramatics for self-expression, might have been taken from the latest prospectus of many a "progressive" sanitarium or hospital for mental disease.

It becomes apparent that the beginnings of psychoanalytic thought in psychiatry had already taken firm hold before Pinel's time. Pinel's distinction, therefore, rests on his conviction of the correctness of the attitudes just quoted, and in his courage in insisting on their introduction into closed institutions of which the dismal, misery ridden Bicêtre asylum in Paris was typical. The personnel of these hospitals, from physician to brutal guards, then, even as frequently nowadays, was apathetic if not actually resistant to the acceptance of changes which would alter their habits of thought. But it is far easier to criticize the quality of the physicians and attendants in mental hospitals than to induce better-educated and cultivated people to undertake the disagreeable task of spending their hours caring for unresponsive and at times dangerous people in dismal, smelly buildings in inaccessible places.

Many thoughts seemingly new to each generation have in some antecedent form been known for centuries. Progress, however, does not subsist on the new alone but also on the readaptation, perfection, and extension of time-tested ideas. This has been true of many of the principles so skillfully organized in Naudeau's slender pamphlet which now are being scientifically investigated by controlled experimentation and psychoanalysis.

A really prophetic comment on the psychoanalytic postulates of the function of sleep, the emergence of repressed psychical material in dreams, and unconscious thinking is found in *Rationalism in Europe* (Volume II, 1865) by the English historian William Lecky.

That certain facts remain hidden in the mind, that it is only by a strong act of volition they can be recalled to recollection, is a fact of daily experience, but it is now fully established that a multitude of events which are so completely forgotten that no effort of will can revive them, and that their statement calls up no reminiscence, may nevertheless be, so to speak, imbedded in the memory, and may be reproduced with intense vividness under certain physical conditions.

But not only are facts retained in the memory of which we are unconscious, the mind itself is also perpetually acting—pursuing trains of thought automatically, of which we have no consciousness. Thus it has been often observed that a subject which at night appears tangled and confused, acquires a perfect clearness and arrangement during sleep.

... In the course of recollection, two things will often rise in succession which appear to have no connection whatever; but a careful investigation will prove that there is some forgotten link of association which the mind had pursued, but of which we are entirely unconscious. It is in connection with these facts that we should view that reappearance of opinions, modes of thought, and emotions belonging to a former stage of our intellectual history. It is especially common (at least especially manifest) in languor, in disease, and above all, in sleep.

In connection with the evolution in the middle of the nineteenth century of the investigation of unconscious life, which Freud later developed, a reference is due to the German philosopher Eduard Hartmann, who at this time published *"Philosophy of the Unconscious* (Berlin, 1867). In this work, with its significant title, he also notes the conflict of instinctual drives that Freud included in the pleasure-pain theory of neurotic conduct: "Love causes greater pain than pleasure," says Hartmann. "Its pleasure is only illusory. Common sense would direct us to steer clear of love if it were not for the fatal sexual drive—therefore it would be best if one allowed oneself to be castrated." However, the strength of this sex drive quite overwhelms whatever advantages might accrue from an asexual or loveless life and gives rise, as Freud has shown, to castration fears and complexes.

This excursion into the past, with its emphasis on certain principles that have survived because of their intrinsic merit, may not be trite or detract from present strivings in view of the vitality and vigilance in psychiatry today. It may actually serve as a source of courage, faith, perseverance, and direction for the increasing number of doctors who carry on the slow, discouraging struggle against mental perturbations.

To be sure, the gentler attitude toward the sufferers from mental illness with which Pinel's name is indelibly linked was accepted slowly abroad and equally so in the forward thinking, socially minded American democracy, less bound by old world tradition. Actually, the austere theocracy of colonial New England fostered the development of absolute criteria of proper and improper conduct, of moral right and wrong, determined by the Calvinistic tradition. This has come in our day to be known as the "New England conscience." It discouraged the expression of emotion and condemned severely the indulgence of many of the instinctual drives and pleasurable natural desires.

The fame of Cotton Mather (1663-1728), the most influential preacher in Boston, rested partly at least on his belief in witchcraft and his advocacy of the relentless punishment of witches. In his voluminous writings he noted the frequency of suicide in New England; but his explanation—"the harsh climate of Boston Bay"—leaves much to be desired. More likely it was caused by prevalent modes of thought, such as his own relentless condemnation as the devil's agent of anyone who dared to propose that tolerance and beauty had a place in the scheme of life. It is probable that the philosophy of suppression and hatred, and the crusades against "sin" influenced these directly or indirectly almost forgotten but numerous instances of self-destruction in New England. The harsh cultural atmosphere that forced its people to restrain themselves so constantly, rather than the climatic environment, is likely to have been responsible for the many episodes in colonial history that would now be called hysteria.

Philadelphia enjoyed a milder climate, more abundant markets from fertile nearby farms, and allowed a gentler behavior toward those who violated set moral codes. Here lived Dr. Benjamin Rush, a signer of the Declaration of Independence, who may well be called the first American psychiatrist. He stood out uniquely not only because of his active participation in the revolutionary political and social movements of the day, but also because of a truly great book, *Medical Inquiries and Observations on Diseases of the Mind*, published in 1812. Rush insists that man, in contrast to the dichotomy of body and soul which most religions of the day maintained to exist, is "in the eye of the physician, a single and indivisible being, for so intimately united are his soul and body, that one cannot be moved without the other." Moreover, Rush vigorously advocated reform in the care and judgment of the criminal and the alcoholic, going so far as to propose the establishment of special hospitals for the treatment of the latter. In recent studies of Rush's work scholars familiar with psychoanalytic psychiatry have assigned to him a place as a precursor of Freud. Fay, for example, makes the questionable assertion that Rush "anticipated the Freudians in the description and even the nomenclature of the phobias" and was "interested in dual personality," [3] and Goodman suggests that Rush in asking psychiatric patients to write out their symptoms "introduced a procedure" called by Freud "mental catharsis" and "anticipated the theory and practice of the psychoanalyst." [4]

Notwithstanding the devotion of some Puritan, Methodist, and other denominational clergymen in New England and other sections (including newly settled frontier parts of the country) in their personal ministry to people suffering from mental conflict, this spiritual borderland had been only tentatively invaded by physicians as fearless as Rush. A striking example of the replacement of the theological approach by the medical to what might still have been regarded by clergymen as demoniacal possession is an account by Dr. L. W. Belden, of Springfield, Massachusetts. He recounts the unusual case of

[3] Fay, James Wharton: *American Psychology before William James*. Rutgers University Press, New Brunswick, 1939, p. 72.
[4] Goodman, Nathan G.: *Benjamin Rush*. University of Pennsylvania Press, Philadelphia, 1934, p. 205.

somnambulism of Jane Rider, a seventeen-year-old Vermont girl.[5] Because of the widespread curiosity that Miss Rider's wanderings had aroused in the community, Dr. Belden decided to publish his medical and psychiatric findings openly rather than in an article in a medical periodical. This matter of publicity, by the way, still constitutes a difficult problem for psychiatrists and psychoanalysts—particularly as to the degree to which the public is entitled to be instructed in psychological vagaries and the methods by which it can best be instructed.

Dr. Belden's popular account did not deter him from including comparisons of insanity and the dream (the dream is a psychosis, said Freud), defining somnambulism in terms of imperfect sleep in which "the mind still believes in the reality of visions by which it is occupied." He also quotes several cases of sleepwalking from the medical literature, including one in which a young Yale student plunged through the glass of a closed window on the third story of a house. Such cases were sufficiently unusual that Dr. Belden thought it necessary to authenticate his excellent observations by the written testimony of several other doctors, including Dr. Samuel B. Woodward, the first president of the American Psychiatric Association and superintendent of the State Lunatic Hospital at Worcester, Massachusetts, where the patient eventually went.

The effects of suppression, which may merge imperceptibly into Freud's concept of repression, in causing physical disturbance in the body is the subject of a book, printed almost simultaneously with Belden's account, by Amariah Brigham.[6] Like Woodward, he was a founder of the American Psychiatric Association. In this work Brigham seeks to prove that dyspepsia is due to a disturbed mind that in turn causes a disordered stomach, that it is psychosomatic. Therefore, the cure must rest

[5] Belden, L. W.: *An Account of Jane C. Rider, The Springfield Somnambulist*. G. and C. Merriam, Springfield, Massachusetts, 1834.
[6] Brigham, Amariah, M.D.: *Remarks on the Influence of Mental Cultivation and Mental Excitement upon Health*. Marsh, Capen, and Lyon, Boston, 1833.

in the restoration of peace of mind. He also remarks that "a more frequent and fatal disease than that of insanity is caused by mental excitement and appears to be increasing with frightful rapidity—I refer to organic diseases of the heart." [7] Recently I came across an almost identical statement in regard to the interrelationship of the "pace of modern living" and coronary heart disease, now detected so much earlier by the electrocardiograph.

Another country doctor of this era, Dr. Andrew J. Ingersoll (1818–1893) of Corning, New York, a deeply religious man, came to recognize from his own theological entanglements the role that sexual repression and doubts play in the development of neurotic symptoms. He not only used the word "unconscious" in approximately the Freudian sense but also appreciated that involuntary forces activated by fear were responsible for such conversion symptoms as constriction of the vagina. "Hysteria," he wrote, "is frequently caused by the voluntary suppression of the sexual life." When he thought that symptoms were hysterical, he investigated freely and frankly the sexual life of the patient and frequently cured serious symptoms, such as a paralysis, by persuading his patient that "since the sexual desire had been bestowed by God, it must be acceptable to man." [8]

It seems probable that the conviction which Dr. Ingersoll exerted therapeutically with his patients rested in his own feeling of intimate communion with God. In this his practice may

---

[7] Brigham, 2nd Ed., London, 1839, p. 33: The terms psyche and soma, and psychic and somatic, both derived from the Greek, were long used independently by Italian, German, French and English medical writers. Also combinations of these words, such as psycho-physical and psycho-organic, appeared frequently in medical literature prior to the introduction of the term psychosomatic by J. C. Heinroth, a German, in 1818. Psychosomatic was adopted quickly by British and other writers. (See Margetts, E. L.: "The Early History of the Word Psychosomatic," *Canadian Medical Journal*, Vol. 63, 1950.)

[8] Brill, A. A.: *An American Precursor of Freud.* Bull. of the New York Academy of Medicine, Vol. XVI, No. 10, 1940.

well have been influenced by the paradoxical philosophy of the nearby central New York Oneida Community, a cult of religious perfectionists with a socialistic, perhaps communistic, program. Its founder and leader, J. H. Noyes, boldly proclaimed that the "sexual organs have a social function which is distinct from the propagative function," and who gave no "quarter to the marriage spirit or to special love."

In the mid-century, revivalists and communities with religiously colored sociologic ideals were numerous and usually short lived. From Brook Farm, which attracted Massachusetts' intellectuals, to Thomas Lake Harris' community founded "under divine guidance" at isolated Mountain Cove, Virginia, the beliefs all reached out for support, more or less, to the rapidly growing sciences. But the cultists and faddists were not alone in their recognition of the effects of emotional release on health. Respected scientists were ready to incorporate it in their thinking and practice. For example, at Harvard University Medical School Professor James Jackson, a distinguished member of the growing group of scientifically trained doctors, remarked in the tenor of psychosomatic medicine:

In the treatment of a dyspeptic, then, more than of most other invalids, it is the first object to ascertain the remote causes of the disease. This requires some cross-questioning; for the patient will often hold back important facts, either because he regards them as unimportant, or because they are such as he does not wish to disclose. If you suspect the last named difficulty, it is well to say to him that you wish to know whether he has had any secret causes of anxiety or trouble; that, if so, it is enough for him to make a general answer. In going over the history of his life from day to day, make him realize that he must not sin for a week, and seek absolution at the end of it by the aid of the apothecary. In this last course such a man loses ground constantly.[9]

Jackson continues with reflections similar to those reported fifty years before in Naudeau's doctoral thesis, with a tinge of

[9] Jackson, James: *Letters to a Young Physician.* Phillips, Sampson & Co., Boston, 1855.

Freud fifty years later, in a reference to sensuality and guilt as the reason for a wide variety of symptomatic complaints.

In many instances, instead of prescribing a medicine, I have found it necessary to give my dyspeptic patient a moral lecture; and that, even though he wore a black coat. My lecture has indeed most often had reference to sensual indulgences. Not infrequently I have had to descant upon the evils and the impropriety, if not the sin, of over-conscientiousness; of too great anxiety to do right, and of distressing regrets from the fear of having erred, unintentionally, in some minute particular. [This is the stern superego of Freud.]

If Freud and psychoanalysis had done nothing more for psychiatry than to insist upon a complete knowledge of the patient's experiences from earliest childhood, his beneficial effect upon it would be incalculable. This, too, had been anticipated by an American psychiatrist, Samuel White (1777–1845), another of the progressive group that organized the American Psychiatric Association. Until psychoanalysis conclusively proved its value few psychiatrists carried into practice the sage procedure advised by Dr. White:

From the cradle to the grave, man's life will be found a series of antecedents and consequents, having a direct bearing on his physical and moral powers. To investigate the human mind, we must trace its history from its infant development, through manhood, to decrepitude. It is by the study of the entire man that we are to learn the deviations from the healthy standard, prostrating those energies and mental endowments.[10]

[10] White, Samuel, *Annual Address on Insanity*. Transactions of the New York Medical Society, February 7, 1844.

2. Anticipations of Freud's Thinking by Novelists and Others in New England

The New England conscience—the severe, unrelenting superego in psychoanalytic terminology—produced one of the finest studies of the effect of responsibility in Nathaniel Hawthorne's *The Scarlet Letter*. It is a description that might be called a psychoanalytic study of the ravages which the sense of guilt wreaked upon the mind and body of a "wearer of the black coat" mentioned by Dr. James Jackson. The book, which dealt openly with an illicit love affair and implied that such existed in Puritan days, shocked the staid Boston community of 1850 and caused great controversy but it had a wide sale. Hawthorne's preoccupation with guilt, from *Fanshawe*, written just after his graduation from Bowdoin College, to his unfinished *Dolliver Romance*, reflects the effort to rid himself of his own unconquerable feeling of guilt through an intermittent series of attempts to "write it out."

Although such writing may alleviate for the author some of his own anxiety associated with a sense of guilt, through a mulling over of the situation, it does not effectively alter his fundamental preoccupation with culpability. The unconscious factors entering into this state of mind persist unchanged and are beyond his conscious control. So, too, in other arts, from the doodling on his program by a bored guest at a banquet to the composition of a symphony, the artist achieves a certain amount of relief from tension. Such activity may also serve as a defense against allowing impulses responsible for such tension to become manifest and permits strongly censored feelings of violence or self-pity to be expressed indirectly and symbolically, or even directly through color, sound, or form. These types of releasing, or creative, activities fall roughly into the category of what is known in psychoanalysis as sublimation. At times they furnish a form of autotherapy or, better, a symptomatic relief without touching the deeper disturbances—perhaps comparable to the temporary easing of the heat of a fever by a cooling alcohol rub, which, however, does not affect the infection of which the fever is only a manifestation.

In Hawthorne's novel, the psychological situation of the minister and the woman, who bears her ignominy for their mutual "sin" silently and alone, pictures the Puritan conscience and concern with guilt. It offers understanding of the situation later developed in an impressive psychoanalytic theory, and the cure of the minister's bodily illness is so prophetically illustrative of the psychoanalytic method that it may well serve as an introduction to the spirit of psychoanalysis.

The Calvinistic minister Dimmesdale of *The Scarlet Letter* is the father of the illegitimate child of Hester Prynne, who, however, does not reveal the fact and protects her lover while she endures all the humiliation of her position as an unwed mother in the virtuous little Puritan village. The minister suffers intense mental punishment from his own sense of responsibility. As a result he develops "psychosomatic" symptoms, namely, tremors and pains about the heart and an alarming wasting away of his body. Finally he is persuaded to put himself in charge of old Roger Chillingworth, a physician, a medicine man, perhaps in modern terminology a lay practitioner, who had lately arrived at the Colony.

Earlier in *The Scarlet Letter* we are introduced to the doctor's skilled technique in situations requiring subtle handling when he is called to relieve the emotional crisis of Hester

Prynne, after the ordeal of her exposure and punishment. He rejected as ineffectual the direct probing into Hester's secret and instead drew up a chair alongside her bed, said very little, and waited for her to speak.

When Dr. Chillingworth was called later to give medical attention to the guilty lover, the tormented young pastor, the latter said what we hear so often during psychoanalysis from depressed patients. He was "well content that his pains and sorrows should be buried in the grave," rather than that the doctor should put his "skill to the proof" in his behalf. But Dr. Chillingworth at once suspected the mental origin of his patient's illness and decided that the pastor's bodily health could be restored only with relief from his mental wretchedness. The technique of his approach is that of the psychoanalyst, and the kernel of his philosophy wholly psychoanalytic.

The sensitive Hawthorne once considered becoming a physician but discarded the possibility because he could not accept the idea of profiting through the illness and misfortune of others. Let us see how this introspective writer recorded lucidly and vividly the clinical course taken for a patient who supposedly lived about three hundred years ago and was afflicted with an obscure debilitating condition that threatened his very life.

Chillingworth scrutinized his patient carefully, both as he saw him in his ordinary life, keeping an accustomed pathway in the range of thoughts familiar to him, and as he appeared when thrown amidst other moral scenery, the novelty of which might call out something new to the surface of his character. He deemed it essential, it would seem, to know the man before attempting to do him good. Wherever there is a heart and an intellect, the diseases of the physical frame are tinged with the peculiarities of these. In Arthur Dimmesdale, thought and imagination were so active, and sensibility so intense, that the bodily infirmity would be likely to have its groundwork there.

This observation brings out with extraordinary clarity that the course of disease is inevitably influenced by the mind and that mental anguish in itself may produce a deceptive picture of physical illness, a theory widely stressed today in psychosomatic medicine (a new term for a very old bit of knowledge). Hawthorne then proceeds to describe the modern, psychoanalytic technique designed to relieve psychological disturbances.

> So Roger Chillingworth—the man of skill, the kind and friendly physician—strove to go deep into his patient's bosom, delving among his principles, prying into his recollections, and probing everything with a cautious touch, like a treasure seeker in a dark cavern. Few secrets escape an investigator, who has opportunity and license to undertake such a quest, and the skill to follow it up.

An attitude of continuous passivity on the part of the physician was formerly, and is still by some, considered to be the most useful and safe in the psychoanalytic procedure, although during the past twenty years many analysts have veered to greater activity in interpretation to and direction of the patient. The older idea is that unless the patient makes his own interpretation of his illness (and this more or less conforms with psychoanalytic theory) the results are not likely to be so permanent. Hawthorne has given us the essence of this passive technique with rare poetic imagery:

> If the physician possess native sagacity, and a nameless something more—let us call it intuition; if he shows no intrusive egotism, nor disagreeably prominent characteristics of his own; if he has the power, which must be born with him, to bring his mind into such affinity with his patient's, that this last shall unawares have spoken what he imagines himself only to have thought; if such revelations be received without tumult, and acknowledged not so often by an uttered sympathy as by silence, an inarticulate breath, and here and there a word, to indicate that all is understood; if to these qualifications of a confidant be joined all the advantages afforded by his recognized character as a physician—then, at some inevitable moment, will the soul of the sufferer be dissolved, and flow forth in a dark, but transparent stream, bringing all its mysteries into the daylight.

Nevertheless, for all his cautiousness, reservation, and forbearance with his patient—a man as uncommunicative and benumbed as Hawthorne himself—the physician's progress was tedious and slow. In this respect it was perhaps no more so than that made by a competent analyst today with a similar situation in which the opposition to cure is great. It may well be questioned whether men like Hawthorne and Dimmesdale (with whom the novelist identified himself) may not have preferred repentance and expiation even unto death rather than to evade them. "No secret such as the physician fancied must exist there, ever stole out of the patient's consciousness into his ear in spite of his close attention and skill." Baffled by his patient's reticence (psychoanalytically speaking, his resistance), the physician sought to come nearer to his patient, and to increase intentionally "the patient's concord with the sagacious, experienced, benevolent old physician." This is the positive transference that appears frequently and spontaneously in the psychoanalytic process.

After a time, because the treatment had reached an impasse, as it so often does in psychoanalysis, Hawthorne's physician adopted a procedure reminiscent of the practice of Ferenczi of Budapest, a friend and one of the most gifted of the early supporters of Freud. During the latter years of Ferenczi's career he abandoned the impersonal technique that Freud insisted upon and became sympathetic and friendly with his patients. He believed that through a more personal contact and with kindly aid to patients he could help them better and quicker to health and happiness. In a similar manner Dr. Chillingworth sought deliberately to foster a growth of intimacy between himself and his patient, and "at a hint from Dr. Chillingworth, friends of Mr. Dimmesdale effected an arrangement by which the two were lodged in the same house." In spite of this closer contact the results of treatment continued far from satisfactory. Suspecting that the minister's "priestly celibacy," presumably a lack of sexual gratification, might be involved in the physical manifestations, the physician said to himself: "This man—pure as they deem him—all spiritual as he seems—hath inherited a strong animal nature from his father or his mother. Let us dig a little further in the direction of this vein!"

With the change in attitude from passive, expectant waiting to increased pressure on the part of the doctor—to active therapy, as analysts term it—the minister began to show a reaction which is an integral part of the psychoanalytic process, stubborn resistance. He became "vaguely aware that something inimical to his peace had thrust itself into relation with him." Impassively, but with firm insistence, the doctor would repeatedly revert in their conversations to the topic of guilt. Finally he evoked from the minister the admission that he, in his role as priestly confessor, had witnessed great relief in others after an unburdening. But still the doctor did not succeed in bringing about a similar outflow of well-hidden thoughts from the clergyman.

Perhaps a year after treatment had been initiated, the doctor, the minister, the wearer of the scarlet A, and her child were by chance brought face to face. The meeting naturally produced strong emotional reactions in all of them. This situation, which had occurred unpremeditatedly, is one that an analyst may occasionally purposively seek to bring about by the use of active therapy (provocation, startling) to arouse reactions in patients with whom the analysis has become stagnant.

The alert Doctor Chillingworth decided to take advantage of the minister's obvious emotional agitation after the encounter. He timed it well. In response to a question from the minister, so familiar in the course of an analysis, as to how the doctor thought he was getting along, Chillingworth did not answer. Instead he asked tactfully, "if all the operation of the strange disorder has been fairly laid open and recounted to me." The patient indignantly protested as many have since during psychoanalysis that the doctor's question was preposterous—"surely it were child's play to call in a physician and then hide the sore."

Nevertheless Chillingworth was not deflected from his conviction of the source of the trouble and observed bluntly to the minister that "a bodily disease, which we look upon as whole and entire within itself, may, after all be but a symptom of some ailment in the spiritual part." This produced another vehement outburst from the minister, who violently denied the right of the physician to occupy himself with troubles of the soul. Thereupon, as often happens when a neurotic patient senses that some obstinately guarded truth is about to be brought to light, the incensed minister angrily announced that he would not lay open to "an earthly physician the wound or trouble in his soul." Finally, "with a frantic gesture, he rushed out of the physician's room."

Wise old Chillingworth was not ruffled by the outburst. "It is as well to have made this step," he said to himself, looking after the minister with a grave smile. "We shall be friends again anon." He regarded the impassioned anger of his patient as proof of the existence of another passion and decided that the minister "hath done a wild thing erenow, in the hot passion of his heart." He suspected that the patient would return when his rage had subsided. And so it happened. "The young clergyman after a few hours of privacy was sensible that he had been hurried into a temper, for which there had been nothing in the physician's words to excuse or palliate." He soon appealed to the physician to continue the cure, which if "not successful in restoring him to health, had, in all probability, been the means of prolonging his feeble existence."

With such a result both the patient and the psychoanalyst of today must occasionally content themselves, at times because of an actual situation outside the analysis that cannot be satisfactorily resolved; at others because the unconscious forces feeding the conflicts have never been sufficiently changed. In the Dimmesdale case, because of the latter difficulty, the problem remained a puzzle, and Chillingworth, musing over it, commented: "a rare case! I must needs look deeper into it, and a strange sympathy betwixt soul and body." So he decided to continue the treatment, for "were it only for the art's sake he must search the matter to the bottom."

So the analyst today in his zeal to uncover the deepest infantile springs of conflict may occasionally consciously or unconsciously succumb to the temptation to slight immediate therapeutic results in favor of the further fulfillment of his scientific curiosity and thoroughness.

We cannot leave our discussion of the psychoanalytic slant in Hawthorne and earlier American literature without a reference to his friend and neighbor in the Berkshires, Herman Melville. Melville idolized Hawthorne and judging from certain of his letters to Nathaniel it may be inferred that his adulation of Hawthorne's work was over-determined. At all events Melville found in him a kindred spirit, struggling wildly with God and the perplexities of life. Like their brilliant contemporary, Edgar Allan Poe, both suffered from periods of despondency and depression.

The hundredth anniversary in 1951 of the publication of *Moby Dick* was signalized by the publication of half a dozen books attempting to clarify many phases of Melville's turbulent life and writings, many of which show intuitive psychoanalytic insight as penetrating as Hawthorne's. Melville has no passages descriptive of the psychoanalytic process such as we find throughout *The Scarlet Letter*, but *Moby Dick* and *Pierre* contain a wealth of allegorical and symbolic material that analysts have assayed with their measures.[1]

Another literary colleague of Hawthorne, Dr. Oliver Wendell Holmes, Professor of Anatomy at Harvard University, had also grasped the importance of unconscious mentation.[2] Unlike Hawthorne and Melville, the many-sided Holmes, essayist, poet, and philosopher, who had studied in Paris, is likely to have

---

[1] See Murray, Henry A.: *Introduction to Pierre*. Hendricks House–Farrar Strauss, New York, 1949.
[2] Oberndorf, C. P.: *The Psychiatric Novels of Oliver Wendell Holmes*. Columbia University Press, New York, 1945.

been acquainted with the work of scholars such as Lecky and Hartmann and of his fellow physicians Elliotson and Moore in England and Brigham, White, and Jackson in America. In his dual role as physician and writer, Holmes produced three novels dealing with the problems of abnormal character: *Elsie Venner*, the story of a schizophrenic girl; *The Guardian Angel*, a study of an hysterical adolescent; and *A Mortal Antipathy*. His understanding is startlingly displayed in *A Mortal Antipathy*, where Holmes describes the psychic factors in allergies, the neurotic and inexplicable fear of young women in an otherwise perfectly healthy and attractive young man. A cure of this phobia occurs through a combination of psychic and physical shocks. The young man, at death's door from "autumnal fever," is dragged from a burning building to regain consciousness in the arms of a beautiful girl. This is, in effect, a rebirth after loss of consciousness.

Holmes not only accepted the unceasing and untrammelled activity of the unconscious mind but also believed that from the unconscious come those irresistible drives that ruthlessly thrust aside our more deliberate thoughts and planning, and those persistent affect-laden urges that lend conviction and power to our deliberate choices and logical opinions.[3] He says:

And so the orator—I do not mean the poor slave of a manuscript, but one who only becomes our master at the moment when he himself is taken possession of, by a sudden rush of fresh inspiration. How well we know the flash of the eye, the thrill of the voice, which are the signature and symbol of nascent thought—thought just emerging into consciousness, in which condition, as is the case with the chemist's elements, it has a combining force at other times wholly unknown!

It is worth-while to repeat that Holmes' acquaintance with the unconscious is not accidental; he demonstrates this in such passages as:

[3] Holmes, Oliver Wendell: "Page from an Old Volume of Life: Mechanism in Thought and Morals." An address delivered before the Phi Beta Kappa Society of Harvard University, June 29, 1870, pp. 260–314.

Unconscious activity is the rule with the actions most important to life. The lout who lies stretched on the tavern bench, with just mental activity enough to keep his pipe from going out, is the unconscious tenant of a laboratory . . . where such fabrics are woven, such problems of mechanism solved, such a commerce carried on with the elements and forces of the outer universe, that the industries of all the factories are mere indolence and awkwardness and unproductiveness compared to the miraculous activities of which his lazy bulk is the unheeding centre.

The picture of a patient reclining on a couch in a psychiatrist's office and allowing his mind to drift from word to word, idea to idea, has become familiar. This mechanism of the free association in thinking, a fundamental postulate of psychoanalysis upon which the therapeutic procedure is largely based, did not escape Holmes. In this connection I shall quote paragraphs scattered throughout his prophetic essay, but here gathered into a sequence, to show Holmes' understanding of uncensored, uninhibited thought association in revealing unconscious thought-flow.

We wish to remember something in the course of conversation. No effort of the will can reach it; but we say, "Wait a minute, and it will come to me," and go on talking. Presently, perhaps some minutes later, the idea we are in search of comes all at once into the mind, delivered like a prepaid bundle, laid at the door of consciousness like a foundling in a basket. How it came there we know not.

At another place in the essay, this idea of unconscious associative thought-functioning is expressed even more concisely:

The more we examine the mechanism of thought, the more we shall see that the automatic, unconscious action of the mind enters largely into all its processes. Our definite ideas are steppingstones; how we get from one to the other, we do not know; something carries us; we do not take the step.

Likewise Holmes' knowledge of the importance of dreams, whose interpretation plays such a prominent part in psychoanalytic therapy, is shown by significant hints of the dream's function in wish fulfillment and the role of the dreamer in the dream he produces. Holmes suggests also that in dream life our problems are solved—a variation of the wish fulfillment function of the dream proposed by Freud—and further that we may unconsciously act in obedience to these solutions in waking life.

The cases are numerous where questions have been answered, or problems solved, in dreams, or during unconscious sleep. Two of our most distinguished professors in the institution [Harvard], have had such an experience, as they tell me. Somnambulism and double consciousness offer another series of illustrations.

This idea of the dream being an evidence of the direction in which the smoke of the unconscious flame is blowing was later advanced by one of the early Swiss psychoanalysts, Alphonse Maeder, and sometimes appears to be verified in the dreams of patients under analysis.

Nor was Holmes alone among Bostonians in his preoccupation with dreams. A contemporary at Harvard, Dr. Edward H. Clarke, Professor of Materia Medica in the Medical School from 1855 to 1872, expressed a similar Freudian view in a book to which Holmes wrote the introduction:

These are some of the characteristics of dreams and are enough to show how singularly and curiously they harmonize with conditions of sleep. They are simply unconscious cerebration of that pattern of the brain over which sleep has no power. Sleep affords the opportunity, within certain limits, for the brain to act of itself and dreams are the result.[4]

Notwithstanding occasional astute references to hypnosis and the psychic factors in invalidism and transient physical symptoms no doctor of unquestionable rank in American medical circles, such as Dr. John Elliotson of England, was willing to risk his reputation in championing the sober examination of hypnotic cures. The defiant Elliotson, a man of outstanding

[4] Clarke, Edward H.: *Visions: A Study of False Sight.* Houghton Osgood and Company, Riverside Press, Cambridge, Mass., 1878.

ability, gave public demonstrations on mesmerism at the University College Hospital in 1838. Because of his use of hypnosis he remained an outcast in the legitimate British medical profession until his death in 1868, but this did not interfere with a successful practice.

Elliotson was not alone among British physicians in studying seriously the phenomena uncovered by mesmerism. A contemporary, George Moore, also a member of the Royal College of Physicians, had chosen as the title for his book *The Power of the Soul over the Body, Considered in Relation to Health and Morals*. In the preface to the second edition he refuses to apologize for the use of the terms "power" and "soul," even though both had been attacked when the book first appeared. The words power and soul, he states, "briefly and pointedly express the twofold nature of man's existence in a manner consonant with revealed doctrine, while at the same time calculated to excite reflection." He prefers the phrase "influence of the mind"; it already "being very familiar to the ear is perhaps more agreeable than the power of the soul"; but he adds that the word "mind also is commonly employed in two senses, the one expressive of the manifestation of a principle, and the other as the name of the principle manifested." [5]

In his chapter on the "State of the Will in Dreaming," Moore, like Clark and Holmes, expresses ideas suggestive of Freud's; for example:

Dreams show us that the state of our spirits takes its character from past experience and habit; they indicate that the soul possesses faculties and properties which are not derived from extraneous influences, and cannot be fully developed in ordinary bodily action; they afford evidence that happiness depends not on physical associations, but on the inherent capacity of that which thinks to form desires, and to obtain satisfaction according to the direction of the will.

[5] Moore, George, M.D.: *The Power of the Soul over the Body, Considered in Relation to Health and Morals*, 2nd Ed. Longmans, Brown, Green and Longmans, London, 1845.

On the other hand, in extra-medical circles, the American mystics and cultists, such as Andrew Jackson Davis and his ingenious pupil, Thomas Lake Harris, combined the methods of the French mesmerists and clairvoyants of the early nineteenth century, "demagnetizing" and "energizing" emotional responses, often definitely sexual, in "counterpartal marriage" and "divine revelations." In effect they made use of conditions akin to hypnosis and the psychological situation of religious awakening, a re-education "directed by Father," for the cure of many symptoms.

About 1850 Dr. Phineas Quimby, an obscure physician of Rockport, Maine, attained a wide reputation for the successful treatment through hypnosis of a great variety of physical illnesses. Among his cures he numbered Mary Baker Eddy who had long suffered from a convulsive disorder; she, in turn, became a mental healer. The peak of healing through faith was reached in a highly successful organized movement called Christian Science, developed by Mrs. Eddy in her book, *Science and Health*, which has had an enormous international sale. Undoubtedly Christian Science removed (healed) many symptoms by denying their reality, by a general questioning of external realities, and therefore responsibility (guilt) for meeting them, and by affording an outlet for repressed urges in emotional satisfaction, in this case not through the sanction of a father substitute but an omnipotent mother. Energy thus released needed no longer to be dispersed in nervousness or invested in morbid activities.

Many momentous social advances occurred during this period, the most significant of which was the freeing of slaves in the South. Several superintendents of lunatic asylums took steps to improve the care of their patients. The most important single effort during this era was that of Miss Dorothea Dix (1802–1887). Born and bred in New England, the daughter of a Unitarian minister, she spent the greater part of her life in this work. Her brave campaign accounted for legislation that gradually freed the mentally ill from almshouses, prisons, public jails, and private ones in the attics of houses where the family hid their insane relatives, along with other skeletons, from the gaze of a censorious community.

Miss Dix, after struggling with the politically minded officials of state after state and achieving results relatively meager for her unwelcome efforts, hoped to make the care of the insane a federal function. She almost succeeded, but the measure to that effect, passed by both houses of Congress, was vetoed by President Franklin Pierce in 1854 on constitutional grounds and as an unsafe precedent. Mr. Pierce thought, perhaps wisely, that provisions for the mentally ill should remain a state function, but the states varied tremendously then, as now, in their interest in the problem and their legal definition of insanity.

Whether mental illness—in its milder form, neurosis, and in the severer one, psychosis—was proportionately less common in America in the eighteenth or nineteenth century than today is pure speculation. Of course no statistics for that time exist. But in the evaluation of statistics of mental illness more caution is needed than in certain other situations when translated into numbers. The term insanity is ill-defined and vague. Of course, the number of persons confined in mental institutions has greatly increased in the last century; so, too, has the number of babies born in hospitals. In each case the proximity of the hospital to a center of population has determined the growth of the percentage of those counted. This number would not indicate whether the total number of insane or babies born had increased in proportion to the population. However, insanity is a relative term and unless a person has been legally so adjudged, he is considered normal for statistical purposes.

With the increase in mental hospitals, and their high cost of maintenance, the problem of mental disease became a matter of public concern. It reached national proportions in 1847 when a group of physicians, largely superintendents of lunatic asylums, organized the Association of Medical Superintendents of American Institutions for the Insane, which eventually changed its name to the American Medico-Psychological Association. For many years it concerned itself more intensively with the question of improvements in the custodianship of the patient than with the nature of his illness; for the overcrowding and inadequacies of mental hospitals have always been great. Psychiatry lacked an essential scientific basis.[6] Procedures used for the treatment of mental illness, such as hypnotism, metallotherapy, static electricity, and hydrotherapy, savored of mysticism and charlatanism. The better medical schools here and abroad were zealously attempting to combat such ineptitudes and eagerly availed themselves of an avalanche of contributions from chemistry, physics, physiology, and biology which could be used specifically in therapy.

With the few striking exceptions I have mentioned the interest of the doctor in psychological medicine had lagged all through the nineteenth century. For that reason Dr. Holmes, fifty years after Belden, considered it preferable to offer his descriptions of psychopathological characters in the form of novels; he thought they would receive a more favorable accord from the general reader than from his apathetic colleagues. And it is doubtful whether these psychological studies would have rated a book review in a scientific medical periodical. Indifference to mental illness by both doctors and the public prevailed, and provision for the mentally ill in most parts of the United States remained pitifully lacking as the following incident that occurred about 1915 will illustrate.

A student from a city of sixty thousand in the deep South developed an acute manic attack while at college in New York State and his well-to-do family came North because of his illness. They related that he had had a similar attack of violent

---

[6] See, however, Bunker, H. A., "Repression in Prefreudian American Psychiatry," *Psychoanalytic Quarterly*, Vol. XIV, pp. 469–477, for observations of Dr. Charles W. Page, a Harvard classmate of James J. Putman and Superintendent of Danvers Lunatic Asylum in 1892.

over-activity while at home at the age of sixteen and had been sent to a jail for two days. When I asked the parents, "Why jail?" they replied with only a slight trace of indignation, "the hospital wouldn't take him so the jail was the only place in the town where he could go."

Surveys made in 1949 indicate that similar, even the same conditions still prevail in the majority of American cities with a population of under two hundred thousand. There, large well-equipped general hospitals still do not accept acutely disturbed mental cases. The crusade of Dorothea Dix for the improvement of the care of the insane begun nearly a hundred years ago has not yet made itself felt in cities like this one in the South or in many other prosperous communities.

The stigma of mental illness despite its attenuation through the popularization of psychoanalysis continues to be widespread. The provision by the state for the mental patient remains far below the minimum standards of medical care and housing, not only in impoverished, sparsely settled areas but even in populous, wealthy states. However, state legislators take their cue from their constituents and cannot be expected to make laws too far in advance of the opinions of the people they represent, or to appropriate large sums of money for the insane or for the disposition of criminals whose minds are affected.

It has taken nearly one hundred years since Pierce's time for the federal government in the last few years to interest itself in mental hygiene as a phase of public health. A partial vindication of Miss Dix's vision has now come in the National Mental Health Act passed by Congress in 1947 as a consequence of the psychiatric experiences with all personnel of the armed forces (including the female auxiliaries) during World War II.

The immense change in public interest in mental health in America, it is fair to say, has been due in good measure to the better understanding of psychic disorders brought about through the labors of a troubled, persevering physician in then far-off Austria, Sigmund Freud. This has taken the treatment of neurotic conditions, and many borderline psychotic states, out of gloomy "asylums" and closed mental hospitals into the outpatient clinics and wards of general hospitals and into the offices of private practitioners of psychiatry, enabling the patient to continue at his customary social life and occupation while undergoing treatment. Possibly of greater importance is the fact that psychoanalytically determined procedures are finding a prominent place in the child guidance clinics of schools. The influence of Freud's work, directly and through psychoanalysts indebted to him, in the teaching of academic psychology, of the theology of various religions and denominations, and of the political and social sciences eventually may produce a more tolerant morality. Perhaps there the ultimate hope for prophylaxis of mental disease rests.

3. Psychoanalytic Theory Crystallizes and Reaches America

In attempting to record the crosscurrents of a discipline of such relatively recent origin as psychoanalysis, and one which is still undergoing constant modification, a writer is at the disadvantage of a proximity that is apt to distort his perspective of relative values. Any description of the psychoanalytic movement is still subject to this handicap of close range vision, although more than fifty years have passed since Sigmund Freud and Josef Breuer published their joint *Studies on Hysteria* in 1895.

The task of evaluating psychoanalysis is more difficult than in the case of other revolutionizing discoveries, such as Darwin's theory of evolution, without which psychoanalysis probably could not have been developed so readily. Its estimation is complicated by the multiple ramifications into ever widening fields of correlated sciences and social endeavor and by its increasing applications as a therapeutic method in many fields of general medicine. The whole situation has been further confused by a misunderstanding from the very beginning of the term psychoanalysis and of its goals, which has persisted among scientists as well as with the public. This is the case today, although to a lesser degree, in spite of—perhaps because of—the vast number of misinformative articles and books that continue to appear on psychoanalysis.

What is probably the first notice of Freud's work in America came from Dr. Robert Edes, who in a lecture on "The New England Invalid" in 1895 [1] makes reference to and accepts "Breuer and Freud's hypothesis about hysteria." This observation shows an unusual alertness on the part of Edes, for Breuer and Freud's *Studies on Hysteria* was only published in 1895, although a previous article on the subject had appeared in 1893. Soon thereafter William James in one of his Lowell lectures on psychopathology in 1896 said: "In the relief of certain hysterias, by handling the buried ideas, whether as in Freud or in Janet, we see a portent of the possible usefulness of these new discoveries. The awful becomes relatively trivial." [2] But James, although a graduate of Harvard Medical School, was not enough of a clinician to put this potentiality to the test in appropriate cases and showed little further interest in Freud's developments. A few years later occasional notices of books by Freud as well as abstracts of articles on psychoanalysis began to appear in American psychiatric and psychological journals which were keenly alert to German scientific literature.

Clinical psychoanalysis in the United States is an importation from Austria via Switzerland, which began about 1906. It has a firmer place as a therapeutic procedure here than in any other country, for reasons which will be mentioned later. However, it is impossible to divorce the early trend in psychoanalysis in America from its evolution in Europe, to which it was most intimately linked until the decade before World War II. Until that time psychoanalysis in America, despite a certain freedom in its therapeutic methods and goals, derived much of its scientific impetus, immediately or remotely, from European sources

[1] Stainbrook, Edward: "Psychosomatic Medicine in the Nineteenth Century," *Psychosomatic Medicine*, Vol. XIV, No. 3, 1952.
[2] Matthiessen, F. O.: *The James Family*. Alfred A. Knopf, New York, 1947, p. 226.
Jelliffe reports that Dr. E. E. Southard (A.B. Harvard, 1899) mentioned to him that James "discussed Freud's initial studies [1893] as early as 1894 in his lectures at Harvard."

and reflectively mirrored the vicissitudes that befell the movement abroad.

The term psychoanalysis was first used by Freud about 1895 to designate both a method he had used to relieve an hysterical patient of her symptoms and the theory of psychology upon which the method was based. Thus psychoanalysis began as a medical procedure. It was a direct outgrowth of the treatment under hypnosis of dysfunctions of the body, such as paralysis of the muscles of the arms, legs, or vocal cords, convulsions, and countless other symptoms, that was being given in the clinics at the Salpêtrière in Paris of J. M. Charcot, called the father of modern neurology, and in Nancy, of H. Liébault and Hypolite Bernheim. Hypnosis, of course, depended upon the discoveries of the fashionable society doctor, Anton Mesmer, who had used "mesmerism" (hypnosis) in Vienna about a century before Freud began his medical career.

The antagonism of his medical colleagues forced Mesmer to migrate to Paris where he puzzled the medical fraternity with the cures he effected where they had failed, using methods which today would be classed as suggestion. His results were so spectacular that the French Academy of Medicine could not ignore them. It appointed a committee of investigation, which reported correctly that whereas the improvements and even cures of Mesmer's patients were authentic, his theory of the cures could not be substantiated. This committee included Benjamin Franklin, publisher, scientist, and diplomat, the superlative Philadelphian, then on a mission in Paris. As psychoanalysis grew directly out of the mesmerism (hypnosis) it may be said that Franklin is the first link between the Freudian formulations and America. The earlier psychoanalysts have recalled how at the beginning they would sit at the head of a couch and place a hand over their patient's brow to facilitate the flow of thought to them through direct contact as in hypnosis. The story of the evolution of the psychoanalytic method from hypnosis has been graphically and intimately recorded by Freud in his *History of the Psychoanalytic Movement* [3] and also by medical historians and other writers.

The frequent grim, distressing fate of rejection and ridicule that many pioneers in science have borne early enveloped Freud as it had Mesmer a hundred years before, and in the same city, Vienna. The practices and theories of each, Mesmer and Freud, provoked the resentment of the formalized thinkers because they ran counter to the habitual medical approaches of their respective eras. Each in a similar way directly defied this medical bias. Mesmer, after fleeing to France and finding the established physicians there as cold to his discoveries as the Viennese, began to train laymen as healers (mesmerists). They included such capable men as the investigative Marquis de Puységur, who studied somnambulism, and Deleuze, a naturalist and philosopher who called attention very positively to the human emotional elements in Magnetism.[4] Freud, faced with a similar medical disinterest in his ideas, welcomed the appreciation which young psychologists and philosophers showed for his thinking, and it followed that he should look upon them as well fitted—indeed at the time best fitted—to test out the curative value of his theories on people suffering from phobias and compulsions.

Freud's unorthodox ideas, in their accentuation of the individual's rights, clashed also with the established religions and governments whose very survival depended upon their authority to control the thinking and mores of the people. Moreover, his utilization of the dream as a means of reaching unconscious thoughts, previously regarded as nonsense beneath the notice of scientific men; his insistence, like Holmes, upon the powerful effect of unconscious mentation on all the activities of normal waking life; his emphasis on the importance of infantile sexuality and the developmental, traumatizing effect of early

[3] Freud, Sigmund: *Selbstdarstellung.* Imago Publishing Co., London, 1946.
[4] Podmore, Frank: *Mesmerism and Christian Science.* George N. Jacobs and Co., Philadelphia, 1909.

sexual experiences in the causation of neuroses later in life, aroused bitter and persistent antagonism not only from physicians, but also from other sources which deny the right of freedom of thought. Fifty years later under Hitler's dictatorship the practice of psychoanalysis was prohibited in Germany, as in Communist Russia today.

Freud's achievements in the fields of neurology, neurophysiology, and neuroanatomy, before he turned to psychological medicine, had won recognition for him at an early age. Among these was the application of the newly discovered drug cocaine as an anesthetic in eye operations. It is perhaps Freud's first scientific link with America, for he turned the idea over to Dr. Carl Koller of New York, an ophthalmologist, who also was working in Brücke's laboratory in Vienna. Because of Koller's development of the use of this drug in his own field, he was credited, in America at least, with its discovery. When Freud concentrated his interest on the study of psychological medical problems, the sneers of his erstwhile friends of the laboratory days, who had enthusiastically praised his valuable contributions to physiology and organic neurology, served to throw him into the solitude of ostracism.[5] The prominent, well-established physicians in Vienna found it convenient to negate and reject his ideas, which involved the wrench and pain of a new adjustment. The intense, local hostility to the man and his work—and the two are so often fused—long delayed the dissemination of Freud's researches not only in Austria, but in neighboring countries as well.

Dr. Josef Breuer (1842–1925), a beloved Vienna general practitioner, first called Freud's attention to the value of deliberate mental unburdening for the relief of symptoms. However, he later found himself in an awkward predicament when a patient, a young girl, insisted that he was the father of her fantasied unborn child. (In psychoanalytic terminology this

---

[5] Jelliffe, S. E.: "Sigmund Freud as a Neurologist," *Journal of Nervous and Mental Diseases*, Vol. 85, June, 1937, p. 696.

reaction would be explained as overstrong positive transference to the physician in an incestuous father role.) Then Breuer decided that the close relationship of confessional therapy was fraught with troublesome, even dangerous potentialities and that it would be prudent for him as a family doctor to withdraw from the field of psychological investigation. That he was probably wiser than he knew is shown by the subsequent difficulties of psychoanalysts in dealing with intense transference reactions of patients. Breuer henceforth limited himself to general practice, in which he enjoyed a long and honorable career and made several original contributions to internal medicine.

All accounts of the development of psychoanalysis credit Breuer with the discovery of the efficacy of psychocatharsis in psychotherapy and the stimulation to Freud's later investigations, but Breuer in his autobiography published in 1925 records this important association in modest words.

In 1880 I observed a sick woman suffering with severe hysteria who presented such an extraordinary course of symptoms that I became convinced that it offered an insight into the deeper levels of psychopathological reactions. The discoveries which we gleaned from this case, Sigmund Freud and myself, were presented first in a short, preliminary communication,[6] then in the book *Studies on Hysteria* by Breuer and Freud. This book, at first rather unfavorably received, appeared last year [1924] in its fourth edition. It is the kernel from which psychoanalysis grew through Freud.

After publication of *Studien über Hysterie* and Breuer's withdrawal, Freud worked out his theories alone, independently and freely, deprived of academic support, but also released from the traditions, restrictions, and obligations that university connections so often impose. During this period of virtual isolation, his private practice was small and allowed him ample time for the study, observation, and reflection so often denied the active university teacher.

[6] Breuer, Josef and Freud, Sigmund: "Über den psychischen Mechanismus Hysterischer Phänomene," *Neurologischen Zentralblatt*, 1893.

Not until more than ten years after Freud's death did it become known that during the period of his supposed scientific solitude he had not been alone. Quite to the contrary, in this the time of his greatest discoveries and severest trials, he had been engaged in a type of analysis by mail with a colleague in Berlin, Dr. Wilhelm Fliess, a noted laryngologist. In November, 1887 he wrote the first letter in the published series to his respected (verehrter) friend and colleague and signed "with warm greetings, Yours, Dr. Sigm. Freud." As the intimacy (transference) of Freud to Fliess grew, the salutation changed to "cherished (teurer) Wilhelm" and was signed "Thy (dein) Sigm." Toward the end, months lagged between the writings, and in the last letter dated Vienna, March 11, 1902 (the 152nd of the series) Freud writes that he has finally received the long deferred title of professor at the University. He also comments bitterly, "I learned that the old world is ruled by authority as the new is ruled by the dollar." [7]

This is a unique correspondence of which to date we know only what Freud has written, which is perhaps the more important in revealing how psychoanalysis began and grew. The letters also reflect Freud's anxieties and railroad phobia, his need for a positive transference, his physical symptoms, and his compulsion to work. It was the latter that enabled him to persist in his creative investigation in spite of his tantalizing doubts and suffering, mental as well as physical. He did, however, feel that he personally profited greatly from his delving into his difficulties with Fliess acting as a re-sounding board. Thus, some ten years after the first letter to Fliess, Freud writes (in letter 106 dated March 2, 1899): "The entire preoccupation (pursuit) has helped my own psychic life very much; I am at this time much more normal than I was four or five years ago."

[7] Freud, Sigmund: *Aus den Anfangen der Psychoanalyse—Briefe an Wilhelm Fliess. Abhandlungen und Notizen aus den Jahren 1887–1902.* Edited by Marie Bonaparte, Anna Freud and Ernest Kris. Imago Publishing Co., London, 1950.

The thought arises how thoroughly Freud considered himself cured and to what extent his subsequent massive contributions and ingenious penetration depended upon the fact that he was still groping with unsolved problems—how much his impersonality continued to act as a defense against self-revelation. No one can read these extraordinary, long, and detailed letters without having his sympathy and admiration for Freud tremendously aroused, especially when one thinks of the courage that must have been necessary to keep this man so undaunted in seeking the truths underlying his illness.

Despite the self-revelation in these voluminous letters, the application of Freud's own psychoanalytic technique to them is not likely to shed much light on the origin of Freud's genius, which made it possible for him to select and combine from his search those elements pertinent to his theory. Freud, like so many other great men whose work changed the course of human progress, Socrates, Copernicus, Shakespeare, Darwin, and Lincoln, will probably continue to live and be judged through the ages by what he produced, quite irrespective of personal difficulties which may have been responsible psychologically for the production.

After his more or less enforced retirement from university circles, Freud's conferences in the last years of the nineteenth century were attended almost exclusively by nonmedical men, whom, as we have learned from the Fliess letters, he did not estimate highly. On the other hand, Freud had reacted to the ridicule of his theories by physicians with understandable bitterness and resentment. Their rejection seems to have reactivated deep-seated feelings of discrimination because of his Jewish heritage, which he had suffered acutely as a boy in the village of Freiberg in Moravia where he lived and as a university student. This prejudice by medical men, as well as his own leanings to laboratory research, may have determined his strong predilection for the theoretical aspects of his work and his subsequent attitude in favoring nonmedically trained persons as therapists. How this position of Freud opposed the American viewpoint and for a time (about 1927) threatened a rupture between the American and European psychoanalytic associations will be discussed later. The problem of "lay analysis" has again become more acute since World War II when chaplains of all faiths, psychologists, psychiatric social workers, and psychiatric nurses in the Army often were called upon to aid in or actually assume the care of mental disorders of soldiers because of the dearth of physicians with psychiatric experience.

About 1903, younger, still unknown physicians joined the small, inconstant, mixed group that had gathered about Freud. At that time and for many years thereafter definite association with Freud or psychoanalysis practically doomed any physician hopeful of advancement at the University Medical School. Professor Wagner von Jauregg, head of the Department of Psychiatry and distinguished discoverer of the malaria therapy for the arrest of syphilis of the brain, saw no good in Freud's ideas. Nevertheless, a number of competent and gifted medical men, who were not too concerned how their professional views might affect their chances for coveted titles at the University, had by 1906 cast their lot with Freud's dynamic psychology, which was coming to be known as the psychoanalytic movement. Among the first to identify themselves with Freud and his school were alert, impatient, intuitive Wilhelm Stekel and I. Sadger, followed only a little later by the rather deliberate and pedantic Alfred Adler—all these Viennese—and Sandor Ferenczi of Budapest, which was then a part of the Austro-Hungarian Empire. All were independent thinkers.

As is so often true when the prophet enjoys little prestige in his homeland, the first authoritative endorsement of Freud's interpretive approach to mental disorders came from neighboring Switzerland. About 1904, Eugen Bleuler, a professor at the University of Zurich and long distinguished as one of Europe's most progressive thinkers in psychiatry, began to test the validity of Freud's theories with psychotic patients, especially schizophrenics, in the closed mental hospital at Burghölzli.[8] Among Bleuler's assistants were Carl G. Jung, a Swiss, and Karl Abraham from Berlin. In 1907, the former, who became an ardent supporter and admirer of Freud, wrote *The Psychology of Dementia Praecox* in which he corroborated Bleuler in showing that Freud's psychoanalytic mechanisms could be demonstrated even more obviously in schizophrenia than in the neuroses.

The observations of Bleuler and Jung opened an entirely new approach to the understanding of the so-called "functional psychoses." Abraham, an extraordinarily keen clinician, who in 1904 had become an assistant at Burghölzli, published a paper in 1907 on the significance of the sexual dreams of youth in the symptomatology of dementia praecox. From that time until his premature death at the age of forty-eight in 1925, he assumed an extremely influential position in the psychoanalytic movement in Europe through brilliant scientific contributions, his skill as a therapist, and his capacity for instruction and organization. Among his more notable articles were his observations on the psychological factors and psychoanalytic treatment of manic-depressive insanity which remain an outstanding study of this psychiatric enigma.[9]

The close association and exchange of views between Freud and the Zurich group did not continue long. Bleuler remained only conservatively sympathetic, but Jung agreed to accept the presidency of the International Psychoanalytic Association at the second Congress at Nuremberg in the spring of 1910. But even at that moment he had begun to question some of Freud's basic postulates. There were differences about the importance of the sexual drives and the conception of the unconscious, which for Jung became a collective heritage of the

---

[8] Bleuler, Eugen: "Freudian Mechanisms in the Symptomatology of the Psychoses," *Psychiatrisch-Neurologische Wochenschrift*, 1906.

[9] Abraham, Karl: *Klinische Beiträge zur Psychoanalyse*. Internationale Psychoanalytische Verlag, Wien, 1921, p. 1.

race whereas for Freud it constituted a personal reservoir of each individual's impressions from the moment of birth.

After the defection of Jung came that of another able member of Freud's entourage, Alfred Adler, who stressed the aggressive features of the instinctual drives and who had originated the terms "masculine protest" and "inferiority complex." Then Stekel, who was seeking shorter and shorter cuts for therapeutic results with psychoanalysis, likewise drifted away. Although the brilliant Ferenczi remained a close and inspiring friend of Freud for many years, shortly before his death he, too, abandoned the strict technique of Freud in favor of a more lenient and assisting approach to the patient. Nevertheless, Freud's position drew a steady and increasing number of sound and experienced adherents from the field of medicine.

When Freud made his first discoveries, the medical profession in America was relying upon the rest cure for neurasthenia elaborated by S. Weir Mitchell, Philadelphia mainliner, perhaps the foremost neurologist of the day. Like Holmes he wrote several novels in which questions of psychological medicine figure prominently.[10] Mitchell's fiction was far more entertaining and popular than Holmes', and his novel *Hugh Wynne, Quaker* became a "best seller," to use a term coined since Mitchell's day. But even in *Dr. North and His Friends*, published in 1900, one looks in vain for the deep "modern" psychological penetration and grasp of Holmes, who belonged to the preceding generation and whose son, Oliver Wendell, Jr., later the eminent Supreme Court Justice, served in the Civil War along with the recently graduated Dr. Mitchell.

The term neurasthenia, a symptom complex first compounded by another American, Dr. George M. Beard, comprised a great variety of anxiety and nervous states, but by 1905 both the diagnosis of neurasthenia and the popular rest cure were gradually falling into disrepute. During the rest

---

[10] Rein, David N.: *S. Weir Mitchell As a Psychiatric Novelist.* International Universities Press, New York, 1952.

cure, which usually lasted six weeks, the patient remained in bed, received no visitors, and was plied with food frequently. It provided a consoling form of treatment for both physician and patient. It relieved the doctor of the burden of investigating integral psychological factors responsible for the psychic disturbance and also of unwelcome reminders of his general ineffectiveness in handling the phobias and compulsions of which patients annoyingly complained. It pandered to the patient in allowing him to regress to an earlier state of helplessness and dependency for which most neurotics unconsciously yearn. The prescribed forced feeding in the rest cure indulged an infantile need for attention and importance; the isolation released him from the stern demands of reality and external conflict to center his interest on himself (really a case of dear me!). It transiently relieved the patient of some of his symptoms and the responsibility for them which had now been condoned by the authoritative physician. At the same time the isolation carried with it some elements of punitive incarceration which would assuage the patient's feeling of guilt. With the prospect of such treatment no wonder neurasthenia and "nervous prostration" (soon dubbed "nervous prosperity") became a fashionable illness which only the rich could afford. The cost of psychoanalysis has given rise to a similar misconstruction of the neuroses as affecting only the opulent. The expensive rest cure failed often, and the neurasthenia recurred too soon after the pamper cure had been terminated by the physician at the end of the fixed period.

Freud referred to Mitchell's work in 1895, but in a manner surprising because of its sharp contrast with the impersonal technique he later adopted. He said:

Moreover, I have made it a practice of applying the cathartic psychotherapy in acute cases with a Weir Mitchell rest cure. The advantage lies in the fact that, on the one side I avoid the very disturbing intrusions of new psychic impressions which may be produced during psychotherapy; on the other hand, I exclude the monotony of the Weir Mitchell treatment during which the patient frequently merges into harmful reveries.[11]

Here Freud takes notice of the painful and sometimes alarming psychic reactions that some patients experience during a psychocatharsis, still an integral part of psychoanalysis. It shows that Freud, less certain of his technique then, was ready to compromise the severity of psychoanalytic revelations by the soothing effect of the rest cure.

I have come across no indication that Mitchell knew of Freud at this early date, but he later frequently expressed his contempt for Freud's "filth." Dr. William Cadwalader of Philadelphia,[12] a nephew of Mitchell, has written to me that Mitchell's opinions about Freud and his work were "so uncomplimentary that I would hate to quote them." But Mitchell did not refrain from expressing them openly. In an address at Chicago in February, 1913 on "The Medical Department in the Civil War," Mitchell in discussing shell shock said, "Today, aided by German perplexities we would ask the victims a hundred and twenty-one questions, consult their dreams as to why they wanted to go home, and do no better than to let them go as hopeless." [13] This opinion of Mitchell is quite representative of the mistrust of Freud by the most influential neurologists and also by the great majority of prominent psychiatrists at that time.

Ten years or more passed after the publication of *Studien über Hysterie* before Freud's writings were extensively noticed by scientific journals here. Among the earliest is a short abstract of the book, *The Psychopathology of Everyday Life* by Boris Sidis in 1906 in the *Journal of Abnormal Psychology*, which

---

[11] Breuer, Josef and Freud, Sigmund: *Studies in Hysteria*. Translated by A. A. Brill. Nervous & Mental Disease Publishing Co., New York, 1895, p. 199.

[12] Personal communications from Dr. Cadwalader.

[13] Personal communication from Prof. Ernest Earnest, Temple University of Philadelphia.

Dr. Morton Prince of Boston had just founded. Until the *Psychoanalytic Review* made its appearance in 1913, this was the only American journal devoted to the study of psychopathology that was at all receptive to psychoanalytic papers.

In the second volume of *Abnormal Psychology*, Ernest Jones contributed a paper on "Rationalization in Everyday Life" and Ricksher and Jung wrote on "The Investigation of Galvanic Phenomena." [14] These two articles appear to have been the first original papers on psychoanalytic subjects in American medical literature. Ricksher's paper dealt with an essentially Swiss application of Freud's use of free association as an investigative method, namely, the reaction of the patient, as recorded by the galvanometer, in associating to a standard list of stimulus words. Quick and violent reactions of the indicator showed that the patient had been emotionally affected by his thought and unconscious associations.

A variation of the same idea, popular for a while, was the association test, in which the patient replied with the first word that entered his mind in response to the standard lists. Certain responses were normal (opposites, such as red in response to the stimulus word blue, or table to chair), but delay in replying indicated that extra time had been consumed in overcoming concern about the word that had first entered the patient's mind. The test had quite a vogue among American psychiatrists and much attention was paid to retarded responses called "complex indicators." Particularly, Dr. Frederick Peterson, Clinical Professor of Psychiatry at Columbia University, had repeated many of Jung's experiments; these he reported in the *New York Medical Journal*, a nonspecialized periodical.[15]

Peterson's role in launching and fostering psychoanalysis is almost forgotten, although in 1909 he wrote that "Freud is perhaps extreme in attributing so great a role to the sexual

[14] Ricksher, Charles and Jung, C. G.: "Investigation of Galvanic Phenomena," *Journal of Abnormal Psychology*, Vol. II, 1907–08.
[15] Peterson, Frederick: "New Fields and Methods in Psychiatry," *New York Medical Journal*, November 13, 1909.

basis of neurosis, but we might grant him half since roughly speaking fifty per cent of the trends, wishes, desires that inspire our activities are for the perpetuation of the species and fifty per cent for self-preservation." As the years passed Peterson showed less and less respect for psychoanalytic ideology and finally wrote a caustic critical article on psychoanalysis called "Credulity and Cures." [16] The scientific reasons for his change of mind are not explicit, but in this instance, as in many others, the adverse stand to Freudian psychology might have been due to personal repugnance to some of its postulates, particularly its emphasis on sex and unconscious incest longings.

Nonetheless, it was Peterson who in 1907 advised young A. A. Brill, who recently had been a student in his classes at Columbia, to transfer his postgraduate studies from Paris to Bleuler's psychoanalytically inclined clinic in Switzerland. He assured Brill that he would profit more from his contacts at Burghölzli in Zurich than at Bicêtre in Paris or at Emil Kraepelin's clinic in Munich, which about this time had reached the height of its reputation as a psychiatric center. Peterson's advice turned out to be most fortunate for the advancement of psychiatry and psychoanalysis in America.

Following his graduation from medical school, Brill had spent some four years on the wards at the Central Islip (New York) Hospital for the insane, had been well trained in neuropathology, and was thoroughly familiar with the descriptive, classificatory approach to insanity generally accepted in America and abroad at the time. In the dynamic psychiatry of Freud, which Brill eagerly absorbed at Burghölzli, he saw the answer to many questions that had puzzled him as he dealt with patients on the wards at Central Islip. Now, the "meaningless" utterances and stereotypes of the chronic insane he had observed took on a new significance. He quickly grasped the fact that if the physician would only take the pains to learn

---

[16] Peterson, Frederick: "Credulity and Cures," *Journal of the American Medical Association*, December, 1919.

their meaning to the patient, he might be in a position to remedy the misconception that had caused the patient to develop these particular symptoms. Brill returned to New York filled with enthusiasm and entered the private practice of psychoanalysis in 1908, thereby originating in America a new specialty, which today occupies more than six hundred physicians.

Although psychoanalytic thought had begun gradually to make its impress upon psychology and psychiatry in New York and Boston, a momentous event for the validation of psychoanalysis the world over occurred in September, 1909 at Worcester, Massachusetts. There, in connection with the celebration of the twentieth anniversary of the foundation of Clark University, at the invitation of its president, Dr. G. Stanley Hall, Freud delivered a series of five lectures "On Psychoanalysis," which are now designated classics. Jung, a staunch supporter, spoke on "Diagnostic Association Studies" and "Conflicts of the Child's Mind." Ferenczi, at the Worcester lectures, says Freud, "would sketch out for me what I would then improvise an half hour later. This was his share in the Fünf Vorlesungen."

Stanley Hall, psychologist, educator, and philosopher, belonged to that group of New England intellectuals whose idealism and honesty have secured for America a distinguished place in the cultural world. He appreciated "the intense emotional response of childhood to every feature of its environment," and that "close contact with Nature in childhood develops rich and rank forms of experience," and that the "survival value of these unconscious experiences is far greater than our current psychology has ever suspected." [17] Like Freud, he had for many years suffered "for his unflinching determination to discover and publish the truth." Back of each may have rested the same strong reaction to the formal restrictions of early training. The strict Puritan discipline, from which Hall per-

---

[17] Hall, G. Stanley: *Recreations of a Psychologist.* D. Appleton and Co., New York, 1920, p. 7.

haps never quite emancipated himself, corresponded to the implication of inferiority under which Freud chafed because of his Jewish origin. Each in his effort to escape plunged into the group of the rebellious minority. In his persistent pursuit of truth, Hall, long engrossed in problems of pedagogy and sex, the author of a classical work, *Adolescence,* boldly called the unapproved Freud to a university rostrum and brought to America the distinction of the first official endorsement of his work.

To Freud, wearied and discouraged by the austerity of his long strife in Austria, the dignified, even warm reception in America by a most distinguished group of physicians and psychologists acted as a reassurance both scientifically and personally. "Psychoanalysis," observed Freud, "was then no longer a delusional fancy; it had become a valuable portion of reality. It was like the realization of a fantastic daydream." With what must have been a long awaited feeling of vindication he also wrote ". . . in Europe I felt myself as an outcast—here I perceived myself accepted by the best men as an equal." [18]

In addition to Stanley Hall, these "best" included Adolf Meyer, psychiatrist, Edward Titchener and William James, psychologists, and James J. Putnam, neurologist. Freud has referred to Hall rather ungraciously as "something of a maker of kings, whom it pleased to throne and dethrone authorities." He had genuine respect for Putnam, but was disturbed by Putnam's tendency to couple psychoanalysis with a definite philosophic system and to use it in the service of moral endeavor. Nevertheless, Putnam was probably the first person in America to avail himself of Freud's ideas in the treatment of three cases, two women and one man, in a special ward at the Massachusetts General Hospital as early as 1904. He and his assistants put these patients in partial or complete hypnosis, and "the conclusion that I draw is not that the 'psychoanalytic'

---

[18] Freud, S.: *Selbstdarstellung, Die Medizin der Gegenwart in Selbstdarstellung.* Felix Meiner, Leipzig, 1925.

method of Freud is useless, for I believe the contrary to be the case, but it is difficult of application and often less necessary than one might think." [19]

The meeting with James left a lasting impression on Freud. However, James' initial respect for psychoanalysis seems to have steadily diminished. We may speculate whether he sensed in the theory some unacceptable factors that may have had a part in his own long and crippling depression in young manhood, for which he vainly sought a cure at several German spas. Perhaps, too, he may have felt vaguely that they were in some way involved in the heart attacks from which he suffered at the time. At all events, in a letter dated September 28, 1909 to his old friend Theodore Flournoy, the Swiss psychologist, he comments:

Speaking of "functional" psychology, Clark University had a little international congress the other day in honor of the twentieth year of its existence. I went there for one day in order to see what Freud was like. I hope that Freud and his pupils will push their ideas to their utmost limits, so that we may learn what they are. They can't fail to throw light on human nature; but I confess that he made on me personally the impression of a man obsessed with fixed ideas. I can make nothing in my own case with his dream theories; and obviously "symbolism" is a most dangerous method. A newspaper report of the congress said that Freud had condemned the American religious therapy (which has such extensive results) as very "dangerous" because so "unscientific." Bah! [20]

It is likely that these sentiments reflect those of the majority of the small but select audience who heard the papers on those September days.

The year before his death in 1910 James wrote: "I strongly suspect Freud with his dream theory of being a regular hal-

---

[19] Putnam, J. J.: "Recent Experiences in the Study and Treatment of Hysteria at the Massachusetts General Hospital, With Remarks on Freud's Method of Treatment by 'Psychoanalysis,'" *Journal of Abnormal Psychology*, Vol. I, 1906–07.
[20] James, William: *Letters*. Atlantic Monthly Press, Boston, 1920, Vol. 2, p. 328.

lucine." He then proceeds in the vein of many other psychologists, philosophers, and psychiatrists of the time, adopting a safe noncommittal position, and repeats that he hopes that Freud and his disciples "will push it to its limits, as undoubtedly it gathers some facts." Then reverting to his essentially pragmatic concepts of life and learning he continues: "It will add to our understanding of 'function' psychology which is the real psychology."

Freud had heard a good deal about Americans and America and had probably formed a rather definite opinion about them before his sole but memorable visit to this country at Worcester. In 1888 his sister Anna had married Ely Bernays, who came to the United States in 1891 in search of wider opportunities than were to be found in his native city of Hamburg. Mrs. Bernays followed her husband in 1892. About the same time Freud had married Ely Bernays' sister Martha. It seems likely that an attachment perhaps a trifle closer than usual between brother and sister persisted between Freud and Anna Bernays. At all events Anna's heart seems to have stayed in her native Vienna and from 1901 until 1912 she went to Vienna with her children practically every summer for reunions of the Freud-Bernays families. Freud learned through this firsthand line of communication from his sister and his American nieces and nephews something of American customs, which he apparently did not approve. "Echt Amerikanisch" (real or typically American) became in the Freud household, as it was in many conservative German families, a synonym for the superficial and flashy. These were qualities that Freud with his thoroughness and scientific background condemned vehemently as he did also some extravagant American publicity of his work.[21]

With such a prejudiced and distorted feeling toward American manners and customs it is not surprising that although

[21] Personal communication from Mr. Edward L. Bernays, a nephew of Freud.

Freud appreciated only too well that the Worcester lectures constituted a signal triumph for psychoanalysis in the world of science, he left America after his brief stay of about two weeks downright dissatisfied with what he had seen and experienced. Various reasons have been advanced for this feeling. Most of them, such as that the food did not agree with his sensitive stomach accustomed to special dishes prepared by his solicitous wife, are superficial. He certainly did not receive such solicitous care during a brief visit to the William James' camp in the Adirondacks or at the now demolished Hotel Manhattan where he stayed in New York. Freud, accustomed to write in the isolation of his booklined study, also resented the bustle and haste of American life and the overdemands of friends and admirers. On the other hand, I surmise that Freud's displeasure in America may have arisen from his *Zumutung* (expectation, presumption) of the dilution of psychoanalysis in America, which according to his criteria certainly has come to pass.

In contrast to the resultant scepticism of William James, Freud's visit had the important result of a more complete conversion to psychoanalysis of Professor James J. Putnam of Harvard University, a personage highly respected in the American intellectual world. Although Putnam, like Holmes a Bostonian Brahmin of long and distinguished lineage, had reached an age when few men are capable of accepting such revolutionary precepts as psychoanalysis proposed, he had previously expressed a lively sympathy for the new psychology. Now, in the spring of 1910, the year following Freud's visit, Putnam had the temerity to present a laudatory paper on "Personal Experience with Freud's Psychoanalytic Methods" at the meeting of the entirely unsympathetic American Neurological Association, of which he had been president. This audacious endorsement by Putnam carried with it the weight of his high professional esteem as a teacher and contributor in many fields of neurology. From then on, no matter how the reactionary neurologist or psychiatrist in America might sneer, slyly or openly, at Freud's theories, he could not afford to ignore the challenge to examine them now that they had been placed squarely before him by one of his greatest contemporaries.

Besides Putnam and Peterson attention was being drawn to psychoanalysis by other respected neurologists and psychiatrists, such as William A. White, superintendent of the federal government hospital for the insane, St. Elizabeth's, in Washington, and Smith Ely Jelliffe of New York, an incomparable extemporaneous orator. They lent the force of their gifts as writers and speakers unsparingly to the approval of psychoanalytic theory. Also Drs. Adolf Meyer and August Hoch, cautious and temperate scientists, insisted on the use of dynamic psychology for diagnosis and treatment of patients at Bloomingdale (now New York Hospital, Westchester Division) and at Manhattan State Hospital. Young Dr. Ernest Jones, educated as a neurologist at London and Cambridge but then teaching at the University of Toronto, who was perhaps the best informed English-speaking analyst at the time, came to the United States frequently to lecture. But over and above these the irrepressible Brill stood out, ever ready to defend psychoanalysis and proselyte tirelessly from the ranks of the younger psychiatrists. Psychoanalysis had begun to take a perceptible hold on American psychiatry as a discipline and a therapy shortly after 1910.

4. A Personal Account of Psychiatry in Medicine at the Turn of the Century

More than forty years have passed since I first became acquainted with and absorbed in psychoanalysis at the Manhattan State Hospital in New York. If this account of psychoanalysis in America from this point on assumes a personal aspect, it may be pardonable because of an active and uninterrupted participation in psychoanalytic affairs during all this time. It also allows a certain latitude in recording events and impressions as the busy years have passed by.

Should there be need of precedent, we have an excellent one in Dr. William A. White's book published in 1933.[1] Although the forty-year periods of the two books overlap, they are not identical; for the field of psychoanalysis comprised a minor feature of Dr. White's manifold psychiatric activities. I should like to quote Dr. White's preface, substituting only the word "psychoanalysis" for "psychiatry":

I undertake to give in outline, and I trust in interesting narrative form, the main facts of the development of psychoanalysis as I have seen them during this period and shall add only such details about myself as are necessary to enable the listener to have some idea of the background and preparation and outstanding tastes of the person through whom the story is presented.

[1] White, William A.: *Forty Years of Psychiatry*. Nervous and Mental Disease Monograph Series, New York, 1933.

Why I went into medicine, or psychiatry, or especially psychoanalysis, no doubt includes the many contributory and intimate conscious reasons that enter into the selection of any occupation when a person is more or less free to make a choice. Of course, there are also unconscious motivations, going back to childhood (in my case in the deep South) and to the ubiquitous family romance, which became more apparent during my personal analysis with Freud some twelve years after my internship at Bellevue. The impatience and unpredictability of my mother, which early mystified me, may have been a determining factor in leading me into a field overladen with perplexities of human conduct. Many years after I had been practicing psychoanalysis, a friend made an amusing observation illustrating how two apparently conflicting tendencies had been combined in my profession. I had casually mentioned to him that in my undergraduate days I had had some success in competitions for positions on the university papers and magazines and had contemplated a career as a journalist. "What are you now?" he asked laughingly. "Nothing but a fellow poking around in other people's affairs to satisfy your curiosity, like any other cheap reporter. Only instead of having to chase all around town to get your news and tediously make a story out of it, you have it all brought right to you and get paid for just listening to it. It's what one would expect of a lazy fellow like you."

Certainly it was not because of any emphasis on psychiatry during my medical course at Cornell University, from which I graduated in 1906, that I decided upon a career in psychological medicine—a most unpopular branch. Psychiatry was just beginning to be recognized as a specialty in the curricula of the better medical schools, and the dozen lectures in psychiatry by Professor Adolf Meyer plus a few afternoons of clinical demonstrations at Manhattan State Hospital constituted the entire instruction in the subject. Notwithstanding the eminence of our teacher, like most medical students at that time—

and perhaps some still today—I thought the whole subject far removed from the tangible signs and symptoms of other illnesses and lacking in the clarity and conciseness of other specialties.

The topic of sex, which psychoanalysis had done much to make factual instead of obscene, was strictly, perhaps studiously avoided by the professors of neurology, medicine, and urology. On the other hand, in the clinics of all of these specialties the students saw day after day the misery wrought by rampant venereal diseases. Only on two occasions, as far as I remember, did any of the instructors make reference, and then only in passing, to those powerful sexual drives which impelled men and women to run the risk of exposure to the ravages of two of the most dreaded and devastating infections of the time, syphilis and gonorrhea. To be sure, the prophylactic measures against both these infections were discovered within the next few years. But the social complications of autoerotic sex drives, outside of marriage and when persistent with married people, remain a major part of the problems with which the psychiatrist has to deal.

After my graduation from medical school at the age of twenty-four, I served on the Second Medical Division of Bellevue Hospital in New York City. The internship ended in July, 1908 after I had become house physician under Doctors Gilman Thompson, Professor of Medicine at Cornell, and C. L. Dana, one of the most distinguished neurologists of the day and a leader in community medical affairs. Both these men, scholarly doctors and keen clinicians, were fully cognizant of the psychic factors in physical illness and the emotional or material gains that a patient achieves, often unconsciously, through illness in the so-called "functional" diseases. Dana usually introduced his lectures to the senior classes in neurology with the remark, "The textbooks for this course will be William Thackeray's *Vanity Fair*, Dr. Conan Doyle's *Sherlock Holmes*, and Dana's *Textbook of Neurology*." Then pausing after the laugh which greeted his words he would add, with a characteristic whimsical smile, "You needn't bother about the last, but be sure to read the first two." In consonance with the emphasis on the socio-psychological aspects of nervousness, Dana had said as early as 1904, "Clinical psychiatry is in fact only morbid psychology."

On the medical, surgical, and obstetrical wards of Bellevue the diagnosis of hysteria was frequently arrived at by the exclusion of any physical basis for the complaints. Because the New York City Psychopathic Pavilion was located on the grounds of the Hospital, Dr. Menas S. Gregory, its director, and his staff were very frequently called for consultation in cases complicated by mental disturbances. Moreover, Dr. Dana's emphasis on the importance of morbid psychology in many forms of illness had attained sufficient recognition so that each physician during his internship on a medical service of Bellevue was required to serve six weeks in the psychopathic wards.

The same intern also spent a similar period on the alcoholic and prison wards, where many patients were admitted obviously deranged. Through these low-ceilinged, dark, overcrowded wards, patients suffering at the same time from medical conditions and psychopathy passed to form a series of never ending, kaleidoscopic, dramatic, unforgettable pictures of human misery. They were the drug addict who became frenzied by deprivation of cocaine or heroin; the hallucinating drunkard; the dulled, restless, self-starved morphine habitué; despairing persons of both sexes and all ages with self-inflicted slashes in their necks and wrists who at the moment were under arrest charged with attempted suicide. Even in those days most judges would dismiss such a charge and order the sufferer to be transferred for observation to the psychopathic ward. Shortly thereafter the laws that made suicidal attemps a criminal offense were revoked.

Usually the psychically determined somatic conditions (and

recollections of cases of monoplegia, aphonia, and a stupor which may have been a catatonia, come readily to mind) were treated with foul-tasting, punitively invested placebos, such as asafoetida and valerian, and by some surprise manipulation, such as a sharp slap or plunging a hysterical patient into a Brand bath (ice-cold). Just then this bath was in vogue for the reduction of the high temperatures of typhoid fever cases which filled the medical wards from August to December. In addition to these, many types of direct suggestion were used for the relief of hysteria. Sometimes we resorted to the previously mentioned Paquelin cautery, today quite obsolete. As an example of the use of this type of device designed to affect the psychology of a patient by surprise, startle, jolt, or deceptive suggestion, let me refer to a woman who thought obsessively that she suffered from a growth in her abdomen. Repeated physical examinations by various doctors, and x-rays, and the nature of her complaints made it practically certain that she suffered from a phantom tumor. No one had thought it worth-while to delve into the patient's history to discover the causes for the symptom or its meaning, nor had the psychoanalytic technique by which such situations are best broached been developed. In the light of present psychodynamics, the obsession (or delusion) might well have been associated with a pregnancy fantasy. Under ether anesthesia, given to the patient in her ward bed, we made a superficial incision into the skin of the abdomen, bound it up with aseptic bandages, and assured her that the growth had been removed. But as might have been expected the symptoms did not change.

In 1951, over forty years later, one of my patients, an internist under analysis for a compulsion to work continuously in his profession, reported an analogous incident. A woman complaining of persistent abdominal distress, whose x-ray films were interpreted by two outstanding radiologists as revealing a growth, was subjected to an operation. The surgeon found nothing abnormal and conveniently left it to the internist to inform the anxious husband. When the husband learned of the fact he became furious and demanded that she be told that three inches of gut had been resected. He insisted that he knew his wife's disposition better than any doctor. After a long conversation with the husband, the doctor convinced him that it would be better in the long run for his wife to know the truth, and he consented. A few days later the doctor informed the wife of the true situation, using to the best of his ability the passive approach he had learned in his own psychoanalysis. She became enraged that nothing had been removed, but she was eventually persuaded that a neurotic symptom is less serious than most abdominal growths, even if successfully extirpated. However, both husband and wife, for reasons which can only be conjectured, refused any immediate psychological discussion of the wife's illness (which may well be a problem in which both share an embarrassing moral responsibility, such as the prevention of conception).

During these formative days of initial close contact with patients the disparity between the descriptions of diseases as written in textbooks and the way in which patients bore these diseases made an indelible impression upon me, as did the vast chasm between theory and practice.

One incident in the treatment of a hysterical condition is unforgettable. A male patient, aged about 35, suffered at irregular intervals, usually about three or four days apart, from what had been diagnosed as hysterical tympanites. This consisted in a sudden distention of his abdomen so that it resembled that of a seven months' pregnant woman. Of course at that time the possibility of unconscious pregnancy fantasies in the male, later detected through the psychoanalytic study of children and dream analysis of adults, was unknown. After observing the patient carefully for several weeks, Dr. Dana, the visiting physician, prescribed that on the next such occasion I should suddenly squirt a siphon or two of ice-cold vichy on the patient's head as recommended by his colleague, Dr.

Thompson.[2] Two siphons had been on ice for several days when at one o'clock one morning I received a note from the nurse that the patient was in an attack. Slipping into my uniform I went down to the half-lit ward to find the patient's abdomen ballooned out as if he were pregnant. We took the man off into one of the side rooms and laid him on the floor. Then I stealthily tip-toed up behind him and let him have the contents of the ice-cold siphon on his head and face. He shuddered and squirmed, but his ballooned abdomen did not respond to the shock and failed to collapse. Being a conscientious intern I repeated the dose, with the same lack of reaction from the patient. As I stood limply there in the dark with the siphon dangling from my hand, looking stupidly at the shivering wretch, I felt very futile and thoroughly ashamed at my own indignity. And yet, if the stream from the siphon had been electrically charged, the shock would not have differed too much from a current practice to influence conduct through insulin or electric shock.

An experience in boyhood possibly had conditioned me against too great a faith in magical procedures. When I was about nine years old and living in the South, a sty developed on my lid. The Negro mammy, in whom I had great faith and upon whom I relied for counsel and comfort when in difficulty, assured me that it would quickly disappear if I stood at the crossroads at nine o'clock at night and said out loud so the Lord could hear me: "Sty, sty, leave my eye; catch the next one passing by." Mustering up all my youthful courage I went to a nearby crossroads and reverently repeated this magic formula—a questionable combination of a prayer for myself and a curse for the prospective recipient of my woe.

As I returned home, a little colored boy passed me emitting a frightening "boo" out of the dark shadow of a tree. Momentarily this increased my conviction that the remedy would

[2] Thompson, W. G.: *Practical Medicine.* 2nd Ed. Lea Boas, Philadelphia, 1902, p. 871.

work. But my sty did not disappear for several days, and my belief in the power of magic was ruthlessly and perhaps permanently shaken.

Now as a young doctor the mystery of the origin and spontaneous disappearance of symptoms that seemed to have neither rhyme nor reason began to puzzle me. The great uncertainties which the most capable older doctors experienced in determining whether some undetected lesion in the bodily organs might be responsible for them also surprised me. The very humiliation which I felt the night that I drenched the victim with vichy made me eager to investigate more rational methods of approach to nervous disorders, of which I was to learn much in the next momentous years of psychiatric advance through psychoanalysis.

Another episode at Bellevue to which my mind has reverted time and again when treating psychiatric patients who showed exceptionally disagreeable traits, such as querulousness, whining, or bitterness toward me, illustrates the uncertainties and injustices that are so often involved in psychiatric situations. Acting as ambulance surgeon, "riding the bus" as the interns call it, was a routine part of the training during the second six months. After the first few weeks, when the thrill and importance of racing through crowded city streets behind a galloping horse and clanging bell had worn off, this work became something of a chore. Generally little actual drama was to be found in the calls. Most of them were for patients who had been sick in their small dark tenement rooms for days, months, and even years and now were being sent by their neighborhood doctors or families for treatment at the hospital or simply to die there.

One summer evening two successive calls turned out to be for drunken men. The first led to a dilapidated wharf on the East River where a stout, red-faced man lay in a comatose stupor with an empty quart bottle of a cheap brand of whiskey at his side. His breath stank with the odor of it. He must have been there all day long in a blistering sun before someone discovered him and reported it to the police. With the help of the driver and the policeman we lifted him onto a stretcher and the ambulance hurried back to the hospital with a seriously sick man. There, he was admitted to the alcoholic ward where he received a warm bath, nourishing food, good nursing and medical care for a week or more before he finally went forth, penniless, to his old haunts, likely to repeat the pattern before long.

The second call, which followed immediately after, ended at a precinct police station where the lieutenant at the desk asked me to look at a fellow in the cell who had a scalp wound. The patient turned out to be a husky young Irishman, now fairly sober and no longer belligerent. He did not budge while I shaved the hair around the wound, cleaned it, put in three or four stitches, and topped it off with a sterile collodion dressing.

He had received this scalp wound as many another man before and since as the result of drinking heavily. Passing unsteadily along the street he made a few uncomplimentary remarks to a policeman on the corner who told him to move on. To this he replied with even less respectful comments. The officer threatened to "run him in." The young man defied him to do so, in positive and profane terms. A scuffle ensued during which the policeman tapped the quarrelsome fellow none too gently on the head with a club. It all ended with the drunkard being arrested, charged with intoxication, disorderly conduct, and resisting an officer in the line of duty. The next day this man with his head dressed in white would be brought before a magistrate who would make a quick disposal of the incident, after listening for a minute or two, in a rough and ready administration of justice by sentencing him to from five days to a month at the workhouse. Obviously, the only mistake, but a grievous one, that the pugnacious young man had made consisted in his failure to imbibe sufficient whiskey to fall into a sodden stupor so that no one could have doubted whether he should be regarded as sick or criminal.

Notwithstanding the lasting memory of these and other situations that involved illness and social values, and perhaps a more absorbing curiosity about the person who had an illness than the illness itself, I had not definitely decided upon making neurology and psychiatry, then joint specialties, my life work. An occurrence just before my internship at Bellevue came to an end may have been a strong factor in my eventual determination to enter this field.

The faculty of Cornell gave a banquet to the graduating class and because the Bellevue house physicians had been helpful in the preparation of demonstrations for the College classes, they were guests. As I was walking from the reception room to the dining hall, I felt a hand placed gently on my shoulder. Looking around, I saw Dr. J. Ramsay Hunt, a distinguished neurologist who had first pointed out the association of paralysis agitans with lesions of the globus pallidus. In an amiable way he asked, "And into what specialty are you going after leaving the hospital?" "Oh, I don't know," I replied, "I've been thinking of pediatrics." Thereupon Hunt turned to Lewis A. Conner, Professor of Medicine, with whom he was walking and said, "Here's a young man who has the making of a neurologist and wants to be a pediatrician." "That's always the way," replied Conner lightly; "they never know what's good for them." And they continued on their way. I had never been aware that Hunt had noticed my work on the wards. But his words sank into my mind. And now it appears to me that in my work as a psychoanalyst I have combined both his and my own original intention, for in this specialty the physician treats essentially a large proportion of grown-up children, at least adults who are still struggling ineffectually with over-strong fixations at a childhood level. Sometimes in humbler moments I think of myself as a skilled nurse transiently assuming the responsibility for adult infants, hoping eventually to release them of the need for childhood supports and anchorages and enable them to stand up to their tasks manfully, "neither as children nor gods, but men in a world of men."

Perhaps an experience that I had immediately after leaving Bellevue accentuated this idea of the evil effects of delayed maturation. Through a rare bit of good luck I was engaged to take a youth of eighteen, an only child, on a European trip, carte blanche. He turned out to be a weak, underdeveloped, undernourished, immature youngster. Although the Binet-Simon Test had not been devised, no standardized scale was needed to determine that his intelligence rating was that of a boy of about thirteen. He had been bandied around from one private school to another, and both his parents and his family doctor were happy to be freed of him for a while. For years he had suffered from a "delicate stomach" and obstinate constipation for which he had been placed on a variety of conflicting but restricted diets by the long list of stomach specialists to whom his neurotic parents had taken him. Because of his spasmodic outbursts of rebellion and sexual precocity his doctors regarded him as an almost hopeless problem. Today, many a doctor, wishing to appear progressive, might label his complaints as psychosomatic.

My embarrassment at having to sit at meals in the steamer's dining room with someone whose diet consisted largely of bouillon, crustless bread, milk and custards, decided me to initiate a change from previous treatments. The "delicate stomach," I thought, had become that way through the constant doctoring and over-attention of his parents; his constipation might be due to a lack of bulk in the bowel and to muscular weakness of the intestinal walls. If his fear of taking food could be overcome, he might perhaps begin to digest well. Pavlov's experiments with the conditioning of dogs' reactions to feeding by the ringing of bells had already found their way into college physiology textbooks. So I began the role of the liberal parent or nurse encouraging him to take one light food after another. To counteract the weakness of the abdominal muscles, I suggested boxing with him. This he eagerly accepted as a bit of manliness that his mother had always forbidden because of his puniness. Our boxing consisted of a feint on my part to the youth's face, which he immediately covered with both his hands. This provided an opening for a few light taps with my open hand on his abdomen. The combination of psychical reassurance that nothing prevented him from at least trying to fight like other boys, coupled with the actual performance of the exercise, worked extraordinarily well. After three weeks he had his first evacuation in six years without artificial aids. When he finally dared to try raw vegetables and laxative fruits, such as strawberries, figs and apples, forbidden in each diet, the cure became complete.

Without underestimating the fact that the essential approach to this delicate youth's problem of health depended upon sound and practical medical training at Bellevue, carrying it out was, I am inclined to think, something of a high-grade nurse's job. The patient is alive today, an over-sixty-year-old boy, an elderly adolescent, who is able to care for himself on a dwindling, inherited income.

During this carefree trip to Europe, at the suggestion of Dr. Gilman Thompson, I made it a point to visit some of the famous watering resorts, each one noted for its beneficial course of treatment for some special illness: Vichy for nephritis, Nauheim for heart conditions, Baden-Baden for nervous disorders, and Carlsbad for diabetes. To these spas many of the wealthier Americans were sent each year by their physicians. Here they benefited from a well-regulated daily life and the psychological changes (among them, the separation of husband and wife) that were recognized as having a profound influence on body function.

I returned to New York with my first patient but still in doubt as to my next step, notwithstanding the fact that the youth's parents were gratified and astonished at the ease with which I had handled their troublesome, maladjusted son. In my dilemma I sought the counsel of the property clerk at Bellevue, a paternal old German, who acted as confidant and advisor to many of the doctors and nurses and who knew not only the secrets and politics of Bellevue but trends in medicine as well. He spoke emphatically in favor of my inclinations, and especially of psychiatry as a field in which the demand for service already exceeded the supply of physicians.

During that period the traditional postgraduate study in Europe was considered a desirable supplement to the American medical training and an advantage if one contemplated entering a teaching career or seeking an appointment in the better hospitals. So I decided to spend this additional time in preparation for practice, although not quite certain whether I would prefer to become first a general practitioner or to aim immediately for specialization in psychiatry. After arriving in Europe I decided to try out my talents in psychiatry and obtained an appointment as volunteer on the neuropsychiatric service of Dr. Theodor Ziehen at the Charité Hospital, the Bellevue of Berlin.

Ziehen had achieved a reputation as a psychiatrist, a neurologist, and a psychologist, but through diffusion of his interests and energy excelled in none of these fields. He acted as director of both the departments of neurology and of psychiatry, and in each the quality of the treatment suffered; for each specialty had expanded to the extent that no one individual could adequately master both. So Ziehen failed to satisfy the needs of any of his assistants and residents, an equal number of whom were interested predominantly in one branch or the other but seldom in both, for the schism of the specialties was well on its way. Indeed the private clinic of Dr. Hermann Oppenheim attracted the neurologists from Ziehen's clinic, in spite of the latter's official University position. The envious professor would make a sour grimace whenever he learned that another of his assistants had surreptitiously visited Oppenheim, whose clinical demonstrations were heavily attended. This was not an uncommon situation in Germany at the time, when the official professorships at the universities did not always go to the outstanding men in the field, especially if they happened to be Jewish, as was Oppenheim.

Ziehen turned out to be an uninspiring, pedantic chief, whose clinical skill compared unfavorably with many of my previous instructors in America. The clinic reflected all the formality and methods of the Prussian Army, whose practice it indeed followed in many respects, both in the etiquette of the medical staff and the discipline of the patients.

Here I met for the first time Dr. Smith Ely Jelliffe, a towering man in his early forties, vigorous and versatile, who was then an instructor at Columbia University's College of Physicians and Surgeons and who enjoyed the enviable reputation among recent graduates of being able to turn so prosaic a subject as pharmacology into a fascinating study. He had spent a short time at the Binghamton State Hospital in 1896, where he first became acquainted with his lifelong friend, William A. White, and had in 1902 assumed the editorship of the *Journal of Nervous and Mental Disease*. Having decided that his major interest had shifted to psychiatry, he had begun another of his *Wanderjahre* by taking a position at Ziehen's clinic at the lowest level, a volunteer. And like a novice he clicked his heels deferentially with German military precision to the *Geheimrat*. Before long, on rounds, the staff who ranged themselves in strict professional rank were paying more attention to the sharp, pertinent observations of Jelliffe than to the discursive, theoretical digressions of the professor.

At the Charité the frequency and difficulty of the decision whether a given symptom was to be treated as organic or functional was again forced upon me. One of these instances, as unique as the case of hysterical tympanites, had an equally pathetic human aspect. A husky, muscular soldier, a raw recruit from the fields, had been referred to the clinic for examination. After he had been pummeled ineffectually by the sergeants on the drill field for several weeks, the military men decided to seek a medical opinion. Was the clumsy country lout malingering, stubborn, or just too dull to obey promptly such simple commands as "forward march" and "shoulder arms"? The particular offense of the awkward soldier consisted in his slowness in starting movements. He was always several seconds behind; but after the drill sergeant had punished him by making him run around the field for a while, encouraging him with a stiff and well-directed boot, he could then step forward in time with the rest of the company, proof positive of the dull fellow's deliberate unwillingness to obey orders. The result of repeated examinations showed that the contrary soldier suffered from Thomsen's disease (myotonia congenita), characterized by the development of painless spasms of the muscles when the patient first begins any voluntary movements. It shows itself in the patient's inability to start movements quickly, but after exercise the spasm relaxes and the muscular response becomes normal. The trouble here lay in the soldier's congenital defect, not in his mind as the sergeant might justifiably have supposed.

The so-called "functional" cases outnumbered the organic ones in the outpatient clinic at the Charité by perhaps three to two, or an even higher percentage. Occasionally we would refer a patient suffering with neurasthenia or a compulsion to a voluntary sanitarium for nervous people, called Haus Schonow in Zehlendorf, a suburb of Berlin.[3] This sanitarium catered almost entirely to neurotics. The garden contained a number of animal pets, among them a donkey that became the scapegoat for the various shortcomings of the patients. This idea of having a living animal as an object upon which patients could lavish affection as well as scorn is one which I have never seen duplicated anywhere. All the present-day methods of occupa-

[3] *Neunter Bericht des Vereins, Heilstätte für Nervenkranke, Haus Schonow*, Zehlendorf, 1907.

tional and recreational therapy such as sports, horticulture, bookbinding, and art, some of which might be regarded as either work or play, were in full operation.

Indeed, these direct forms of therapy quite overshadowed suggestive psychotherapy, and psychoanalysis was of course unknown. In fact, the prejudice against psychoanalysis was so great that at the meeting of German neurologists in October, 1910, physicians who conducted sanitaria were obliged to declare officially that they had nothing to do with psychoanalysis. Similarly, at a convention of German psychiatrists in Breslau in 1913, Professor A. Hoche of the University of Freiburg who led the opposition to psychoanalysis declared that such "intellectual rooting like a pig" ought to be repulsive to everybody.[4]

The statistics of the therapeutic successes at Haus Schonow parallel those of the best contemporary sanitaria. For instance, of one hundred and fifty cases diagnosed as neurasthenia, ninety-four were discharged as cured or improved and fifty-six unimproved; and in cases diagnosed as alcoholism one hundred per cent were cured or improved, which perhaps may merely prove the unreliability and vulnerability of statistics then as now.

After a few months at the Charité in Berlin I was happy to receive a similar appointment as volunteer at the Psychiatric Clinic in Munich, directed by Emil Kraepelin, then regarded as the world's most distinguished psychiatrist. At the University of Munich neurological cases were assigned to the medical service under Friedrich Müller, an internist of international reputation. The comfortable, leisurely, almost lax atmosphere of Kraepelin's clinic, and the direct, informal, at times gruff, abrupt manner of Kraepelin offered a welcome relief from the grim austerity of Berlin; but the approach here, as there, consisted almost exclusively of a description of symp-

[4] Bjerre, Poul: *History and Practice of Psychoanalysis*. Richard Badger, Boston, 1916, p. 66.

toms with emphasis on classification into one of the two great groups of functional psychoses, manic-depressive and dementia praecox. Kraepelin's great contribution had been in the separation of these two syndromes while at Heidelberg a decade previously. This differentiation had proved of incalculable value to the families of patients from a practical angle, because of the usually favorable prognosis of the manic-depressive cases and the likelihood of chronicity in dementia praecox. Knowing the probable outcome of the illness, the family could begin early to readapt itself to needs in living, counting with a reasonable certainty on the return or permanent absence of the sick member.

A goodly proportion of the admissions to Kraepelin's clinic were victims of Munich's seductive beer, which seemed to induce confusional states, torpor, and mental dullness of a type that I had never seen in the alcoholic wards of Bellevue Hospital, where the acute delirious forms of alcoholic intoxication predominated.

Among Kraepelin's assistants were the genial Alzheimer, discoverer of the disease (pre-senile psychosis) that bears his name, and Felix Plaut, one of the earliest serologists to amplify the work of Wassermann. Just at this time the interest in dementia praecox had been overshadowed by the assistance that the Wassermann test had brought to the diagnosis of mental disease. It enabled the clinician to determine that excitements and stupors were part of the picture of paresis caused by syphilitic infection and not the manifestation of a transient functional mania or a deteriorated schizophrenia.

At neither place, Berlin or Munich, had there been more than a fleeting comment on Freud's work. Ziehen spoke once, briefly and disparagingly, almost scoffingly, of it in the presentation of a case of hysteria, and Kraepelin, also, in his clinical demonstration only once gave casual notice to Freud in referring to the mechanism of projection. He made use of this concept in ascribing the delusions of infidelity, common in alcoholics, to the sexual impotency that the alcoholic experienced as a result of heavy drinking. When the sodden drunkard, of whom there were many at the Munich clinic, returned to his home after drinking innumerable glasses of heavy beer and failed in intercourse, he projected his own feeling of inadequacy and guilt upon his wife, accusing her of promiscuity. This mechanism, frequently repeated, gradually developed into a delusion of the wife's infidelity.

Dr. Louis Casamajor, later Professor of Neurology at Columbia, passed through Munich in the spring of 1909 on his way back to America from Vienna, where he had been studying neuropathology under Marburg. It was he who first specifically called my attention to the work of Freud. At a popular Munich beer-hall, where a little group of American students habitually gathered in the evening, he reported in his enthusiastic manner that "a fellow named Freud in Vienna has the goods on hysteria." He advised me to get hold of one of Freud's books at once as they were a most important contribution to psychiatric understanding. But Freud's works were not easy to obtain in Munich at the time. Finally I found a copy of *Drei Abhandlungen zur Sexualtheorie* (*Three Contributions to the Theory of Sex*) which contained so many unfamiliar terms and concepts that I found it confusing, unintelligible, and so difficult to read that I soon laid it aside.

Being under the influence of my teachers at Bellevue and in Munich, I paid no further attention to Casamajor's prophecy. Instead of attempting to get in contact with Freud in Vienna to learn more of the new theories before returning to America, I went to Berne to see Dr. Paul Dubois whose work *Les Psychoneuroses* had been translated by Dr. Jelliffe and Dr. William A. White in 1905, and whose contributions to questions of the influence of the mind on the body had made a great stir abroad and in America.

Dubois received me with great courtesy at his cheery sanitarium not far from the center of Berne. When I asked him about his method for the treatment of neuroses, which he called a method of persuasion and education of the reason, he explained in general terms that he did not practice direct suggestion but that with the method of persuasion the patient accepts the views of the physician whom he trusts and admires. Thus he learns to appreciate the logic of the doctor's reasonings through the latter's sincerity. But in the end Dubois said in effect, "My method is me," indicating what is often the case, that the happy results of the psychotherapist are frequently due to his personality as well as to the method he uses. Dubois, at that time an aging man with a full grey beard, gentle voice, and considerate manner, was ideally suited to play the role of the understanding, patient father or grandfather who could successfully persuade his children to abandon their fears, and then re-educate them to self-reliance. The great influence that such a personality can achieve through transference later became clearer when I understood through psychoanalytic psychology the dynamics of the identification of the therapist with a trusted older figure.

The stay in Europe proved eventually to be far more profitable than I had estimated at the time, for it gave me a familiarity with the German language and psychiatric literature, so important when psychoanalysis began to permeate psychiatry. Psychoanalysis remained essentially an Austrian (German) development for over twenty years, and American psychoanalysts depended, largely, for guidance and instruction upon German literature.

On the other hand, living with the German doctors in hospitals at Berlin and Munich and learning from them their estimate of contemporary leaders helped me to establish new standards of judgment. It also lessened for me the importance to be attached to heavy and involved German thinking on psychiatric problems expressed in cumbersome writings; these German residents also were unable to grasp them clearly and spent much time in profitless disputation over diagnosis. Later, American psychiatry attuned to social issues soon began to appeal to me as a working force for human betterment.

5. Psychoanalytic Psychiatry Takes Root at Manhattan State Hospital

In May, 1909, I returned to New York better instructed but neither stimulated nor inspired by the psychiatry I had seen in Europe. So I sought the opinion of Dr. Menas S. Gregory, a startlingly diminutive man who was wide awake and amazingly keen as a diagnostician. In 1904 he had organized the New York City Psychopathic Service at Bellevue, which was his lifework until he was superseded in 1934 through one of those political upheavals that occur every now and then in hospitals, with shifts in alignment of scientific positions and personal ambitions. Gregory advised me to continue my training in psychiatry as a resident at Manhattan State Hospital on Ward's Island before launching a private practice.

Such counsel in itself constituted something of an innovation in the preparation for specialization in psychiatry, for many of the "nerve specialists" (as they were euphemistically called) who cared for "nervous patients" outside of private sanitaria had drifted into their careers with little formal training or even experience. About 1910, perhaps not more than a dozen "brain specialists" or "alienists" were engaged in private practice in a city as large as New York. There were probably not more than another dozen in the rest of the United States. Gregory, whose manner was exceedingly positive, perhaps a compensation for his short stature, was emphatic about my need for a residency and in his recommendation of Manhattan State as the most stimulating and progressive psychiatric center in the country at that time.

It did not take long for Gregory to persuade me, and in May, 1909 at Ward's Island I came into contact for the first time with psychoanalysis in actual practice. When I had been at Ward's Island for a day or two one of the younger men on the staff came to me and said in a hushed voice, "Did you bring your rubber-soled shoes along?" and I inquired, "Why do I have to have rubber-soled shoes?" "You have to have some sneakers anyway," he replied seriously. "Why?" And he whispered, "To sneak up from behind and catch those hidden complexes." I laughed perfunctorily, but I must confess that abroad I had not heard such terms as Oedipus, Elektra, or inferiority complex.

At a time when the two leading clinics in Germany, linguistically identical with and geographically adjacent to Austria, had ignored Freud's work, at Ward's Island the dynamic psychology of psychoanalysis was being used day in and day out to clarify the psychiatric syndromes of committed patients. The credit for this perceptive attitude is due largely to two men, already mentioned, Dr. Adolf Meyer and Dr. August Hoch, whose work still lives in the thinking of many of the young psychiatrists whom they instructed and in turn in the latters' students.

Dr. Peterson, mentioned in connection with Brill's studying at Bleuler's Clinic, served as Chairman of the New York State Lunacy Commission from 1902 to 1906. In this capacity he was influential in establishing the New York State Psychopathological Institute (now the Psychiatric Institute) for research in psychiatry, namely: "To assist the State hospitals in their endeavors to progressively advance in the fulfilment of their most important functions, that is, the study and treatment of the patients entrusted to their care." The selection of Meyer,[1]

[1] See Meyer, Adolf: *Seventh Annual Report of the Psychiatric Insti-*

a neuropathologist of great repute and an acknowledged leader in scientific psychiatry, to head the new Institute was also largely due to Peterson.

Meyer, a Swiss who had come to this country in 1896, had gone to Kankakee, Illinois, and from there to the Worcester State Hospital in Massachusetts as director of psychiatry. In 1902 he became the first director of the new psychiatric institute at Ward's Island and soon thereafter was made Professor of Psychiatry at Cornell.

Hoch, also a Swiss by birth but largely American trained, had spent several years at McLean Hospital in Massachusetts and Bloomingdale Hospital at White Plains, New York as special clinician.

Dr. William L. Russell records that the first reference to psychoanalysis at Bloomingdale is to be found in the annual report of 1907, but adds, apparently to soften any implications of an endorsement of psychoanalysis by this conservative hospital, that it was "probably not the Freudian pattern thereof." [2] However, at the time only Freudian psychoanalysis existed. The modifications of Freud's ideas proposed by his early followers were not formulated until several years later. Russell makes this statement about psychoanalysis in praise of Hoch's efforts to change the largely custodial attitude toward the patients then prevalent at Bloomingdale into one of scientific therapy.

In this 1907 report of the Bloomingdale Hospital, Hoch himself wrote:

That which we then call the mental disorder, is nothing more than the becoming dominant of such conflicts in various forms of peculiar abnormal reactions and faulty attempts at adjustment. These mani-

---

tute, 1908-1909. State Commission in Lunacy, 21st Annual Report. J. B. Lyon Co., Albany, 1910, pp. 107-123. This shows the psychoanalytic orientation at the Institute at that time.

[2] Russell, William L.: *The New York Hospital. A History of the Psychiatric Service, 1771-1936.* Columbia University Press, New York, 1945, p. 387.

fest themselves in delusions, hallucinations, peculiar acts, and the like. In each case, therefore, a careful psychoanalysis is necessary, not only for the purpose of research, but for the diagnosis as well. By diagnosis we no longer mean merely that which can be expressed in a single word, but we mean an understanding of the actual struggles and difficulties which are hidden under the perplexing array of mental symptoms. It is becoming more and more evident that for a proper management and treatment of those forms of insanity which we have in mind, such a knowledge is indispensable, and that to be satisfied with anything less is a procedure to be put on the same level as a treatment without any diagnosis at all, i.e., without adequate indications.[3]

This statement epitomizes a new attitude in psychiatry that changed practice in America not only in mental disease but also in sociological judgments and legislation which so often derives its force from them. A new era in sociological appraisals due to psychoanalytic investigations had begun.

Perhaps even more significant is the fact that Hoch was invited to come to Bloomingdale because of his work along these lines of dynamic psychiatry at McLean, also a voluntary hospital, from 1897 to 1907. It is certain that he used the mechanisms of psychoanalysis frequently in his studies there.

The first state hospital in which psychoanalysis was used regularly for diagnosis and treatment was Manhattan State, beginning about 1908. There Meyer and Hoch, both liberal psychiatrists, followed Kraepelin's descriptive psychiatry and nomenclature. However, they had maintained close professional associations with the Swiss Clinic at Zurich, and neither accepted Kraepelin's formulations uncritically. Meyer had found that the symptoms manifested by many so-called "functional" patients fitted into neither of the great groups of nonorganic mental disorders, dementia praecox and manic-depressive insanity, that Kraepelin kept shuffling and reshuffling in his efforts to establish them as definitely separate entities. Moreover Kraepelin's emphasis on a strict division of all

[3] *Op. cit.*, pp. 386–387.

psychoses into endogenous or exogenous groups discouraged his co-workers from examining mental disorders from inside out or to give due weight to the effect of individual social and cultural influences upon the origin and course of the illness. In this sense Kraepelin's classifications, valuable as they were in the matter of prognosis for recovery, fostered a far-reaching negative effect in clinical ideology and treatment.

Meyer reiterated that a full collection, if not necessarily an investigation, of "all the facts" in the life history of a patient should always be assembled. He and his assistants found that the data corresponded so remotely with Kraepelin's elaborate descriptions that he felt obliged to acknowledge this insufficiency. He classed these cases as "allied to manic-depressive psychosis" or "allied to dementia praecox," a truer appraisal of the clinical picture than an arbitrarily imposed Kraepelin label. Where Dr. Meyer's grasp seemed wanting was in the correlation of a wealth of laboriously ascertained facts with the meaning of the clinical picture that the patient presented. Facts without theory, just as theory without facts, are not enough. Here the new theories of Freud, supported by facts if one were trained and sufficiently alert to observe them, supplied new keys to open wide doors that afforded vast new, amazing, and inspiring vistas into human conduct.

Although Meyer understood psychoanalytic theory he seemed never quite able to reconcile himself to some of its fundamentals, especially the examination of sexual aberrations and the early sexual trauma in the development of neuroses. So whereas Meyer never completely accepted Freud, he did not reject him. He credited psychoanalysis with focusing a new and searching light upon psychotic syndromes. Meyer, a shy, reserved little man, grave and serious, always slightly apart from his environment, never used psychoanalysis as a therapeutic technique. He demanded that the staff at Ward's Island become familiar with the dynamic approach as an aid in interpretation and diagnosis.

Hoch, approachable and accessible, was better attuned clinically to psychoanalytic thinking than Meyer. As early as 1907 he presented a paper before the New York Psychiatric Society on "The Psychogenic Factors in Some Paranoiac Conditions, with Suggestions for Prophylaxis and Treatment," the very title indicating the author's orientation in psychodynamics. In this article he maintained that "paranoid states were based upon conflicts and unhygienic ways of dealing with them and that the psychogenesis could be clearly traced when the facts were really accessible." [4] When Meyer resigned in 1910 to become the director of the newly built Phipps Clinic in Baltimore and Professor of Psychiatry at Johns Hopkins, Hoch succeeded him at Ward's Island and continued the program of psychoanalytic psychiatry.

So it happened that in 1909, in order to keep abreast of the spirit of staff conference presentations of newly admitted patients to Manhattan State Hospital, I again read and now partly grasped Freud's *Three Contributions to the Theory of Sex* and also attempted to understand his *Traumdeutung* in German. Dr. George H. Kirby, the Clinical Director, as well as Dr. Macfie Campbell, who in 1908 had published an article entitled, *Psychological Mechanisms with Special Reference to Wish-fulfillment*,[5] encouraged the Freudian approach consistently. Although Meyer and Hoch instituted no formal instruction in psychoanalysis, most of the staff learned it the difficult way, through working gropingly with patients once a diagnosis had been made. This may have been hard on the patients but was certainly far better than the routine history-taking and relative disinterest that had preceded it. This antedated the visit of Freud to Clark University in 1909 and also, of course, the time when the analyst had gained an insight into the workings of

---

[4] Hoch, August: "The Psychogenic Factors in Some Paranoiac Conditions, with Suggestions for Prophylaxis and Treatment," *American Journal of Insanity*, Vol. LXIV, 1907–08, p. 189.

[5] Campbell, Macfie: *Psychological Mechanisms with Special Reference to Wish-fulfillment*. New York State Hospital Bulletin, 1908.

psychoanalysis through his personal analysis and planned instruction.

The staff of the Hospital at that period included a number of men whose names have since become well known in psychiatry. In addition to Kirby, who acted as Director of the New York State Psychiatric Institute from 1917 to 1931, and Campbell, later Professor of Psychiatry at Harvard, there were David Henderson, now Sir David and head of the Edinburgh Royal Infirmary in Scotland, and Clarence Cheney, who succeeded Kirby at the Psychiatric Institute, at that time more interested in pathology. Also notable were John T. MacCurdy, subsequently Instructor in Psychology at Oxford University, Morris J. Karpas, and, for a brief stay, Trigant Burrow. Karpas, who died in France of a coronary attack during World War I, was a warm admirer of Brill. He would militantly, almost fanatically, apply psychoanalytic interpretations, not only to the actions of all the patients on the wards but also to his associates. This habit is not unknown among present-day psychoanalysts. All of these men were profoundly interested in the new psychology, although in their later careers only Karpas continued affiliation with psychoanalytic organizations.

To complete the picture of this blossoming of psychoanalytic psychiatry some forty years ago, a reference must be made to the advance in the understanding of mental illnesses due to organic changes in the central nervous system. Aside from improved techniques in staining nerve tissue and in autopsy examinations, a tremendous aid in diagnosis came from the Wassermann test for syphilis, which had reached America late in 1908. Shortly thereafter the spirochete in the brain was discovered as the cause of dementia paralytica or paresis. Controversy arose as to whom the credit for the discovery should go, to Dr. Hideyo Noguchi of the Rockefeller Institute or to Dr. Joseph Moore at the Pathological Institute on Ward's Island. This was finally attributed to Noguchi.

The Wassermann test and the cell count of the spinal fluid

enabled psychiatrists to differentiate quite accurately patients afflicted with general paresis from the befuddled chronic alcoholics, senile psychotics, arteriosclerotics, old, dilapidated schizophrenics and manics, any of whom at times might show a clinical picture similar to that of paretics. The introduction of the arsenical preparations for the cure of initial syphilis proved very effective in the prevention of paresis and also for the arrest of paresis years after the initial syphilitic infection.

Observation of the extreme degrees of mental illness prevalent in a closed mental hospital gives the physician a perspective of the likelihood for success with the patient less profoundly disturbed and still living in the community. The study of the psychotic is probably the best means of convincing the novitiate in psychiatry of the truth of psychoanalytic mechanisms. In working with deteriorated psychotic patients the postulates of Freud become so obvious and undeniable that one who (like myself in 1909) still doubts the diagnostic as well as therapeutic value of psychoanalysis will be forced to admit the validity of psychoanalysis. As an illustration I should like to refer to a case of dementia praecox, a middle-aged patient with whom I came in contact shortly after entering Manhattan State.

This patient spent much of his time expectorating on his hand and wiping the saliva on his clothes, the walls, or the furniture. When this was impossible for him, he would blow his breath onto his hand and fling the hand away from his body into the air. Before the advent of psychoanalytic mechanisms this would have been regarded as a nonsensical stereotypy. But because of the deeper insight that the psychoanalytic study of dementia praecox had made possible, this preoccupation of the patient became clear. It was a means that he had devised to rid his body of the filth and disease he fancied existed in him because (he thought) he had contracted syphilis. The negative Wassermann reaction would prove this idea a delusion. However, the most obvious way of ejecting from the system such a dreaded invader as the recently discovered spirochete would be to blow, spit, urinate, or defecate it away. The bizarre repetitive motions served a purpose and thereby eased the anxiety and guilt associated with such a delusion which had the value of a reality.

Dr. Trigant Burrow, who stayed at Manhattan State only a short time, was among the first to call attention to the operation of psychoanalytic mechanisms in group activity. His work after leaving Ward's Island may be regarded as precursory to the present-day gathering together of people in groups of various sizes for psychotherapy, a trend that is becoming increasingly popular for both children and adults.

Burrow was especially concerned about the artificial situation that exists in individual psychoanalytic therapy in which all external impacts are excluded and for the hour only the psychic interplay between doctor and patient is operative. He had the idea, if I understood him correctly, that if a number of people could be brought together and allowed free expression, the effect of continuously active, external stimuli brought into the psychological situation would produce reactions immediately analyzable. Subsequently Burrow formed groups for analysis at which he was present but which he claimed were leaderless. When I asked him whom the participants in the group paid, he replied that it was he, of course. To this I commented that such a group could not be leaderless because both consciously and unconsciously the participants would regard the person whom they pay for service as the leader—the person to whom they look for help and direction. In group therapy today, the role of the leader is acknowledged and his qualifications for leadership are duly appraised.

Dr. Ernest Poate, also at Ward's Island, had a flair for writing mystery and was one of the first writers to introduce psychoanalytic mechanisms into the solution of weird stories which he contributed profusely to the pulp magazines. This type of story retains all of its popularity after forty years. It furnishes an escape medium from realistic problems into a fanciful world for even the well-educated and intellectual. At that time the general public was already becoming acquainted with some of Freud's ideas and terminology through popular articles in the general press, but the flow of novels and short stories with a strictly psychoanalytical background did not follow until many years later.

The presence of many younger men, with their enthusiasm and varied interests in psychoanalysis, living together on Ward's Island afforded mutual help in the professional conversation at meal time and after-hour discussions. The interchange of experience fostered a communal striving to learn the essentials of the psychogenesis of schizophrenic, depressive, and above all, the mixed forms of neurotic illnesses. The latter, usually because of economic difficulties, inevitably find their way into the closed mental hospitals. These zealous endeavors were reflected in case presentations at the State Inter-hospital Conferences and in such papers as Karpas' "Contribution to the Etiology of Dementia Praecox,"[6] read in part before the Ward's Island Psychiatric Society in 1909. It was based entirely on ten cases admitted to the Hospital, and in his study Karpas was guided by Jung's statement, "In dementia praecox a performed mechanism is loosened which normally and regularly functionates in the dream." Interest in psychoanalysis at Manhattan State did not represent a strife against authority, as was so often the case and is even today, but conformity to it.

It was such encouragement of psychoanalysis that was responsible for a study of suicidal flight which I presented at the Ward's Island Society about 1911 as indicative of the extent to which the new techniques of psychoanalysis were in use. The very fact that neither Karpas' paper nor this one, containing numerous sexual details, represented a novelty to the staff illustrates the extent of their psychoanalytic orientation. The orig-

---

[6] Karpas, Morris J.: "Contribution to Our Knowledge of the Etiology of Dementia Praecox," *New York Medical Journal*, December 5, 1908.

inal which lay buried away in my records for forty years follows.[7]

The character of the flights of this patient is distinctive in that they present nothing savoring of the aimless peregrinations of the imbecile and half-witted, of the confusion attendant upon the vagaries in delirious and toxic states, of the haze and amnesia associated with the fugues of hysterical patients and epileptics, or of the persistent determination that forces some patients afflicted with paranoia or with paranoid dementia praecox to travel for days and weeks to accomplish some definite purpose. Indeed, this direct form of escape from intolerable situations seems to occur less frequently today than in the past century, although the migratory families who live in the cabin trailers of their automobiles are reminiscent of the attempts to elude responsibilities of the hoboes and gypsies of an earlier day.[8] We may possibly account for this by an appreciation, conscious or unconscious, on the part of the patient, that flight is less likely to be successful and also by the fact that those who wish to escape the duress of authority (especially juveniles) can or are forced to find refuge in institutions and homes provided for their care and guidance.

The superficial symptoms of the patient to be described resembled most closely the "dromomanie" of French authors. This case was reported partly because it is an unusual type of fugue and also because there have been revealed certain childhood impressions and other psychologically significant expressions that seem to some extent to account for the tragic symptoms to which the patient fell prey. Although the facts were obtained by psychoanalytic methods, the case was not analyzed because of the limited amount of time available for such work. As a matter of fact, for more than a year before the death of the patient a policy of laissez faire had been adopted.

[7] Oberndorf, C. P.: "Study of a Case of Suicidal Flight," *Psychiatric Quarterly Supplement*, Vol. 24, pp. 11–22, Part 1, 1950.

[8] Joffroy, A. and Dupouy, R.: *Fugues et Vagabondage*. Felix Alcan, Paris, 1909.

Only two terminations seemed possible to me at the time: an accidental suicide, paradoxical as the term may seem, or dementia praecox. (Suicide by drowning in the East River occurred on October 26, 1912.) Before admission to Manhattan State Hospital in October, 1910, the patient had been committed to mental institutions for two periods of about four months each, in 1909 and again in 1910, because of an uncontrollable impulse to wander, with attempts at self-destruction at the end of his fugues.

Heredity: The patient's paternal ancestors for at least three generations are said to have been "perfectly normal." The mother, who had suffered from depressions, had been confined to an asylum before her marriage. She continued to be subject to these depressions throughout her life and finally died in Manhattan State Hospital from an intercurrent disease. As the mother advanced in years the depressions increased in frequency and severity, and during several of them she would mysteriously disappear for days. The patient, the last of seven children, was born when "mother was getting worse and worse." He presents an intricate psychopathic personality.

Personal history: The patient, who was born in Wales in 1891, had lived in America since the age of two. He was graduated from a New York high school in 1908 and then entered Harvard University on a Pulitzer Scholarship, a high distinction. In disposition he was always retiring, preferring the company of books to association with friends, and was sensitive to a fault. At times he would exhibit very transient periods of exhilaration during which he "sang and joked like other boys." Although he seemed to prefer to keep to himself, his personality appealed to people and he attracted many friends. Some years before his first admission to a mental hospital he had formed an attachment to a young girl to whom he wrote ardent letters, though she replied only in friendly terms. He was not addicted to intoxicants or smoking, nor had he suffered from venereal disease.

Mental disorder: The first evidence of abnormality manifested itself in March, 1909 when he suddenly left college for Providence, Rhode Island, where he boarded a steamer for his home in New York City. Upon his arrival here he consulted his family physician, whom he told of his practice of "self-abuse," he was sent for a rest to his grandmother's farm in Vermont where he remained for only three weeks before returning to Harvard. Shortly thereafter he became disturbed again. He destroyed his family photos, school pennants, papers, and pillows, saying he had no further use for them. After telling a friend that he had purchased a steamboat ticket for New York with the intention of jumping off the boat, he set fire to some of his own belongings but destroyed nothing of his landlady's. Following this episode he again returned to the Vermont farm where he remained only eight days before he tried to walk to Rutland, about eighteen miles distant. In May, 1909, when he was eighteen years old, he again disappeared and could not be traced for a few days until he was picked up in Chicago by the police, who notified his relatives.

He was treated at a hospital for the insane until October, 1909. Upon his release, after working for six weeks, he suddenly vanished and was not heard from until he wrote from Buffalo, where he had visited Niagara Falls with the idea of drowning himself "but lacked the courage."

On December 27, 1909 he went to Danbury, Connecticut, where after registering in a hotel under an assumed name, he bought eight ounces of chloroform with which he attempted suicide. He failed in this attempt also and was returned to New York to Middletown State Hospital from which he escaped in July, 1910. His relatives sent him to a farm on Long Island where he remained only a few days; then he suddenly made his appearance at Port Jervis where the police took him into custody as a vagabond.

The physical examination of the patient was negative. He was well-built, active, good-looking, and made an exceptionally good impression.

The patient attributed his desire for suicide to his inability to overcome the habit of masturbation.

The desire to do away with myself comes as a result of a relapse into the habit which occurs about every three weeks. The very fact of having that relapse makes me disgusted with myself and things in general, especially myself. At those times more than others I have a fear that this habit is going to cause my life to be a failure.

Examination: The investigation was undertaken through a word association test which furnished many clues; through requesting the patient to write a list of his favorite colors, foods, actresses, plays, and books, which I found an excellent means of determining a patient's predilections; through dreams that were analyzed to a limited extent only; and finally through forced fantasies in hypnoidal states.

Inasmuch as the patient was an unusually good hypnotic subject, I was able to ascertain facts in the hypnoidal as well as in the waking state. On the whole, the thoughts expressed in the latter condition were more spontaneous and thought association seemed to go farther.

As a matter of experiment I repeated the association test that I had performed in the waking state upon the hypnotized patient and found that the average time for reply to the stimulus word was slower, the number of retardations greater but usually on the same words as in the waking state, and the explanations of the retardations less satisfactory. When the patient was asked to jot down his impressions in doing the association test while hypnotized, he wrote the following:

First, my mind was slower to react and seemed more anxious to make no blunders; second, my mind was not absolutely free to act as it wished because of the fact that I had been over the test before and finally I was far from being so eager and alert to throw myself into the thing.

By using these methods we discovered underlying factors that might account for the unusual symptom-complex. His recollection of his father, who died when the patient was only five and a half years old, had become very indistinct. He was strongly attached to his mother, however, and recalled that even during the intervals when she appeared normal she had repeatedly threatened to take her life. He described his younger sister as "looking very much like mother."

The earliest event that the patient can recall occurred when he was five years old. His mother had lain in bed all day afflicted with one of her attacks, so that when his father returned in the evening the household tasks remained untouched. During a violent quarrel which ensued the father dragged the mother, half-dressed, out of bed and threw her downstairs. The patient, huddled together with the other children at the foot of the stairs, became very much frightened at the struggle he witnessed and began to cry bitterly. His older sister and brother attempted to console him.

When the father died about six months after this incident, the children were sent to the farm in Vermont. During the first winter the patient, who was not quite six years old, slept regularly with his younger sister, five years older than he. On only one occasion did they attempt coitus, but for several years they excited each other by mutual genital stimulation. He recalled that once while he and his younger sister were coasting when he was about eight, she tumbled and lay on the ground for some time pretending that she was dead. Not realizing it was a joke he became greatly frightened; he remembered his intense satisfaction because she had not died.

A male cousin, about six years older than himself, taught him manual masturbation at the age of eight, and he found the sensation decidedly pleasurable. Stimulated by this new knowledge, and at his cousin's suggestion, he again proposed intercourse to his sister, but she, having now grown older, indignantly rebuked him. The entire family had been piously raised, and he felt he had proposed "something almost sacrilegious." Nevertheless, the rebuff did not deter the patient from continuing frequent masturbation. When shortly after this he attempted to induce a younger boy to masturbate, the latter became alarmed and told his mother, who reported the fact to the patient's aunt. His aunt impressively told him that the thing she heard he was doing would "make him crazy if he ever did it again" and made him solemnly swear not to do so. This warning was sufficiently impressive to make the patient cease masturbation for about six years—that is, until he had reached the age of fourteen—although he was constantly struggling to restrain sexual impulses.

In 1905 his mother died, and as she had always been a companion to the patient, he found himself more and more isolated and solitary. Now he resumed masturbation, but the momentary pleasure immediately transformed itself into a panic that the habit might ruin his life. He sought sublimation by applying himself more assiduously to his school work, but one morning when the principal publicly addressed the students on sex hygiene, particularly condemning masturbation, the conscience-stricken patient wrote a letter to the principal explaining his own difficulties and begging forgiveness. The principal asked him to come to his office, encouraged him to combat his desires, and suggested as an aid the application of cold, wet cloths to the genitals and long walks in crowded, well-lighted thoroughfares. Nevertheless, the impulse did become overpowering during his loneliness and the long walks were little help. He attempted to overcome his difficulties by studying even more diligently and made excellent records. In school he maintained pleasant and active, although never very intimate, relations with his schoolmates.

As a celebration at the happy termination of his school

course, he went on an excursion with his sisters to Niagara Falls. At the first sight of the torrent he thought that he might commit suicide. He and his younger sister jumped onto a rock a little distance from the bank where she suggested that they might slip into the rushing current together.

He entered Harvard the next fall with some reluctance; he feared that being away from the home environment might make the struggle with masturbation more severe. College life proved a distinct disappointment—he failed to find the sociability and free conviviality that he had imagined would exist there. He was harassed by his habit and by a constant fantasy of seeing his sisters nude when he returned home at Christmas. After the Christmas vacation he yielded to masturbation with such abandonment that because of the resulting exhaustion he could not attend lectures and allowed his work to go undone. At this time he decided to leave college, fearing that the cause for his scholastic decline might be discovered.

From then until his admission to the hospital one and a half years later, the patient ventured upon fourteen distinct flights of varying lengths, all fundamentally similar in that they were compulsive, often had no definite destination, involved no mental confusion but always with the idea of suicide at the end. It will suffice for illustration to describe the general characteristics of the first and fifth flights.

Having decided to leave Harvard for good late in March, 1909, he first masturbated and then set fire to a long English theme over which he had been working for three months—to burn his bridges behind him, he said. He recalled minutely all events subsequent to this, even to the good breakfast he ate, the trolley he took to the station, and the train that he boarded for Albany with the intention of going to Niagara Falls. As he left Cambridge he began to feel less tense, and a rather unnatural elation gradually replaced his depression, so that toward the end of the trip, which took an entire day, he wavered more and more in his purpose of going to Niagara Falls and of committing suicide.

By the time he reached Albany he had become obsessed by an intense desire to return home. The thought then came to him that he had traveled to Niagara Falls the previous summer with his sister on the Hudson Day Line. He sauntered to the river bank where he felt compelled to take a boat back to New York. On his arrival there he sought a restaurant that he had visited the summer before with his sister. Not wishing to alarm his sisters by his sudden appearance, he went first to the family physician to whom he had confided the secret of his masturbation the year before. When the younger sister learned, through a friend, of her brother's unexpected appearance at home, she immediately left work to see him. In her presence the patient "felt relieved."

After the patient's fourth flight he was sent to Bloomingdale Hospital. Here he learned to swim—perhaps his desire to learn may have originated in a subconscious attempt to eliminate the possibility of suicide by drowning. After his discharge from the hospital in October, 1909, an episode occurred in which the patient and sister played "flirtation," and the patient finally forced his sister in her negligee to the couch where she yielded to his passionate kisses. Immediately after their embraces he left the house to pace the streets for hours.

The fifth, a typical flight, followed not long after the foregoing incident and was accompanied by an act of destruction: this time of a scarfpin in the form of a wishbone with an opal at the junction of the two bones (the symbolism is evident). Like all the other flights it was preceded by masturbation and a suicidal impulse. This impulse was partially, although not completely, relieved by long wandering during the night in Westchester County. The next day after withdrawing his savings from the bank, he traveled all night to Cleveland, Ohio. After masturbation the suicidal impulse became more insistent than ever. Instead of attempting suicide, however, the patient cut a slit in the hair-stuffed mattress of the bed in his dingy hotel room and buried his watch and fountain pen in the rent that he had made; he covered the aperture and left both articles in the mattress. (Again, note the symbolism.) He scrawled a postal card to a distant friend in Philadelphia, saying goodbye forever. He then went by rail to Niagara Falls, where he intended to cross to the Three Sister Islands, the point he had selected for throwing himself into the water. However, his courage failed him again. He journeyed afoot all the way to Buffalo and found himself free from his dejection at the end of his long walk. He worked for a week in Buffalo but after the usual cycle started again for Niagara Falls on foot in a blinding snowstorm. He became more contented and relieved as he walked and at the end of the long, hard trip he no longer felt inclined to self-destruction.

Paramount features of the case are: (1) The destruction of personal property precedes the beginning of a flight. (2) The cause for the wandering is definitely attributed to the desire to escape from the habit of masturbation. (3) The object of the flight is nearly always suicidal. (4) The patient is entirely clear throughout his wanderings. (5) The fugue usually diminishes his depression.

It is striking that the patient never attempted suicide without first wandering from the place where he masturbated, and that although he had started with the intention of self-destruction on perhaps eight or ten occasions he had never accomplished his aim.

Naturally, such an involved case, the study of which must necessarily be incomplete and in which many unconscious influences can only be surmised, admits a wide range of interpretation, but it seems evident that the patient's malady is quite definitely related not only to hereditary influences but to the childhood impressions and episodes already described. The sexual instincts first aroused at the age of five and a half years apparently strongly affected his sexual longings throughout life. The sexual excitement in childhood was not only premature but also frequent and prolonged, so that it made a tremendous impression on his mind. The sister acted the role of the aggressor in most of their early indulgences, which might be natural in view of her seniority, but the patient never played the passive role consistently.

Although manual masturbation at the age of eight was distinctly gratifying and the urge for intercourse had already been aroused by his sister, he might perhaps have continued to puberty or beyond in comparative calm had not other factors influenced his sexual life. Notable was his cousin's suggestion that heterosexual relations with his sister might afford greater enjoyment than self-abuse. The sister's indignant rebuff of his proposal impressed upon him the idea that intercourse was ethically unpermissible, and this not only aroused an enormous sense of guilt but removed as the sex object one who had already probably become typified in his mind as a sexual ideal. Heterosexuality thus became abhorrent.

To satisfy his longings, which had been aroused so early and which evidently found fruitful soil in an inherited psychopathic constitution, he again resorted to onanism but this outlet was soon blocked by his aunt's admonition about insanity. Even to a psychopathic child this warning might not have meant too much, but this boy had already begun to acquire a vague idea of his mother's insanity and to appreciate from constant observation of his mother's moods the agony that insanity entailed. The logical conclusion was, as he expressed it, "If masturbation produces insanity and ruin, I must never do it again," for insanity had a connotation of self-destruction.

For five years he successfully combated his impulses until his mother died just as he reached puberty, when the conflict became progressively more severe. The aunt's warning was perhaps partly weakened by the removal of the mother through death; the fear of the revelation of his habits to her was removed. When he finally yielded, a flood of fear and remorse overwhelmed him, dominating him and returning after each indulgence.

It does not seem improbable that the patient's love became

centered in his mother from the time he observed her maltreatment at the hands of his father. This mother, however, was an intangible personality and, in her illness, foreboding to a child. It is not a far step to conjecture that he soon transferred this love to the younger sister, who not only "greatly resembles mother" and whose emotional constitution was similar to his own, but who from childhood had always been thrown into intimate contact with him socially and physically. The patient stated that he first consciously connected the personality of his sister and mother when he was about eleven, and the physical resemblance between the two had become more manifest. The assumption that he early began to identify his sister with his mother seems likely and is within reason although it is not proved.

Later, the advice of the school principal, who occupied an exalted position in the boy's mind, offered relief from his tortures. His therapeutic suggestions consisted not only of applying water (with the idea of drowning) but also taking long walks (fugues), both of which ideas were rigorously followed for over a year. The final moment in the development of the obsession for suicide is perhaps due to the suggestion of his sister at Niagara Falls that they might slip in together.

When the patient had been removed from the proximity of his sister without being able to repress his habits, the thought of freeing himself from what he believed would eventually produce mental disintegration seemed impossible. Instead of leading his sister to ruin, he destroyed her image and then prepared to wander, with the idea of suicide, in many instances to the spot where she had remarked on their death together (expiation). But as he progressed on his trips a feeling of relief came over him. Perhaps this was a result of the suggestion of the therapeutic effect of walking; or perhaps the hardships to which he exposed himself reduced the amount of guilt and induced the solace that masochistic substitutes sometimes yield. However this may be, the fact remained that notwithstanding all manner of sacrifice to reach Niagara Falls, the patient's courage uniformly failed him at the crucial moment because his thoughts invariably turned toward home, which to him meant the abode of his younger sister.

It has perhaps been noticed that before starting his first flight it was not the photograph of his sister that the patient destroyed but a long theme, the contents of which, curiously enough, he had spent three months in preparing. He states that it contained the same subject matter as a previous short theme in which he substituted a female character for a male. I have been unable to bring the subject matter to his memory even during hypnosis but he thinks that it was strongly reminiscent of George Eliot's novel *Adam Bede*.

Supplementary note (1950). The paper ends somewhat abruptly with a reference to *Adam Bede*. Eliot's novels, representative of the "free thinkers" of the Victorian era, often dealt with the question of illegitimacy. Adam Bede had been in love with an upright young girl who kills her illegitimate child. Here then we have incestuous love, with which the patient was preoccupied, and an identification with Adam.

My own, a novice's, attempt to cure this patient of his severe compulsion by psychoanalytic psychotherapy was, as already indicated, unsuccessful. My service at Manhattan State Hospital was part time, and I saw the patient approximately one hour a week during which I clumsily explained mechanisms involved in his illness and tried to alleviate his overwhelming sense of guilt. But I was allowed to maintain an office in New York, and in the spring of 1912 the patient became sufficiently stable and calm to be allowed to come on parole to the city where he took a room at one of the Y.M.C.A. dormitories. I attempted to continue the treatment at my office, but at the end of the first week the patient again attempted suicide by poison and was returned to the hospital. Thereafter he received practically no therapy as he was transferred to a chronic ward.

As I have already mentioned, he died through suicide by drowning in the fall of 1912.

Interest in the study of fugues, which had been very active (especially among the French psychiatrists), waned about the time of the reading of this paper, and the subsequent literature on this topic is not too extensive. Recently, however, Fisher and Joseph,[9] approaching this topic with psychoanalytic knowledge, presented cases in which they divide the fugue episode into two stages: (1) the patient acts out unconscious fantasies that are in conflict with the superego; and (2) the patient attempts to defend himself against and resolve the guilt generated by the events of the first stage. These two stages may be seen in the case just described, although the word "conscience" takes the place of the term "superego," which did not come into use in psychoanalytic terminology until 1923. In this case, the patient acted out to escape the conflict with his superego. His flights and all the incidents that occurred during them illustrate very distinctly the domination of guilt through separation of the individual from the scene of his sinful fantasies.

As I think about this patient I am not sure that the result would have been different had he presented himself to me today and under the most favorable external circumstances. Because of the intensity of his sense of guilt, his defense in compulsive flights from the scene of incestuous fantasies was one that would be difficult to alter even with increased experience in psychoanalysis and the management of patients. I am inclined to think that even today, after the patient had made his second or third suicidal attempt, the average psychoanalyst would be unwilling to assume responsibility for him and would likely refer him for self-protection to a closed institution. Now, as then, a spirited discussion might take place in a staff conference about whether the diagnosis should be schizophrenia, psychopathic

---

[9] Fisher, Charles and Joseph, Edward: "Fugue with Awareness of Loss of Personal Identity," *Psychoanalytic Quarterly*, October, 1949.

personality, compulsion neurosis, or even recurrent depressions of the manic-depressive type. The result for the patient would not have changed.

Papers such as Hoch's "Constitutional Features in the Dementia Praecox Group," [10] Macfie Campbell's "Psychological Mechanisms with Special Regard to Wish-Fulfillment," and Meyer's "The Role of Mental Factors in Psychiatry," [11] and the case just described depended upon familiarity with interpretative psychiatry at Manhattan State Hospital. These new time-consuming methods of examination annoyed many of the older physicians who had become habituated to the routine of custodial care. They growled and chafed, and offered plenty of quips about Fraud and Junk, but could not too openly defy what their leaders had approved. Yet I recall a staff meeting in 1910 at which one of the grizzled physicians who had been on Ward's Island for twenty-five years or more was asked by Dr. Kirby for his opinion of a case in which much psychoanalytic interpretation had been introduced. He cleared his throat and snarled, "Well, if you really want to know, it is my impression that since we added stenographers to the staff at this Hospital, it now takes a full hour to say what we could formerly say in five minutes."

These veteran physicians, reliable old-timers, men of good intent and kindly disposition, who had conscientiously trod the long, dismal halls that housed the chronic cases, saw no need to change their comfortable old shoes for the "gum-soled" ones that suddenly became useful and desirable. They found it almost impossible to adjust their pace to the new order, which

---

[10] Hoch, August: "Constitutional Features in the Dementia Praecox Group," *Review of Neurology and Psychiatry*, August, 1910.

[11] Meyer, Adolf: "The Role of Mental Factors in Psychiatry," *American Journal of Insanity*, Vol. XLV, 1908, p. 48.

sought to replace their accustomed "you must" to a patient with an inquiring "why?" of the origin of the patient's actions.

An honorable place for such men still exists, for only a small percentage of patients who dwell behind the locked doors of mental hospitals are amenable to the therapeutic approach of psychoanalysis or psychoanalytic psychotherapy. This was brought home to me when I recently visited one of the newest New York State hospitals. Architecturally well planned, it has plenty of air and light, but the inevitable barred windows and halls chilled one with the cold smoothness of modern tiles and concrete. The hospital was filled for the most part with people so crippled in mind that they will never pass beyond its well-guarded gates. The wards and dayrooms were overcrowded with the idle, aimless people whom I knew so well at Manhattan State forty years ago.

The histories of many would record that they had had the benefit of psychoanalytic therapy and of a few of a long psychoanalysis. One such patient who was under my care for about five years and was subsequently treated for about the same length of time by two other accredited analysts has for five years been confined to a state hospital. The modern case records contain many psychoanalytic terms, Rorschach tests, with psychoanalytic interpretations, encephalograms, Wechsler-Bellevue intelligence tests, and a considerable amount of laboratory work. The histories of those in the chronic ward, in spite of this amassing of data, do not differ much from those at Manhattan State in 1912. One change is noticeable. Then, among the notes of the chronic patient's condition, one would be apt to find at not too frequent intervals: "The patient is disinterested, apathetic, sits alone, will not work, and is deteriorated." In contrast to this, in 1950, the notes read: "The patient is disinterested, apathetic, sits alone, and will not work and is regressed."

The amiable physician who assisted me in my examination of a case during my visit to the hospital had had twelve years' service there. He told me, with a wistful smile of resignation and regret, "I guess I'm fixed here for the rest of my life." But this care of the chronic mentally ill continues a necessary work, with few rewards and little applause for those doctors and attendants who devote their lives to it. Whatever benefits psychiatry and psychoanalysis may be contributing to the prevention of mental disease, the effects are not yet appreciable in state hospitals. This may not apply to private sanitaria patronized by the well-to-do, who can afford more prolonged treatment of a psychoanalytic character. I am sure that many such happy instances exist.

One way by which the deadening isolation of the average mental hospital might be somewhat relieved and vitalized, when they are not too far removed from large cities, is through part-time employment of men in general or psychiatric practice in the adjacent towns. Such an arrangement would diminish the unhealthy gap between the hospital, remote from the impact of life, and the demanding world outside. At the same time such a plan would give the extramural physician training in psychological medicine from which his patients in general medicine might well profit. The question of split loyalties, which is the basis of many hospital superintendents' disinclination to part-time service, would, in most instances, be more than offset by the advantages.

This feeling may have a personal bias. When I had been at Manhattan State about five months, I resigned, youthfully impatient to enter private practice. The clinical director said that he regretted my leaving and we reached an agreement by which I spent my mornings and certain afternoons at the hospital. I am incalculably indebted to Manhattan State for the opportunity to really round out my psychiatric education. This schedule continued for over three years, until it was terminated by a regulation of the State Commission requiring that all members of the staff reside on the hospital grounds. In recent years this rule has been liberalized a bit in New York and other states, and there is an increasing tendency to locate mental hospitals sufficiently near large medical teaching centers to permit university teachers to visit them frequently.

The first patient whom I treated strictly by psychoanalysis in private practice, a woman of thirty-five living in a village in rural New Jersey, came to my notice in July, 1909 while I was acting as locum tenens for the local doctor. The analysis was reported before the New York Psychoanalytic Society in 1910 as "A Case of Hallucinosis Induced by Repression." [12] The patient suffered from visual hallucinations of skulls and squirming snakes in an otherwise clear mentality. She was treated in sessions of an hour twice a week from July, 1909 to June, 1910 and continued to consult me about once a month from 1912 to 1915. She is still alive at the age of seventy-seven without having had any recurrence of her mental symptoms. Her case served as the basis for the fictionalized story "Christmas Card" in my book *Which Way Out*.[13] In the light of my present knowledge I would consider this a transference cure which, however, has persisted for over forty years.

After I had been at Manhattan State Hospital a short time, I presented a paper on "Cases Allied to Manic-Depressive Insanity" at one of the New York State Inter-hospital Conferences in 1910. The paper reviewed cases originally so diagnosed after four months' observation on the wards, of which some had recovered but others had become chronic. It was typically the effort of a novice and contained many unseasoned observations which Dr. Adolf Meyer as the senior discussant of the paper treated none too leniently. However, luckily for me, as it turned out later, I had quoted in the paper from Cicero's *De Senectute*.

At the end of the meeting I was standing alone in the hall,

---

[12] Oberndorf, C. P.: "A Case of Hallucinosis Induced by Repression," *Journal of Abnormal Psychology*, February, 1912.
[13] Oberndorf, C. P.: *Which Way Out*. International Universities Press, New York, 1949.

not at all pleased with my initial performance before a psychiatric group. Suddenly a lively little man with a Van Dyke beard bustled up to me with a warm smile and outstretched hand. "My name is Brill," he said. "I like a fellow who quotes from Cicero." Brill was known to me as a semi-official spokesman for psychoanalysis in America. The gesture was characteristic of Brill's frankness, directness, and cordiality now shown to one whom he had seen for the first time. It marked the beginning of a friendship that ended only with his death on March 2, 1948.

Although residence on the grounds had been customary in the State Hospital Service, through a break in tradition, already mentioned, I was permitted to spend part time at the Hospital. At the same time I became associated with the outpatient Neurological Clinics at Cornell Dispensary and the Neurological Institute, which had just been established in a converted building on 67th Street, east of Lexington Avenue. Here three brilliant neurologists, Joseph Collins, Joseph Fraenkel, and Frederick Peterson, each headed a service. But none of them, not even Peterson, felt favorably inclined to psychoanalytic psychology and before long I discontinued my connection there. The limited remaining time I spent in private practice, which, thanks to Dr. Dana, was active from the start and has continued relatively free of struggle and anxiety.

As I look back at my initiation into psychoanalytic medicine at Manhattan State Hospital, I am sure that Freud's complicated theories would not have made so deep an impression upon me had they not been so easily discernible in the actions, mannerisms, and utterances of psychotic patients. One needed only to know the code supplied by psychoanalytic mechanisms, such as identification, its force and its enormous range, symbolism, overcompensation, projection, and displacement, to see in formerly meaningless manifestations expressions of secret yearnings and unconscious wishes and vital strivings. These incongruous actions made the interpretation of bizarre mystifying dreams seem plausible. "The dream is a psychosis" says Freud.

To be able to take apparently totally unrelated symptoms and finally bring them together into an intelligible whole, or even loosely connected fragments, had the fascination of a picture puzzle and putting it together gave one a satisfying feeling of partial understanding and accomplishment. About fifteen years ago a patient suffering from depersonalization expressed a similar idea concerning the function of the psychoanalyst. She complained of "living in a tomb" where she "felt the terrible agony of having all the outlets of my energy stopped—a worse suffering than the pain ensuing from a contact with the world." She once remarked to me in her characteristically toneless voice, "Anything which a patient in his clumsiness may construct in his mind, a psychiatrist with his skill and training should be able to unravel."

Of course this is still not always possible. At times the very intricacy of the psychic disorder and the inability of the patient, even with the best of intentions, to cooperate with the doctor prevent this. It is, nevertheless, an ideal toward which psychiatry and psychoanalysis keep courageously striving. The challenge in itself has become an inspiration for further careful inquiry into the factors entering into the frequently unsatisfactory results obtained in psychiatric and psychoanalytic therapies.

6. Clinical Practice and Organization of Psychoanalysis Expand, 1910–1920

When Brill went to Zurich in 1908, the Burghölzli Clinic, which was in close touch with the Viennese psychoanalysts, was engaged in a successful attempt to supplement Freud's extramural work with the neuroses and other more serious types of mental disorders. This activity of the Swiss group led to a meeting of the central Europeans interested in psychoanalysis at Salzburg in April, 1908 and to the formation of the International Psychoanalytic Association with Freud, naturally, as its first president. Here, too, plans were made for the establishment of the *Jahrbuch für psychoanalytische und psychopathologische Forschungen*, the first psychoanalytical publication, under the direction of Bleuler and Freud and edited by Jung.

Ernest Jones, who had treated his first patient in England by the psychoanalytic technique as early as 1905, and Brill, whom he had met for the first time at Zurich, journeyed together to Budapest and then to Vienna for a visit to Freud. It would be difficult to find men of more contrasting backgrounds than these two English-speaking pioneers in psychoanalysis, drawn together by their interest in the newly revealed universal psychological phenomena. Jones, born in Gower, Glamorgan, Wales and educated at Cambridge, was a master of English diction; and Brill, who had come from a small town in Galicia, an almost penniless *émigré* to America at the age of fifteen, was a self-made man who had battled his way up and who still retained a strong foreign accent. Yet these men became friends, traveled together, and later attended the Salzburg Congress.

Psychoanalytic activity was beginning to be hailed as a "movement," the very term indicating the extent to which the advancement of Freud's ideas had assumed the aspects of a cause or even a crusade with Freud's supporters.[1] In the announcement of the Third Psychoanalytical Congress (held in Weimar on September 21 and 22, 1911) written by Stekel, we find sentences such as frequently appear in the proclamations of religious sects and political parties:

> We can say with pride, that our teaching, which is the teaching of Freud, is daily gaining more supporters and marches forward continuously. *La vérité est en marche.* . . . We feel in these days like brothers of an order which demands from each single one sacrifices in the service of all. . . . Our Congress is not pointed to the public, it is a confidential (vertrauliche) gathering.[2]

These devoted and zealous men considered themselves proud standard bearers of a vanguard with a mission to convert to new theories that promised a clarification of all forms of human motivation and a therapeutic method of demonstrated value. Some thought it might eventually reveal the secret of the soul itself. They sought to strengthen the confidence of both the medical and lay public in Freud's postulates by quotations, short and long, from celebrated writers and from philosophers, which illustrated the Freudian mechanisms. Indeed, the opening paper at the Weimar conference, by Putnam, bore the title "Concerning the Significance of Philosophy for the Further Development of Psychoanalysis."

---

[1] Freud, Sigmund: *Zur Geschichte der psycho-analytischen Bewegung, Zweite Auflage.* Internationale Psychoanalytische Verlag, Vienna, 1922. (Many facts in connection with the movement abroad are taken from this account.)

[2] *Zentralblatt für Psychoanalyse,* Vol. I, 1911, p. 53.

That there is no dearth of such material in any literature has been previously shown in the quotations from American sources. The early volumes of the *Zentralblatt für Psychoanalyse* (1911–1913) contain excerpts from the letters of the French poet Baudelaire, boldly revealing his incest complex, from the German philosopher Schopenhauer, who had preceded Freud with the idea of repression, and from others who recognized the force, power, and truth of thoughts from the unconscious as compared with conscious mentation. An example of "superstition of evident sexual origin," based on the positions in coitus, is drawn from an American source, Mark Twain's *Huckleberry Finn*. A drowned person who was thought to be Huckleberry's father had been found floating on his back. However, as the dead person was floating on his back Huck said to himself that it could not be a man and therefore not his father—it must be a woman—"I know'd mighty well that a drownded man don't float on his back but on his face so that I know'd that this warn't pap but a woman dressed up in man's clothes." [3]

The virulence of the opposition of the protected Viennese academicians provoked among these ardent disciples of Freud a solidarity, perhaps a feeling of martyrdom, for which no need existed in America after Clark University had offered a forum for the dignified consideration of the thoughts of Freud. So the term "psychoanalytical movement" which had only a brief currency in America continued to be used in the German literature. This served as the title for a periodical devoted to nonmedical aspects of psychoanalysis, *Die Psychoanalytische Bewegung*,[4] edited by A. J. Storfer, a journalist in the Vienna group. It began publication in 1929 and ended abruptly in 1933 with "the worsening of economic conditions" and political upheaval in Austria, due to Nazi pressure.

Brill, who always invested his ample energies fully into what-

[3] *Zentralblatt für Psychoanalyse*, Vol. III, 1913, p. 98.
[4] *Die Psychoanalytische Bewegung*, Vols. I–V, edited first by A. J. Storfer and later by Eduard Hitschmann, Wien, 1929–1933.

ever he undertook, had absorbed much of the Viennese spirit of fighting a battle, perhaps to an extent unnecessary here and arousing rather than allaying opposition. He was well endowed professionally to carry on the exposition of psychoanalysis in America. He returned to New York in the spring of 1908, having completed a translation of Jung's *Psychology of Dementia Praecox*,[5] with boundless faith in the psychoanalytic theories and their therapeutic possibilities. Soon thereafter he entered private practice. He possessed to an unusual degree talents needed by a psychiatrist: broad sympathy and quick empathy with the patient, rare intelligence, and dogged persistence to ferret out obscure psychological causes. So although as we have seen psychoanalysis was cradled in Boston, it was raised and grew up in New York.

Ernest Jones, who had become Professor of Psychiatry at the University of Toronto in 1908, writes that the American Therapeutic Congress in New Haven, before which he read a paper in May, 1909, "was, I think, the first medical body in any country to be addressed on the subject of psycho-analysis" and his "the first paper in an English speaking country to actively support psycho-analysis."[6] Whether one considers this opinion as tenable is dependent upon whether or not one regards early papers such as Hoch had unobtrusively presented in New York as active support of psychoanalysis. But, above all, the irrepressible Brill was busily engaged in contributing articles on psychoanalysis to American medical periodicals and advocating it at medical meetings. And, what was far more important, Brill before long demonstrated in some stubborn cases

---

[5] Jung, C. G.: *Psychology of Dementia Praecox*. Translated by A. A. Brill. Monograph, *Journal of Nervous and Mental Disease*, 1909. (Published by White and Jelliffe as one of the first monographs of the Journal.)

[6] Jones, Ernest: "Early History of Psycho-Analysis in English Speaking Countries," *Internat. J. Psycho-Analysis*, Vol. XVI, Parts I & II, 1945.

that had been unsuccessfully treated by prominent physicians with other methods over many years that psychoanalysis worked well—at times spectacularly—in curing a great variety of illnesses.

Jones, who met with more bitter and entrenched antagonism and prejudice to psychoanalytic postulates at the conservative University of Toronto than existed in Boston and New York, resigned his professorship there. He returned to London where, in 1912, he founded the British Psycho-Analytic Society. With his departure all representation of psychoanalytic thinking in Canada temporarily ended. Dr. David Slight, as Professor of Psychiatry at the University of Montreal, attempted in the middle thirties to reintroduce psychoanalysis but met with little success. Today it has almost no academic recognition and very few adherents in private practice in the Dominion, although a study group of the Catholic Order of Dominican Brothers has been formed in Montreal recently.

From 1908 to 1913, by far the largest program of training in psychoanalytic psychiatry in the world flourished at Ward's Island. The staff there knew well of Brill's activities in New York, that he had been designated by Freud at that time as translator of Freud's works, and that he appeared regularly at medical meetings to defend psychoanalysis. However, little contact existed between this independent worker in the City and the staff at Manhattan State Hospital until he called together a group at his home to form the New York Psychoanalytic Society on February 11, 1911.

The influence of the extensive psychoanalytic interest at Ward's Island is indicated by the fact that fourteen of the twenty-seven members who had joined the New York Psychoanalytic Society by October, 1912 had been in the immediate past or were still on the staff of Manhattan State Hospital. (See Appendix.) Others had served in other New York State hospitals.

Reflecting this spirit of thorough medical preparation, the New York Psychoanalytic Society functioned in the pattern of other specialized neurological or psychiatric organizations in New York to which most of its members also belonged.

Whenever a new organization is established there are always a certain number of men who are willing to lend their names to it, sometimes merely because they fear they may be missing an opportunity to be known as progressive or to link up with a possible success. For this reason the original membership of the New York Psychoanalytic Society mounted within a few months to twenty-one. As one reviews this list it is apparent that a goodly number of the members had little acquaintance with or sustained interest in psychoanalysis. All, however, were physicians, most of them with long intramural experience with the mentally ill.

The Report of the Carnegie Foundation on Medical Schools in America (1910), this the work of Dr. Abraham Flexner, revolutionized American medical education gradually, exposed the notorious proprietary medical schools, and raised the standards of those that were associated with universities. Both state and university authorities carefully guarded the advances that had been attained through this support and perhaps for this reason regarded skeptically the new method of psychoanalysis that seemed to hover precariously on the borderline between speculation and science.

Brill of course became the first president of the fledgling organization; Dr. B. Onuf, also a State Hospital alumnus, the vice-president; and Dr. Horace W. Frink, former House Surgeon at Bellevue Hospital whose interest in hypnosis had led him to psychoanalysis, the secretary. The first report of the Society's activities in the recently founded *Zentralblatt für Psychoanalyse* mentions that four monthly meetings were held before the summer of 1911. The papers presented reflect the typically clinical range of the members' activity: A. A. Brill, "A Fragment of the Analysis of a Compulsion Neurosis"; E. W. Scripture, "Freud's Theory of Sex"; C. P. Oberndorf, "Demonstration of a Case"; and H. W. Frink, "Analysis of a Mixed Neurosis."[7]

Scripture entered the field of psychological medicine after having been director of the Yale Psychological Laboratory, which like similar university laboratories was applying to the study of mental life methods adopted from the physical sciences. The term "resistance" was in use in psychological laboratory experimentation in differentiating two analogous sensations, resistance and heaviness, with their variations in intensity. It may be that Freud adopted his term resistance (Widerstand) from the German academic psychologist who provided America with the pattern of laboratory experimentation toward the end of nineteenth century.[8]

After the first few sessions of the Society the attendance at the regular meetings became extremely uncertain; at times not more than half a dozen physicians were present. From 1911 to 1915 the nucleus that could be counted upon to provide scientific material for the programs dwindled to Brill, Frink, and Oberndorf, all in private practice, and Karpas, who was soon to leave Manhattan State to begin private practice. In 1915 Adolph Stern, who had been a resident physician at Central Islip State Hospital, joined the Society and soon became absorbed into this nucleus. The meetings were held at Dr. Brill's home and my own until 1920. Because there were so few of us in those days the gatherings lost formality and assumed the nature of an intimate study group where, in addition to the topic of the evening, problems of technique and opinions on recent articles and books were talked over far into the night. No matter how skeptical physicians may have been about the theories

[7] *Zentralblatt für Psychoanalyse*, Vol. I, 1911, p. 432.
[8] Scripture, E. W.: *The New Psychology*. Walter Scott Ltd., London, 1898, p. 263, with a reference to Goldscheider and Blecher, "Versuche über die Empfindung des Widerstandes," *Archiv für Physiologie*, 1893, p. 536.

that this small group of psychoanalysts were sponsoring, there could be no question of the thorough medical and psychiatric training of the nucleus or of their competence to treat patients by accepted methods had they so chosen.

I do not wish to imply that only half a dozen men were present at all the meetings or that others did not at times present papers or participate in the discussions. Among the others were Doctors Jelliffe, Hoch, and J. H. Conant. During this period, too, Dr. Putnam, always impressive by his calmness, dignity, and wisdom, occasionally came from Boston to lend the weight of his authority to the discussion of some of the papers presented by the New York group at neurological, psychiatric, and general medical meetings.

As early as 1910 Freud had observed that in the practice of psychoanalysis "every analyst's achievement is limited by what his own complexes and resistances permit." [9] Because of this, about 1913, a new question had been placed flatly before the New York group: the proposition, then so startling, that the analyst himself submit to analysis as a part of his preparation. Of course, the fundamentals of psychoanalysis had been discovered and the foundation of its practical use had already been laid by men who themselves had never had a formal analysis. These were Freud himself, Ferenczi, whose range was wide and deep, and Abraham, whose clinical insight and originality far exceeded that of most men who have since been analyzed. Certainly before the introduction of the analysis of the analyst there had been published many observations that still retain their value undiminished today. I refer to those of Federn, Jones, and Silberer, who wrote so exhaustively on problems of mysticism and its symbolism in 1914; Rank, who made such an important contribution in the application of psychoanalysis to the investigation of myths; Stekel, whose quick flashes concerning the psychoanalytic meaning of symptoms in health

---

[9] Freud, Sigmund: *The Future Prospects of Psychoanalytic Therapy.* Collected Papers, Vol. II. Hogarth Press, London, 1922.

and disease were unique. Reports of happy therapeutic results achieved by unanalyzed physicians were profuse and detailed.

The new concept of didactic analysis seemed definitely sound. It was intended to help rid the analyst of his own psychological blind spots and enable him to regard his patient with less bias and prejudice favorably or unfavorably. In other words, it had become apparent that the emotional response called counter-transference, a result of the patient's activation of unconscious feelings in the analyst, interfered with his interpretation and evaluation of the patient's attitude and ideas. A process designed to enlighten the analyst of his own vulnerability seemed highly desirable.

The idea had taken form in 1908 when the Burghölzli staff, living in the same quarters, had indulged, semi-humorously, in the questionable entertainment of analyzing each other's dreams. But the formal analysis of the analysts did not receive encouragement by the International Psychoanalytical Association until its second meeting at Nuremberg in 1910. Although the New York analysts appreciated the advantages of the procedure, each of us was reluctant to disclose his conscious and unconscious motivations to one of his friends and competitors. "There is something in the misfortunes of our friends which does not displease us," reflected one of the cynical French philosophers, and there was in America no one else to whom we could turn for analysis other than our intimates.

Carl Jung, who was about to break definitely with Freud, visited New York briefly in 1911 and 1912 at the invitation of Doctors Jelliffe and J. W. Maloney [10] to deliver a course of lectures at the newly established medical school of Fordham University, a Catholic institution. At the time Jung had a number of followers in New York, notably Dr. Thaddeus Ames and Dr. Beatrice Hinkle [11] who, like Frink and me, were at-

[10] Jelliffe, Smith Ely: "Glimpses of a Freudian Odyssey," *Psychoanalytic Quarterly*, Vol. II, 1933, p. 323.
[11] Hinkle, Beatrice M.: "Jung's Libido Theory and the Bergsonian Philosophy," *New York Medical Journal*, May 30, 1914.

tached to the Cornell Clinic and used a type of psychodynamic psychology in treatment. Ames subsequently became a member of the New York Psychoanalytic Society but continued his affiliation with religious bodies. As late as 1938 he wrote an introduction to *Pastoral Psychiatry* by Bonnell, minister at the Fifth Avenue Presbyterian Church since 1935. This church, as well as several others in New York, such as St. Mark's In-The Bouwerie, has maintained counseling clinics which often resort to psychoanalytic psychiatry for a clearer insight into the problems that parishioners present.[12] Ames' deep interest in religion may account for his early inclinations toward Jung's deviations from Freudian psychoanalysis.

This visit of Jung offered an excellent opportunity for the New York analysts to undergo with one of Freud's still accredited supporters the very brief personal analysis then considered adequate for the analyst, but none of them did so. The members of the New York Psychoanalytic Society were aligning themselves with Freud in his controversies with Jung and Adler, and so far as I can recall Jung was not invited to address the Society. Jung's theory of a collective unconscious and his disavowal of the importance of the sexual drive and its derivatives never attracted a large number of psychotherapists in America, although a few of the members of the American Psychoanalytic Association were first analyzed by the Jungian and later by the Freudian technique.

When Dr. Paul Federn, one of Freud's associates, came to America in May, 1914, I availed myself of the opportunity to begin a didactic analysis with him. Many years later he told me that Dr. Jelliffe had done the same. The attempt ended quickly after only a few sessions, with the threat of World War I in Europe, which led to Federn's hasty departure. The analytic sessions were conducted rather informally in Dr. Federn's hotel room. I slumped on an uncomfortable sofa while

[12] Bonnell, J. S.: *Pastoral Psychiatry*. Harper & Bros., New York, 1938, pp. 136–139.

Federn sat beside me. During our hour he would drone two or three times, "Sie haben doch eine kleine Neurose" ("I'd say you do have a bit of a neurosis"). It seemed to console and reassure him that the analytic sessions were justified. Up to that time I had not encountered this question of making a justification for analysis, for all the patients who came to me were suffering from urgent and distressing symptoms.

It happened that at the outbreak of World War I I found myself marooned in Zurich and sought to utilize the time by starting in analysis again, with Dr. Alphons Maeder, then a prominent figure in the psychoanalytic world. Maeder did not seem concerned about the question of neurosis but concentrated his psychoanalytic endeavor almost exclusively upon dream interpretation, in which he had a reputation for great skill. This attempt, too, ended abruptly when I was fortunate enough to obtain passage back to America in September, 1914 just before the German Ulans came almost in sight of Paris and of the port of Le Havre from which the ship to America slipped out silently at night without lights.

During this summer of 1914 a chance incident again impressed the superiority of the psychoanalytic method dramatically and indelibly on my mind. In Paris I attended the clinic at the Salpêtrière of Joseph Jules Dejerine, a vigorous, genial man, considered to be one of the ablest and most progressive psychotherapists in all France. His success, like Dubois', seemed dependent upon his personal influence, although the hearty Dejerine typified the French man of the world, the Boulevardier, in contrast to Dubois, the gentle, cultivated teacher. Perhaps they were strong father and kind (motherly) father images, respectively.

The case presented that day turned out to be an agoraphobia in an anxious-looking, middle-class housewife of perhaps forty years. Dejerine spent much time in describing to the assembled doctors, very vividly, fears in general and this woman's fear in particular. When he had finished, the woman, who had been waiting in impatient resignation during his lecture, asked, "But Professor, what shall I do?" He replied, "You have nothing to fear on the streets." "I already know," she said, "that the streets are not dangerous." "But now I tell you, you have nothing to fear." Unimpressed, she persisted humbly, "I know it. If there were danger on the street I would ask for a gendarme—not ask monsieur le professeur." Dejerine had exhausted his resources. For a moment they looked at each other vacantly. Then she turned in great despondency to walk slowly out of the room. The professor followed her a step or two, laid his large hand on the shabby black shawl covering her slender shoulder and said softly, "You must have courage, courage." She proceeded on her way out of the room shaking her head hopelessly. Surely, I thought, psychoanalysis had something more encouraging to offer to patients suffering from such psychopathology.

A compatriot of Dejerine, Pierre Janet, had a few years before introduced the term psychasthenia into psychiatric nomenclature as an entity different from neurasthenia and it enjoyed a brief vogue in this country. Somehow the prefix "psych" instead of "neur" before asthenia seemed to lend prestige to the mental factors operative in those forms of nervousness from which patients suffered who flocked to the few and inadequately manned outpatient neurological clinics of the university and other hospitals. Also Janet, a contemporary of Freud, belonged to the French school of psychiatry, which because of Charcot's extraordinary reputation still occupied a preferential position with some neurologists who stubbornly resisted the separation of psychiatry from neurology.

Janet ascribed neurotic disturbances generally and also psychasthenia to a diminution of psychic tension. His ideas were more comprehensible and hence more acceptable to the average neurologist because of the importance he placed on the external, material causes and the powerful effects of deprivation. He had little to say about sexual aberration and the protest of the repressed urges that Freud constantly pointed out. In his therapy, Janet depended largely on the manipulation of the psychological and environmental assets and liabilities of his patients and never acquired an approach in any sense dynamic.[13]

[13] Janet, Pierre: *La Medicine psychologique*. Flammarion, Paris, 1924, p. 286.

7. The Impact of Psychoanalysis on Medical Education and the Public, 1910–1920

As was and still is customary for younger physicians needing experience in a particular specialty, the men who formed the core of the New York Psychoanalytic Society attached themselves to the neurological clinics treating a great variety of organic and functional nervous disorders. The rather meaningless term "neuropsychiatrist" had not yet been coined.

From 1909 Brill worked at the Vanderbilt Clinic of Columbia University. Frink and I were instructors in neurology at the outpatient clinic of Cornell Medical School, and Karpas had a similar position at New York University. Because of the generally lax supervision by the faculty of the ambulatory patient clinics, no one inquired very closely how patients were being treated. To most of the neurologists of higher rank in these departments psychoanalysis remained a hazy, somewhat disreputable subject. When it came to the instruction of students, no one at the Cornell Medical School raised objections to the teaching of the general principles of psychic dynamics in the neuroses unless sex was mentioned too often and too openly. To that extent the psychoanalytic concepts could be used unquestioned in classroom instruction to explain symptoms of neurasthenia and psychasthenia, such as anxiety, insomnia, mild depressions, exhaustions, and phobias. With the tacit consent of Dr. Dana, Frink and I became increasingly bold in using psychoanalytic mechanisms in the presentation of cases to students. From time to time after the teaching hour some young man or woman would stay to ask questions or request references for further information about psychoanalysis (among them two keen students, Monroe Meyer and Abram Kardiner). Brill carried on a similar educational campaign unofficially at Vanderbilt Clinic and Karpas at New York University.

At that time in America, psychoanalytic treatment in private practice and in the outpatient clinics was generally conducted face to face; none of us had placed the patient in the recumbent position which has since become so characteristic of psychoanalytic procedure. Dr. G. Lane Taneyhill of Baltimore was one of the first psychoanalysts in this country to use the couch. He recommended it to me in 1917, pointing out its more obvious advantages, such as the relaxation and freedom it affords both the patient and the analyst because they need not face each other. When I protested to him that the disadvantage of being unable to see the patient's facial reaction outweighed everything else, he responded: "If you watch the patient's feet as he lies on the couch and get accustomed to his telltale movements, these will reveal to you as much as his face."

In my very brief contacts with Federn and Maeder both had used the recumbent position but I was not convinced of its advantages until after my own experience in analysis with Freud from September, 1921 to February, 1922. Upon adopting it I found that Dr. Taneyhill's observations were true in the main and that not only the crossing and uncrossing of the feet, but also the breathing, both costal and abdominal, the pulsation of the arteries of the neck, the blushing which flushes the forehead, tell quite as reliably as the eyes and the lips what the patient does not or cannot put into words and confirm or refute his utterances. Perhaps even more revealing than any of these is the quality of the voice to which, as time went on, I paid closer and closer attention.

In 1913 I established at the Outpatient Department of Mount Sinai Hospital in New York what probably was the first psychiatric clinic connected with a general hospital. Many of the hospital officials doubted the feasibility of such a clinic; they thought that mental patients because of their excitability or general behavior would disturb the patients of other departments. Of course, nothing of the sort actually happened, and the stigma then (as to a lesser degree now) attached to mental illness was diminished by the fact that it was possible for these patients to pass the admission clerk routinely and be assigned by the same procedures as medical and surgical cases. However, to admit that a general hospital treated psychiatric cases annoyed the head of the neurological service of which the new clinic was a part. For almost ten years it continued as the unofficial psychiatric clinic to which difficult mental patients from other neurological clinics could be referred for psychotherapy. My title remained "adjunct neurologist." Finally in 1920 psychoanalysis and psychiatry had become sufficiently important, and hence respectable, to permit the physicians in the clinic and hospital to be designated as psychiatrists and the outpatient service to be called the Mental Health Clinic. As chief of the clinic I was able to foster, almost unmolested, the practice of psychoanalytic psychotherapy whenever it seemed appropriate for the ambulatory cases and also for those cases that I was frequently called upon to see on the wards of the hospital. This enabled me to bring psychoanalysis directly to the attention of the visiting staff and interns.[1] Whereas a few, especially the surgeons and neurologists, scoffed and made sarcastic remarks about the implications of sexual elements in the illness, the majority listened politely and reserved decision.

[1] Oberndorf, C. P.: "Substitution Reactions," *New York Medical Journal*, October, 1914. (The material for this paper came from the Neurological Service of Dr. Bernard Sachs at Mount Sinai Hospital, where, as in the case of Putnam at Massachusetts General, many cases of neuroses and even psychoses were constantly under treatment.)

Another focus of psychoanalysis in America existed at the Johns Hopkins Medical School in Baltimore, Maryland, where for seven consecutive years from 1917 to 1925 Dr. G. Lane Taneyhill gave elective courses in psychoanalysis to third and fourth year medical students. They are the first regularly catalogued courses in any medical school for which students received the usual credits toward a degree. A goodly number were sufficiently interested to choose these courses. Paradoxically, the courses were offered under the department of neurology rather than psychiatry, for Dr. Adolf Meyer, Professor of Psychiatry at Hopkins, did not encourage his students to examine too closely the psychoanalytic theories. Nevertheless, after completing their residency at Phipps Clinic, several of his most valued assistants, Phyllis Greenacre, Bertram D. Lewin, Clara Thompson, Leo Bartemeier, and others, joined the ranks of the psychoanalysts.

In neighboring Washington, notwithstanding the fact that Dr. William A. White's extremely popular books, *Outline of Psychiatry* and *Mental Mechanisms*, were entirely psychoanalytically oriented, the staff at St. Elizabeth's Hospital seems to have received relatively little instruction in psychoanalysis. White's assistants included Bernard Glueck, who translated Adler; Nolan D. C. Lewis, now director of the New York State Psychiatric Institute; and Harry Stack Sullivan, who later made an adaptation of psychoanalytic concepts in a formulation which he called the "analysis of interpersonal relationships." In any case, with the exception of E. J. Kempf, the author of *Physiology of Attitude* and *Emergence of Ego-Organization*, no one from Washington, other than White, became a member of the American Psychoanalytic Association before 1920.

In Boston, where psychoanalysis received its first attention in America before it flowered in New York, a few men, including Dr. Isador Coriat and L. E. Emerson, a doctor of philosophy, met occasionally with Dr. Putnam, who during the last years of his life gave his attention almost exclusively to the philosophical and ethical implications of psychoanalysis. These meetings ceased with his death in 1918, not to be revived for nearly ten years.

In addition to these centers of local activity, national movements to aid in the advancement of dynamic psychiatry were under way. In Washington, on May 2, 1910, a few psychiatrists, dissatisfied with the programs of the American Medicopsychological Association (now the American Psychiatric Association), largely devoted to questions of hospital administration, formed the American Psychopathological Association to provide a forum for the discussion of the scientific problems exclusively. Morton Prince of Boston, whose studies in dissociated and multiple personality came close to the Freudian theory of unconscious conflict, became the head of the new organization.

The American Psychoanalytic Association came into existence at Baltimore on May 9, 1911, three months after the New York Society had begun its meetings, largely through the efforts of Ernest Jones. He persuaded the somewhat reluctant Putnam to accept the presidency. All of the founders belonged to the American Psychopathological Association, but the object of this new national organization was to afford psychiatrists interested in psychoanalysis, residing outside of New York City, an opportunity for annual scientific contacts. The membership as reported by Jones, its first secretary, consisted, in addition to Putnam, of Doctors Trigant Burrow, John T. MacCurdy, Adolf Meyer, G. Lane Taneyhill, all of Baltimore, Ralph C. Hamill of Chicago, and S. Alexander Young of Omaha, Nebraska. At the next meeting of the American Psychoanalytic Association which was held in May, 1912 this membership was increased and extended to include Brill and Jelliffe and not long thereafter others from New York.[2]

Because of this interlocking of membership of the two or-

---

[2] *Zentralblatt für Psychoanalyse*, Vol. III, 1913, p. 103.

ganizations, the third meeting of the American Psychopathological Association in 1913 is reported by Dr. Trigant Burrow, the secretary, to have been "practically a psychoanalytic meeting." Subsequently this organization gradually shifted its predominating interests to other forms of psychotherapies and to social psychology although psychoanalytic papers have continued to appear with varying prominence on the programs up to the present time.

Thus psychoanalysis began in America nearly fifty years ago as an integral part of medical practice, differing radically in this respect from its position in Vienna. Notwithstanding a generally unreceptive attitude on the part of many, perhaps most, psychiatrists, American psychoanalysts never regarded psychoanalysis as a distinct discipline, but as essentially a branch of psychiatry and medicine. Most of its advocates held teaching positions and appointments at important hospitals, as they continue to do.

To be sure, psychoanalysis introduced a strange and unfamiliar terminology, called jargon by its opponents, but actually this did not differ too startlingly in its novelty from the nomenclature used in the Wassermann test and arsenical preparations that came into psychiatric practice about the same time. Indeed, new words must be coined whenever any discovery is made. This happened when the newfangled "horseless buggy" of 1905 appeared and again when radar and atomic energy gave rise to a new vocabulary in recent years.

Possibly the unfamiliarity of editors of established psychiatric and neurological journals with the terminology of psychoanalysis, as well as their understandable resistance to many of its postulates, made them reluctant to accept articles for publication. Morton Prince's *Journal of Abnormal Psychology* was practically the only exception. Abroad a similar difficulty in publication led to the establishment of special journals controlled by psychoanalysts. The *Zentralblatt für Psychoanalyse* was founded in 1911 by Freud and edited by Stekel. As American collaborators we find the names of Brill and Putnam. After two years Freud and his strongest adherents withdrew from the *Zentralblatt* and organized the *Internationale Zeitschrift für Psychoanalyse* which appeared regularly until 1941 when it was forced to discontinue because World War II had scattered its editors. The *Zentralblatt*, which continued under Stekel's sole editorship, survived for only two years. The previously mentioned *Jahrbuch für psychoanalytische und psychopathologische Forschungen*, in which many of the most scholarly early psychoanalytic investigations appeared, also ceased publication when Jung, Adler, and Stekel broke with Freud about 1912.

White and Jelliffe, each with unusual literary and editorial gifts, met at the Binghamton State Hospital in 1896 where both were preparing for their future lifework. They formed a friendship and their names were coupled together in publications in the psychiatric field until White's death in 1937. They began the publication of *Monographs on Nervous and Mental Disease* in 1909. The first issues included translations of works on psychoanalytic topics such as "Selected Papers on Hysteria and Other Psychoneuroses" by Sigmund Freud (translated by A. A. Brill) and Jung's "Psychology of Dementia Praecox" (translated by Frederick Peterson and A. A. Brill). White and Jelliffe also established, in 1913, the first psychoanalytic periodical in English, *The Psychoanalytic Review*, a quarterly which significantly opened with a contribution by Jung instead of by Freud. It has been published continuously to date, at first in the face of many difficulties and with considerable personal sacrifice on the part of the editors. After the death of Jelliffe in 1945, Dr. Nolan D. C. Lewis assumed the editorship.

By 1919 psychoanalytic principles had permeated psychiatric thinking in America to an extent unknown anywhere else. Consequently in October, 1919 Ferenczi, then president of the International Psychoanalytical Association, pointed out that the "remarkable increase" in psychoanalysis in America and England during the past few years made it desirable to establish an official organ of the International Psychoanalytical Association with special reference to the English-speaking members of the profession. He invited Dr. Jones, then an editor of the *Internationale Zeitschrift für Psychoanalyse*, to undertake the task. Jones, in turn, asked Brill, Frink, and me to become associate editors of the new quarterly, the *International Journal of Psychoanalysis*. Like the *Zeitschrift* it became an official organ of the International Association and has continued to cover the psychoanalytic field for English-speaking writers and readers. In 1950 it dropped its designation as "official organ" of the Association, but it publishes the proceedings of the Association in its *Bulletin*.

The first number of this journal contains a good, although not entirely complete, bibliography of the original literature and translations in English to that date.[3] The American references indicate that during the preceding ten years many and diverse periodicals had opened their pages to psychoanalysis. In addition to the *Psychoanalytic Review* and *Journal of Abnormal Psychology*, the list included others with high scientific standards, such as the *American Journal of Psychology*, the *American Journal of Insanity* (now the *American Journal of Psychiatry*), and the *American Journal of Sociology*. On the other hand many accepted material uncritically, such as the *New York Medical Journal*, the *Medical Record*, the *Denver* (Colorado) *Medical Times*, and the *Woman's Medical Journal*. If one considered only these latter, it would be immediately evident why Freud had been fearful about the fate of psychoanalysis as a science in America. It degenerated completely to "wild analysis," that is, the misconception and gross misapplication of his laborious researches in psychopathology.

Following Freud's visit to Worcester, therapeutic psycho-

[3] Read, Stanford: "Review of the Recent Psychoanalytic Literature in English," *International Journal of Psychoanalysis*, Vol. I, 1920, pp. 68–85.

analysis slowly began to attract the partial or full support of the directing physicians in institutions for the insane and of competent practitioners of psychiatry in the East. As early as 1913 Freud's contributions were presented in a textbook intended for medical students by Francis X. Dercum, Professor of Nervous and Mental Diseases at Jefferson Medical College, Philadelphia, a city where psychiatry long remained under the control of such extremely conservative men as William G. Spiller, Charles K. Mills, and Charles W. Burr. Although Dercum repeats the frequent accusation of the time that "unfortunately Freud and his followers have been obsessed by the single factor of sex," the method and theory of psychoanalysis, especially dream interpretation, receive adequate attention.[4]

Before long Freud's terminology, Oedipus complex, libido, regression to the infantile, infantile traumata, was advisedly adopted or unwittingly copied into psychiatric case reports, sometimes by avowed opponents. However, the number of men who fully accepted and carefully followed the development of psychoanalysis abroad or devoted most of their energy to actual analytic work continued small from 1910 to 1920. Freud ascribed the generally cordial reception accorded his theories in America to the "absence of embedded scientific tradition and the slight weight of official authority" and thought that "precisely for these reasons it is clear that the fight for psychoanalysis must receive its decision where it has encountered greater resistance, namely, at the site of the older centers of culture."

The uneven course of psychoanalytic progress in Europe and the personal dissensions, defections, and repudiations of Freud's work by former collaborators were quickly echoed in America. The first scientific offshoot from Freud's psychoanalytic postulates by Alfred Adler in 1911 aroused sufficient in-

[4] Dercum, F. X.: *A Clinical Manual of Mental Diseases*. W. B. Saunders and Co., Philadelphia, 1914, pp. 356-363.

terest to warrant the translation of some of his works by Americans.[5] Adler regarded neurotic striving as a compensatory reaction to overcome an actual organic inferiority or even a feeling of organic inferiority. The patient became ill, not primarily because of the way in which he handled his instinctual drives, but also because of fictitious goals which he kept futilely striving to attain. The expression, "suffering from an inferiority complex," became a popular byword in this country. Nevertheless Adler's approach did not attract sufficient support to warrant its adoption as a starting point for clinical therapy by many physicians, either with adults or children. Freud acknowledged the credit due Adler in calling attention to the importance of the aggression component present in all instinctive drives and to the inclusion of ego strivings as components of the sexual instinct. He also accepted Adler's conception of the transferring of love to the ego, thus investing part of the ego instinct with sex libido, in his speculative work, *Beyond the Pleasure Principle*.[6]

Some of Jung's reformulations of psychoanalytic theory, which led to his resignation from the International Psychoanalytical Association in 1914, followed his visits to America. His predication of a collective unconscious seemed to cater to American predilections, for it evaded those disagreeable and repellent notes in Freud's "personal unconscious" in regard to incestual relationships and sought to soften Freud's clashes with conformative religious and ethical standards. Jung's later works [7] contain so much of spiritual, mystical, and quasi-theological admixtures, which he engrafted on Freud's basic theories in the attempt to defend "religious instincts," that it

---

[5] Adler, Alfred: *The Neurotic Constitution*. Trans. by Bernard Glueck and J. E. Lind. Moffat, Yard & Co., Boston, 1917. Also, *Study of Organic Inferiority and Its Psychical Compensation*. Nervous and Mental Disease Monograph Series, 1917.

[6] Freud, Sigmund: *Jenseits des Lust Prinzips*. Internationale Psychoanalytische Verlag, Wien, 1921, p. 51.

[7] Jung, C. G.: *The Psychology of the Unconscious*. Trans. by Beatrice Hinkle. Moffatt, Yard & Co., Boston, 1916.

is questionable whether his concepts would still come within any broad definition of psychoanalysis. His theory and procedures have appealed strongly to the inexactitude and fantasy of many laymen.

Notwithstanding the goodly number of psychoanalysts in America and the felicitous introduction of analysis to academic psychology by Dr. Hall,[8] American contributions fundamentally affecting the underlying principles of analytic science were meager during the second decade of the century. There was no dearth of articles in medical periodicals recording therapeutic successes with the method, illustrating Freud's mechanisms, or corroborating his contentions in regard to the function of the unconscious, only too often echoes of work previously published abroad. There were recapitulations of his theories in book form, some lucid, scholarly, complete in their scope, and accurate,[9, 10, 11, 11a] but a flood of others were fragmentary, loosely written accounts. There was also a plethora of discursive articles touching on the practicability of analytic application and disputatious refutations of some particular aspect of the general psychoanalytic theory, rarely carried to the point of proof.

Perhaps the most noteworthy and original among American contributions before 1920 are E. J. Kemp's attempt to correlate psychoanalytic mechanisms in terms of the reactions of

[8] Hall, G. Stanley: *Life and Confessions of a Psychologist.* D. Appleton & Co., New York, 1924, p. 410: "Now, when I have diligently read and kept tab on nearly all of its [psychoanalysis] important literature to date . . . and having given courses on various aspects of it since 1908, my sense of its importance . . . has steadily grown."

[9] Frink, H. W.: *Morbid Fears and Compulsions.* Moffat, Yard & Co., Boston, 1918.

[10] Brill, A. A.: *Fundamental Conceptions of Psychoanalysis.* Harcourt, Brace & Co., New York, 1921.

[11] Read, Stanford: "Bibliography and Review of Recent Psychoanalytic Literature," *International Journal of Psychoanalysis,* Vol. I, 1920, pp. 68–113.

[11a] Holt, Edwin B., *The Freudian Wish and Its Place in Ethics.* Henry Holt & Co., New York, 1915.

the autonomic nervous system,[12] L. Pierce Clark's unconvincing study of the mental content of epileptics during and following attacks, as well as his analysis of the epileptic personality,[13] Trigant Burrow's emphasis of a "primary subjective phase" in the infant chronologically preceding the Oedipus situation,[14] and the extensive though biased critique of psychoanalysis by J. T. MacCurdy.[15] Jelliffe [16] ventured boldly into the field of organic diseases, such as thyroid disturbances, cutaneous eruptions, and even disease of the spinal cord, and evaluated them according to the dynamic-economic principles of Freud. These investigations were brilliantly anticipatory of some of the most recent in the field of psychosomatic medicine, but as presented at the time they seemed merely inconclusive speculations to many of his colleagues. Jelliffe, however, writes in 1933 [17] that in a recent letter to him Freud generously referred to them as "that medicine of the future for which you are preparing the way," perhaps meaning that Freud was again turning to the collaboration of psychoanalytic psychology with physiology and biology for additional advances in medical practice. However, when Jelliffe first met Freud in Bad Gastein in 1921, his "eclectic Americanism" brought him "some slight disfavor."

Most of the American contributions elicited little comment abroad nor did they receive real consideration here. Never-

[12] Kempf, E. J.: *The Autonomic Functions and the Personality*. Nervous and Mental Disease Monograph Series, No. 28, 1918.
[13] Clark, L. Pierce: "The Psychobiologic Concept of Essential Epilepsy," *Journal of Nervous and Mental Disease*, May, 1923.
[14] Burrow, Trigant: "Character and Neurosis," *Psychoanalytic Review*, February, 1914.
[15] MacCurdy, John T.: *Problems in Dynamic Psychology*. Macmillan, New York, 1922.
[16] Jelliffe, Smith Ely: *Emotional and Psychological Factors in Multiple Sclerosis*. Reprint, Association for Research in Nervous and Mental Disease, 1921. Also, "The Psyche and the Vegetative Nervous System," *New York Medical Journal*, April 5, 1922.
[17] Jelliffe, Smith Ely: "A Freudian Odyssey," *Psychoanalytic Quarterly*, Vol. II, 1933, p. 328.

theless, America was rapidly becoming the proving ground of practical psychoanalysis. With the widespread practice of psychoanalysis by physicians variously equipped, its feasibility in the hands of the medical man with psychiatric training and average skill and intelligence, and its adaptability under such limitations to help the patient suffering from various forms of neuroses and psychoses, Freudian medical technique was being broadly and freely tested.

By 1920, psychoanalysis, along with the Montessori system of free initiative in the education of young children then in vogue at progressive schools, had become popular topics for discussion among "advanced" thinkers. They tossed about such terms as "fixations" and "repression," and psychoanalysis became an excuse for uninhibited conversation about sex at polite dinner parties. Literary circles and press clubs invited the few psychoanalysts to talk before them, hoping for a new sensation. "Let's unshackle our libido, loaf half dressed upon the Lido," chirped a rhymester in the Columbia University's humorous magazine, the *Jester*.

A leading New York book store carried nearly two hundred popularly written books bearing directly or indirectly on the subject. As typical of these may be mentioned *The Child's Unconscious Mind* by Lay, a teacher in the Flushing (New York) High School, which summarizes that "emotion is a constant factor in all mental activities" and that "the education of the will is the removing of obstacles existing in the unconscious." [18]

Then, as sometimes now, psychoanalysis and sex were considered identical, and, because of this sexual connotation, patients often regarded it a disgrace to admit that they were being treated by a psychoanalyst. I recall that about 1920, when my office was located on a quiet West Side street, one of my female patients met a friend in the neighborhood who asked her

---

[18] Lay, Wilfrid: *The Child's Unconscious Mind. The Relation of Psychoanalysis to Education. A Book for Teachers and Parents.* Dodd, Mead & Co., New York, 1920.

where she was going. "To see the doctor," she replied. "Which doctor are you going to?" "Dr. Oberndorf." "What kind of a doctor is he?" "A psychoanalyst." "Oh, Mary how can you go to such a man! I understand psychoanalysts do nothing but have sexual relations with their patients." And my patient, who was quick-witted and sharp-tongued, replied: "Isn't it terrible —and just think of poor Dr. Oberndorf with eight patients a day!"

During the last years of World War I, interest in psychoanalysis fell to a low ebb in America, as it had already done in Europe. War and wartime psychiatry can have little consideration for the individual, his rights, or his purely personal problems. During those war-torn years Freud, now past sixty, was able to withdraw to his studies. He published some of his most penetrating and inspired theoretical papers, "Zur Einführung des Narzissmus" in 1914 and "Trauer und Melancholie" in 1917, which deepened our knowledge of two major types of psychotic illness and extended the scope of the therapeutic possibilities of psychoanalysis. During this war period he must have also laid the groundwork for two other of his most original later works, speculative and philosophical rather than clinical: *Jenseits des Lustprinzips* (1920) and *Massenpsychologie und Ich-Analyse* (1921).

The New York Society continued to meet regularly during the war period, but with reduced enthusiasm. Frink and I, designated as essential teachers by the Army, had taken over most of the instruction in neurology at Cornell, for Dr. Foster Kennedy, the associate professor, a British subject, had volunteered in 1914. Brill, too, contributed his share as a civilian consultant at Plattsburg; and Captain, later Major, Karpas had left for France.

In 1919 the feeling against Germany was still running high. The annual meetings of the American Psychoanalytic Association, which had been allowed to lapse for two years because of the war, were resumed in that year at Atlantic City.

There, Dr. William A. White, one of the most effective American propagandists for psychoanalysis, possibly still affected by the lingering national hatred of everything German that had even prohibited the teaching of German in public schools, gave way to a surprising outburst. He indignantly proclaimed that "the time has come to free American psychiatry from the domination of the Pope at Vienna"—a proposal strongly reminiscent of the universal and ineradicable Oedipus relationship and the dethronement of the father.

White endorsed a movement to abolish the American Psychoanalytic Association and to have its functions combined with the American Psychopathological Association. This would have placed psychoanalysis in a subordinate role. Those who fought to preserve the Association argued heatedly the need for an independent organization that could authoritatively initiate, sponsor, and direct psychoanalytic activities in America. They insisted that the specific nature of advanced psychoanalytic problems requires a degree of familiarity with the literature and practice that makes such problems suitable for discussion only in a special society. The few members present, probably not more than fifteen, were evenly divided on this issue, and no final action was taken.

At the meeting held in the spring of the following year in New York, the same group—White, MacCurdy, and L. Pierce Clark, a prolific writer on psychoanalytic topics—pressed the question of dissolving the American Psychoanalytic Association. The proponents and opponents, again evenly divided, were bitter. After a fiery and prolonged discussion Dr. Adolf Meyer rose and stroking his beard, a characteristic mannerism of his when in deep thought, said in his quiet voice: "I think that the contributions of psychoanalysis to the understanding of psychiatry have been sufficiently great that there should be some organization in this country to guide its destinies." The weight of his opinion swayed the vote for the continuation of the Association. I believe, however, that had the vote gone the other way, Brill, Frink, and I would have immediately formed a new national society.

With the defeat of this last attempt to destroy psychoanalysis as a special branch of psychiatry, with the increased attention to psychiatry that had been created by the mental disorders of "shell-shocked" soldiers in the war, and with the reestablishment of communication with Vienna (interrupted for six years), a new era for psychoanalysis was about to start in America.

8. Recollections of Psychoanalysis in Vienna, 1921–1922

The proposal of the analysis of every analyst to increase his clinical proficiency, first mentioned about 1912, had gained increasing approval, and in the summer of 1919 Adolph Stern went to Vienna, now war-crippled, cold and hungry, for a personal analysis with Freud. Frink and Monroe A. Meyer followed him in the fall of the same year. Frink came back to New York early in 1921, but Meyer remained in analysis with Freud for a full year longer. On September 1, 1921 when Freud's summer vacation ended, four other members of the New York Psychoanalytic Society, Doctors Leonard Blumgart, Albert Polon, Abram Kardiner, and I, began our didactic analyses with Freud, then aged sixty-five. This made five American physicians in training and reestablished an intimate connection between European and American influences that had been interrupted for seven years by the war.

My decision to take the time out from a full schedule of practice to conform with this new ideal did not come easily. In the twelve years of practice there had been numerous instances in which both the patient and I were content with the results attained. Very probably I could have continued, as Brill and others did, without submitting to an analysis. Also, I knew that I was running counter to my interests at Cornell and Mount Sinai. Dr. Dana had cautioned me not to spend too much time with Freud when he granted my leave of absence from Cornell. Dr. Bernard Sachs at Mount Sinai, whose virulence against psychoanalysis had mounted steadily, reluctantly signed my leave from duty as chief of clinic of the unofficial psychiatric clinic of the Department of Neurology. Nevertheless I stuck to my determination.

Vienna was just recovering from Austria's disastrous defeat and the courses at the University were still not well organized or attended by foreign graduate students upon whom many of the poorly paid professors depended to supplement their depleted incomes. Psychoanalysis, being independent of University jurisdiction, had not been affected by the drastic political upheaval. It is told that at this time one of the University professors met Freud on the street. After a few casual comments he remarked enviously, "I hear, Herr Doktor Freud, that you have so many American students studying with you." "Yes," replied Freud, and then said the Professor, "How odd—the Americans are supposed to be such practical people." "Yes," said Freud, "but there are also among them a few who are idealists." The seven Americans who had come to Vienna were indeed practical clinicians but also idealists in that they hoped for improvement in their methods of the treatment of neurotic illness and were seeking at a considerable expenditure of time, effort, and money to perfect themselves in the procedures that Freud had offered.

Freud had established as his rule that a patient under analysis should be seen six days a week. With the five American doctors and the late Dr. John Rickman and James Strachey of London, who has translated much of Freud's work, plus two patients, there were nine in all, and consequently he saw them only five times a week. I think that Freud considered this decrease in the number of daily visits an undesirable concession forced upon him in an emergency and undertook to work with so many only because he felt it an obligation to pass on his method to these psychoanalysts from abroad. They would carry his scientific ideas accurately to wider audiences in America and Britain.

The analytic situation that confronted Freud at the time, the rivalry of five professional brothers, seeing much of one another day by day, for the favor of the father, was not an easy one to handle and has never been presented under similar conditions to any other analyst. From hour to hour he heard associations in which one or the other brother figured. The opinions of the fully grown sons as to Freud's skill in handling this competitive striving showed wide, at times amusing, variations.

People continue to ask me, as they do all others who knew him, for impressions of Freud. I shall try to give my impressions—from memory, for I made no notes. By 1921 Freud's reputation had grown to considerable dimensions. My own admiration and respect—shall I say awe of him—was very great, and it was with a heart quickened with expectation and anxiety that I hurried in the twilight down the narrow Berggasse for my first six o'clock appointment. Accustomed as I was to the pretentious addresses of prominent New York specialists, and also of their European counterparts, the modesty, almost dinginess, of this little side street surprised, perhaps disappointed, me. At least it was not what I had anticipated. Likewise, the building in which Freud lived bore no resemblance to those small villas surrounded by well-kept gardens in which other European medical men of note whom I had visited on earlier trips abroad, especially at the spas, were likely to reside. His office and home were one flight up over a cooperative grocery store. This had been his home for twenty-five years and here he continued to live until the disgraceful day in 1938 when Nazi troopers after virtually making him prisoner finally allowed their hostage to proceed to the haven provided for him in London.

The reception room of the Professor was a high-ceilinged, dark, narrow, rectangular room facing a courtyard. It was plainly, simply furnished, with stiff-backed chairs against the wall to the right, a table with a worn plush cover in the middle of the room, and a white tile stove to the left as you entered.

The large steel engravings added to the unpretentious formality, perhaps one might say severity. The scarcity of coal in Vienna, which had begun during the war, made it so difficult and costly to obtain fuel that the temperature of the stove was not sufficiently warm to relieve the general chilly impression of the room.

Promptly at the appointed time of the first visit the door leading to Freud's office opened, and he appeared. To me, Freud looked his sixty-five years, a stooped, gray man with a well-trimmed, almost white beard. The outstanding feature and the lasting impression, as I now remember, were his deep-set eyes—brown, steady, with a penetrating, burning look. Despite the general effect of old age, his movements were quick and precise, his voice crisp.

Freud greeted me affably, said he had heard much good of me, and asked a few questions about friends and acquaintances in America. At Brill's suggestion, I had brought along a box of Havana cigars, for the Professor was an inveterate smoker. He took them appreciatively, saying it was the only gift from a patient that he would accept as an exception to his long-standing rule. Then he indicated that I should lie down on the couch in a corner of the office; he walked to a chair at its head, sat down and, to my discomfiture, disappeared from view. Although I had had a very brief experience with the reclining position with both Maeder and Federn, Freud's unceremonious removal of himself proved definitely disturbing to me. Possibly I would have preferred to prolong the short, social, conversational contact to study my man. Freud read English with ease and understood spoken English well, but he did not speak or write it fluently. He conducted the analyses of most of the Americans and British in their mother tongue, by now no longer the "pidgin English" in which he had given his course in neuropathology to Americans some thirty-five years previously. He seemed pleased when he found that we could proceed with the analysis in German.

The qualities of the Professor that remain fixed in my mind are his generally impersonal, detached manner, his uncanny ability for discovering the weak points in a position and of pointing them out lucidly, at times pitilessly, and his incredible capacity for hard work. An elderly man, and not in too good health, during the winter of 1921-22 Freud saw "analysands," a word coined to designate analysts who were being analyzed, six days a week from seven or eight o'clock in the morning to noon or later. Then after an intermission of two or three hours, he resumed his work from three o'clock to seven or eight in the evening. I was told that this had been practically his unvarying habit, an almost cloisteral routine, for many years and one from which he did not depart until driven out of his home by the political exigencies.

At the meetings of the Vienna Psychoanalytic Society held at 9 P.M. he would regularly appear showing little evidence of fatigue as he presided attentively over the proceedings. He would close the discussion of the papers with penetrating, sometimes caustic comments, which like a cool blast of air cleared the mist from many a foggy picture or blew the dust from some old portraits offered as new. These words of the Professor were usually authoritative and final. It was the moment for which his co-workers and students seated about the long table seemed to have been waiting all evening and many a head would nod in assent to the words he uttered. Perhaps it was this veneration by the group, which contained several men capable of independent thinking, that gave to these meetings the atmosphere that Freud's critical analysis of the paper of the evening was not open to question and that gave to Freud's comments an impression of infallibility that he may have had no intention of encouraging.

Nevertheless, at that time the Inner Circle of the Seven Rings—revealed for the first time, I think, by Sachs [1] in 1944—

---

[1] Sachs, Hanns: *Freud, Master and Friend.* Harvard University Press, Cambridge, 1944.

had already come into existence. It had remained a secret as Freud had intended it.

At the Hague in September 1920, [writes Sachs] Freud called six of us together [Karl Abraham, Max Eitingon and Sachs of Berlin, Rank of Vienna, Ferenczi of Budapest, and Jones of London] and unfolded a plan. "Henceforth we would form a coordinated, anonymous group whose duty would be to direct the ever-widening movement by joining together and acting according to preconcerted plans." All of us accepted the plan with enthusiasm. It gave to a practical, commonsense arrangement the spice of a schoolboys' secret society—just enough of it to make it attractive without becoming ridiculous.

Retrospectively, the idea of a secret cabinet seems to have been ill-advised, to say the least. Its purpose to direct the use of a body of scientific knowledge could, of course, not be carried out. Despite the fact that America already had forged to the front as a center of psychoanalytic activity, Freud included no American among the chosen ringwearers. Although Freud said in 1926 to Max Eastman that John Dewey "is one of the few men in the world for whom I have a high regard," [2] perhaps he realized that the American experiential psychology of Dewey left little leeway for authoritarian regulation and that the distance and the previous course of development of psychoanalysis in America would not be favorable to any control from Europe. Of course the whole scheme soon proved unfeasible. Within a few years (1924) the trusted Otto Rank had publicized widely his intention to direct psychoanalysis into channels not approved by the cabinet chosen by Freud. Also without consultation with the Ring, he advanced a theory that neurotic symptoms were caused by the trauma of birth.

Not long thereafter Ferenczi published what many consider his most important work, *Versuch eine Genitaltheorie*. He also began his defection from Freud by openly adopting a more lenient and personal attitude toward the patient during analysis.

[2] Eastman, Max: *Heroes I Have Known*. Simon & Schuster, New York, 1942, p. 267.

In commenting on this in his obituary of Ferenczi, Freud writes, "His need to heal and help had become imperious. Probably he had set himself aims that today are not to be reached with our therapeutic means." [3]

Although psychoanalysts continue to refer to "classical" or traditional analysis in their writings, it is not so simple to say just what is covered by these terms. If they mean by this an attempt to uncover unconscious childhood memories and trace back the formation of the patient's reactions in terms of libidinal investment, by the method of free association, with the patient lying on a couch for periods of fifty-five minutes five times a week, this was Freud's method with me. But like any method, its minute to minute application depends on the person in charge and the character of the object to which it is applied.

After my analysis had been in progress for about two weeks, during which I gave profuse memories of my life, many dreams, and rattled off associations easily, Freud said to me, "What shall I do with you—you have no neurosis." The number of hours Freud had devoted to me when he made this comment was more than double that which I had spent with Federn seven years before. His opinion differed from Federn's, that there was "a bit of neurosis." The inference to be drawn is that the criteria of these two psychoanalysts as to what constitutes a neurosis or a neurotic manifestation did not agree. To this very day the definition of neurosis and the appraisal of neurotic behavior fluctuates tremendously, not only with psychiatrists and analysts of the many so-called "schools of thought," but also at different times and in different localities with those following any one system. None of us relishes the idea of harboring a neurosis, because of its origin in an unconscious sense of guilt, and I would have wholeheartedly subscribed to the opinion of Freud even had he not been the master.

[3] Freud, Sigmund: "In Memoriam S. Ferenczi," *International Journal of Psychoanalysis*, Vol. 14, 1934, p. 299.

I believe that had not I been an established analyst presenting myself to Freud as a student to learn more of his theory, he would have quit with me then and there. As it was, we continued to work with no definitive objective but with the analysis of my problems and personality, certain characteristics in which, such as stubbornness, passivity and persistency, ambition, envy, procrastination, improvidence, if tenaciously indulged might act as a detriment to effectiveness in social adaptation or in work.

Many years later when Paul Federn had come permanently to New York and I told him at a luncheon what Freud had said about the absence of neurosis in my case, he exclaimed, "Just think, in those days we knew nothing of character analysis." This had become a popular psychoanalytic term for people who were not well adjusted but showed no outstanding incapacitating symptoms. Be that as it may, my own analysis continued for one hundred hours, at that time considered adequate as a didactic analysis for a physician in no great conflict about his course in life.

During my anticipatory "character analysis" Freud may have been less meticulous in following his prescribed technique than he would had he been dealing with a severe neurosis. At the time it was still considered desirable to conduct the analysis with the patient undergoing periods of sexual abstinence with the idea of bringing out latent anxiety. Freud did not suggest this denial to me, nor did he forbid me anything in the way of recreation or amusements, or ask me to undertake any assignment which might have evoked latent anxiety or repressed resentment toward him. However, from some of my American colleagues under analysis at the same time, I learned that Freud did use active therapy, such as sending a man who feared the dead to visit a cemetery at midnight. On occasion his activity in therapy showed itself in biting criticism of the analysand's lack of cooperation in the analysis or his conduct outside of it.

After about three months the analysis lagged until it came

almost to a dead halt. Then I remarked to the Professor, "If you touch a fox terrier with a pin point, he jumps. When you have a rhinoceros like me, you've got to use a spear." He responded only with his characteristic dry chuckle but did not choose to resort to either active therapy or increased activity in his conduct toward me. Indeed the Professor remained consistently impersonal in his attitude, and this I think may have militated against the development of a feeling of warmth for him.

On the other hand, at times he became communicative and talked over questions of general interest with me on the level of colleagues. Some of his remarks may be recorded almost verbatim, so clearly do they stand out in my mind. Speaking of the social handicaps and precarious position of the Jews, the pitiable victim of which he was later destined to become under the Nazi persecution, he said, "It is a great misfortune to be born a Jew but it is better not to evade it."

Throughout the five months Freud hardly ever made a reference about himself or his family nor did his voice take on a friendly tone. Perhaps he was bored generally by having such a heavy and possibly unstimulating schedule. In view of the anxieties from which he had so long suffered, graphically described in his letters to Fliess, it may be that this impersonality acted as a protective armor against his own uncertainties and the unwelcome intrusions of the daily and analytic routine into his far more important scientific work and prolific writing.

Only on one occasion did he show anxiety, and this might well have been realistically valid fear. On a cold day in December, 1921 the desperate poor people of Vienna rioted, and in a frenzied outburst smashed windows of the well-stocked stores in the fashionable Kärntner Strasse, and plundered and looted them. I had been at an auction at the time to buy some Dürer prints and only learned of the riots when I came out. The taxi driver told me he would have to make a detour around the riot scene (Unruhen) in the center of the city in driving me to my hour with the Professor.

Dr. Freud appeared agitated and pale when he ushered me into the office. As soon as I had lain down he said with a quivering voice, "I hear there have been riots in town." I replied that I had heard so, too, and began with free associations on other subjects. That evening I went around to some of the taverns in the neighborhood to try to find out what it was all about. I heard plenty of loud complaints about the miserable conditions in Vienna but only one explanation: "That fellow Wilson (or sometimes the damned Americans) with his fourteen points is responsible for it all." However, what surprised me most was Freud's unwonted tone of astonishment and alarm in his voice when I told him of my tour of investigation at the hour with him the next day. "What," he commented, "you went out that night alone?" Possibly Freud may have thought my curiosity to have been foolhardy or stupid. He appeared to have little patience with dullness and stupidity in any form. One day he remarked, "Stupidity and sickness are the most costly things in the world; when they are combined in one person it becomes almost hopeless."

Many anecdotes are told of Freud's sharp wit and laconic replies, one of which has to do with what Freud may have regarded as typical American stuff and nonsense. An American physician making a rapid tour of European medical centers, registering for a brief course here and there, to return to a small town as a specialist, had obtained an appointment with Freud. When the latter met him at the door, he began cheerfully, "Dr. Freud, I am Dr. Smith of Plainville, Ohio. I have heard so much about you, so I wanted to see you, shake hands and have a few words with you before returning to my country." Freud looked at him appraisingly and with one gesture and two words filled all of the visitor's requests. He grasped his hand and said "Pleasant journey" in less time than it has taken me to tell it.

Frequently Freud voiced his distrust of America and American customs and standards, although during his brief visit in 1909 he really saw very little of America—even of New York.

He particularly disapproved of the subservience of American men to their womenfolk, concerning which I think he had a distorted notion. He criticized sharply the tendencies of American analysts to ally themselves with psychiatry and medicine in general and had sensed the opposition in America to his own position.

Some disagreement existed at this time (1922) between Freud and Brill, his staunchest protagonist in America. When it began, how deep it went, or why it occurred I never learned. Certainly they were far apart on the question of lay analysts. Be that as it may, shortly after beginning the analysis when I remarked that Brill, like other American analysts, had not used the couch, Freud said in annoyance, "In this important matter, too, he has deviated." On the other hand it was evident that Freud had become impressed with Horace Frink's talents as an analyst and his devotion to "classical" analytic procedure. Here was an American, born and bred, who had mastered Freud's theory and could be relied upon to follow it implicitly in practice.

At that time Freud regarded anxiety as a manifestation of free-floating (sexual) libido. As an illustration of his emphasis on sexual fulfillment as an essential to happiness, as compared with the effect of the culture and social patterns, I may refer to the following incident. He had analyzed simultaneously an analyst and a woman who had been the former's patient. They had fallen in love with each other. Both were well known to me. One day while I was lying on the couch, Freud said to me in a tone of satisfaction, "Dr. X and Mrs. Y have been married in America." Basing my reply on a personal knowledge of their backgrounds, social aspirations, and ambitions, I answered, "That will never work out. Their aims in life are so different." And Freud replied, "But not if she is satisfied sexually." I answered, "Even so." But the point was not argued further.

Long before his death Freud's position as one of the most fertile and versatile minds of all time had been firmly established. The scope of his conceptions of unconscious mentation, which he had intrepidly worked out and modestly offered to medicine, had come to touch and clarify nearly every phase of human endeavor. Further, he had expressed these ideas in a prose so clear, powerful, and imaginative that it had won for him one of the highest distinctions for a German writer, the Goethe prize in literature. He and his collaborators had proven that the method that he had developed could become an instrument of amazing force in aiding innumerable persons suffering from disordered thinking to become more sound, effective, and happy.

At least two American physicians who were in analysis with Freud some ten years later have reported their experiences, Doctors Joseph Wortis of New York and Roy R. Grinker of Chicago. Both were analyzed by Freud in the last decade of his life. Their impressions are no doubt influenced by their personal reactions to the Professor, but to each Freud seems to have freely voiced opinions about persons, psychoanalytic trends, and current events.

Both record that at this time, when Freud was about seventy-eight, he "often made disparaging remarks about America and Americans" and about American women, whom he described as a phenomenon going against culture ("eine kulturwidrige Erscheinung").[4] Grinker states that "Freud did not forget or forgive easily" and that when he was sick and unhappy at Putnam's Adirondack camp, he received no more sympathy for his intestinal cramps than "that's too bad." He still blamed Americans for their lenient reception of Jung's efforts to soft-pedal the personal unconscious and the sexual factors in psychoanalytic theory.[5]

More than a decade has passed since Freud's death. Like many other truly extraordinary men, Freud as a person is becoming a

[4] Wortis, Joseph: "Fragments of a Freudian Analysis," *American Journal of Orthopsychiatry*, Vol. X, p. 843.
[5] Grinker, Roy R.: "Reminiscences of a Personal Contact with Freud," *American Journal of Orthopsychiatry*, Vol. X, p. 850.

figure as controversial as his theories were during his lifetime. Several studies have appeared, such as Fritz Wittel's *Freud and His Time* [6] written nearly twenty years before the death of the subject. In recent years (1947) we have had Emil Ludwig's envious criticism of Freud, who dared to invade Ludwig's own field, biography, with new criteria, such as he applied in his study of Leonardo da Vinci. Ludwig's book, *Doctor Freud*,[7] was closely followed (1947) by Helen W. Puner's gossipy attempt to apply Freud's own methods to explain an inscrutable man whom many met but few came to know intimately.[8] Although Freud had protested on several occasions that there was no need for people to interest themselves in his personality and that only his work should be examined, an early and analytically gifted collaborator of Freud, Siegfried Bernfeld, now of San Francisco, has sought to clarify the origin of Freud's genius through careful research into his early intrafamilial relationships. The value of all these biographies has been immeasurably lessened by the hitherto unsuspected personal revelations in the previously mentioned letters of Freud to Fliess, published in 1950. Surely many "lives" of Freud will follow, now fortified by the study of his self-analysis, one of which so clearly documented that it will become authoritative.

Another outsider who came into close contact with Freud not many years before his death was Olem Nemon, the Yugoslav sculptor, for whom Freud posed in many sittings beginning in 1933. An intimate friendship developed between them. Nemon describes Freud at the beginning of the sittings as "sulky and distant" but later more communicative. Nemon first showed the statue to the famed man's maid, who offered the criticism that he had made the Professor look too cross.

---

[6] Wittels, Fritz: *Freud and His Time*. Liveright Publishing Co., New York, 1931.

[7] Ludwig, Emil: *Dr. Freud*. Hellman, Williams & Co., New York, 1948.

[8] Puner, Helen Walker: *Freud & His Mind*. Howell, Soskin Publishers, Inc., New York, 1947.

When Nemon related this to Freud, he commented, "But I am cross. I am cross with mankind." When the statue, which now stands in the New York Psychoanalytic Institute, was finally finished, Freud regarded it closely and made one of his characteristic laconic comments: "I am glad you made me look sufficiently cross."

9. Theoretical and Practical Status of Psychoanalysis at the Beginning of the Third Decade

During the ten years of the practice of psychoanalysis before going to Vienna I had had a gratifying number of successes, some of them quite startling. This may have been beginner's luck. I ascribed these good results exclusively to the theory and method of psychoanalysis, not to any aptitude on my part in handling patients. The favorable outcome of those days was due at least partially to my enthusiasm and conviction of success, which may have been conveyed to the patient and unconsciously absorbed by him. The stay in Vienna gave me ample time for reflection and aroused my first serious scepticism about the possibilities of the mighty psychoanalytic process to achieve results in the conditions for which it seemed particularly designed, compulsion neuroses and phobias. Possibly at the beginning I was far too enthusiastic at having an implement at my disposal so vastly superior to the vichy-siphon, the weirdly crackling static electricity machines of the New York dispensaries, or the stereotyped prescription of ten drops of tincture of nux vomica before and a teaspoonful of a mixture of triple bromides after meals given almost indiscriminately to every patient who was nervous or neurasthenic.

I had a similar feeling of futility about the use of hypnosis. Symptoms that would often vanish quickly and completely under direct suggestion would reappear after a few days. They could usually be dissipated again by fresh hypnotic suggestion to which the patient often became disastrously habituated. A particularly pathetic example was a callow young man of thirty, who had become a professional hypnotic subject for stage hypnotists who gave demonstrations of this phenomenon in vaudeville performances. He had developed the capacity for autohypnosis during which he would involuntarily become amnestic and "lose himself" for days and weeks.

Perhaps my expectations from psychoanalysis may have been unjustifiably sanguine. I may also sometimes have unconsciously underestimated how far my therapeutic results fell short of the ideal of structural personality changes set by psychoanalysis. Here I am reminded of a comment made to me some ten years ago by a former president of the New York Psychoanalytic Society, who nostagically remarked, "I wish that I might again have the good results with patients which I attained when I did not know so much psychoanalysis." Perhaps any procedure if it becomes too codified leads to classifications, receipts, and formulas, which in turn tend to produce stagnation and routine.

Whatever shortcomings I had in curing patients by psychoanalysis before going to Vienna, I attributed to my inexperience and not to any flaw in the postulate that neurotic symptoms resulted from unconscious factors and that they would disappear when these factors were made conscious, intelligently interpreted to the patient, and thoroughly worked through. The more experienced physicians of Vienna, through their continued contact with Freud, versed in handling resistance and transference, would surely know how to avoid disturbing situations which had appeared in my own psychoanalyses. However, I found that these men, too, were confronted with insurmountable difficulties similar to one which had developed in a patient just before this trip abroad.

A young married woman had been referred to me because

of mild depression, indifference to her baby and home, and dissatisfaction with her marriage of three years' duration. She improved quickly on the basis of a positive transference, and the progress continued until the investigation of her frigidity disclosed her strong, mainly unconscious homosexuality. She reacted to the examination of this intolerable sexual component by a severe depression during which she became retarded in her thinking, self-accusing, and so inaccessible that further psychological treatment was quite impossible. After a brief hospitalization the depression lifted and she regained her norm.

When I returned from Vienna I found this patient, now no longer depressed, eager to resume analysis. I hesitated and warned her husband and her family physician that further analysis might result in another depressive reaction. She and her husband wanted "this thing cleared up." I proceeded with the utmost caution in the treatment, but as soon as homosexuality appeared in her dreams, possibly activated by the treatment, she became profoundly depressed and was again hospitalized for half a year. As a postscript it may be recorded that she recovered from this depression also, but it recurred in a mild form about seven years later. This time I refused to treat her analytically and another psychiatrist cared for her successfully by the usual supportive measures.

Theoretically, then as today, such a result should and could have been avoided by postponing to a more propitious moment any consideration of the homosexuality, although it seemed a powerful force responsible for her neurotic unhappiness in marriage.

Unfavorable responses to therapy such as this were seldom, if ever, described in the clinical cases reported in the *Zeitschrift für Aerztliche Psychoanalyse* or the *Psychoanalytic Review*. This tendency to withhold the publication of unsatisfactory results persists in current psychoanalytic journals, although it would seem quite as important scientifically to examine the instances in which we fail as those in which we succeed. A careful review and discussion of such cases might eventually provide us with new insights into the weaknesses of psychoanalysis as a science and its therapeutic limitations.

Even as I write this book (1953) a similar problem confronts me. About five years ago I undertook to analyze an extremely intelligent and cultured woman of thirty for a compulsion to eat, "stuff in food," even after her appetite had been satisfied. An unhappy marital situation existed because of her husband's absorption in his research work in nuclear energy and his neglect of his wife. I interpreted the compulsive intake of food as a substitute for the lack of love, following a pattern in childhood when her mother was "mean" to her. Through analysis of the origin of the patient's scorn of her husband's intelligence and the use of her mind as a weapon of offense against her husband, a great improvement in their love relationship occurred. But this change did not decrease the intermittent overeating with its embarrassing obesity.

At Vienna the clannishness of the psychoanalytic group and their slight participation in medical affairs as compared with that of American analysts surprised me. Possibly this was not of their choosing. So far as I remember, only Paul Schilder had an appointment as docent at the medical school. The appreciation in America of the value of psychoanalysis for the clarification of psychiatric situations appeared far greater than in Vienna. An annotated bibliography of American articles and books on psychoanalysis for the years 1920–22 contains over 250 titles and a list of 7 translations of 7 books by Freud, Kolnai, Sadger, and Stekel.[1]

I also became acutely aware of two paradoxes, one of which involved the newly endorsed analysis of the analyst. It became apparent that unless the latter suffers from some urgent conflict it is difficult for him to tap those important forces which blend to make up his personality but which are only partially con-

---

[1] Frink, H. W.: "Die Amerikanische Psychoanalytische Literatur," *Internationale Zeitschrift für Psychoanalyse*, Vol. 10, 1924, pp. 57–86.

scious to him. Hence the prospective analyst, of whom a thorough analysis was now demanded, could not be too normal but must be afflicted with a persistent (and neurotic) conflict sufficiently burdensome to induce him to wish seriously to change his personality.

On the other hand, it is questionable whether a very deep psychoanalysis can thoroughly alter the structure of a severely neurotic personality. This later became apparent in at least one of the New York physicians under analysis with Freud in 1922, and was probably realized by Freud at the time. With the benefit of our increased experience we screen this type of candidate today and he is likely to be rejected by the Admission Board of an accredited psychoanalytic institute as unsuited to become an analyst. Even a long personal analysis probably would not free this physician from distortions and fixations that seriously impair his capacity for the interpretation of transference, resistance, and identification, basic elements in psychoanalytic therapy.

A second paradox or inconsistency I noted in Vienna concerned the rule, uncompromisingly followed by most of Freud's colleagues, that the patient be seen six times a week. Any interruption would affect progress toward cure. If this continuity were as important as it was asserted to be, it seemed incredible to me that when the doctor (or possibly even the doctor's wife) decided on a certain date for his summer vacation, that all his patients at that time could safely dispense with this continuum. At times I had twinges of conscience at having interrupted the analysis of all my cases so indiscriminately when I came abroad for six months. The fact that upon my return to America none of my patients seemed to have suffered very great relapse through my absence lessened my belief in the need for daily visits by all patients.

I found also that considerable disagreement on theory and practice persisted in the Freudian group, even after the major dissidents—Stekel, Adler, and Jung—had gone their independent ways. Soon, too, I heard for the first time a witticism that the colleagues seemed particularly to relish: "die Nach-Analyse der Analyse," the second analysis with another analyst after the first or original analysis had been presumably completed. The Viennese masters had not been able to avoid unsatisfactory outcomes any more than the relative novices in New York. Although this unfortunate fact gave me a certain malevolent consolation, it proved disquieting to my fond hope that psychoanalysis would invariably and unquestionably benefit appropriate cases. Perhaps this is too much to expect of any form of medical treatment.

When I remarked upon this discomforting fact to Freud during an analytic hour, he reverted to an anecdote, a device with which he was fond of illustrating his ideas. In a small Galician village where Jews were not allowed to own dogs, a Jewish man came to the rabbi complaining, perhaps as I had to Freud, that the dogs of his Christian neighbors snapped and bit him when he passed down the village street. The rabbi after long consultation with the Talmud and deep deliberation announced, "If dogs attack you, lie down on the ground and pretend that you are dead." On the next occasion when the dogs came at him yelping and snarling, the man promptly flung himself in the dust of the road and simulated death. Nevertheless the dogs bit him so viciously that he jumped up and ran to the rabbi indignantly telling him what had happened and asking him to explain the failure, in practice, of his advice. Then the latter said, "Yes, you know that is the way to deceive the dogs, and I know it, but the dogs don't know it." An explanation of this type did not solve the therapeutic problem of influencing the "unruly dogs" in the patient's unconscious to live at peace with those conscious forces, the severe censors, which attempted to suppress them. It seemed to beg the question.

About 1920 many of the foremost analysts thought, as some do today, that the remedy for these disappointing therapeutic situations lay in longer treatment and deeper penetration into the unconscious. However, I was not convinced that better results would necessarily follow. I remained in doubt about the best way of avoiding and overcoming those periods of standstill that are so trying in therapy for the physician and for the patient.

In all discussions Freud seemed to regard the therapeutic results of analysis of secondary importance to determining the origin and structure of the illness. Possibly this may reflect Freud's first interests after graduation from medical school, which were not therapeutic. With all his absorption in psychological impacts as a cause for dysfunction, he never forgot the earlier lessons of physiology and biology. In the light of recent advances in endocrinology, one of his comments upon the influence of glandular secretion on character development and mental illness—especially schizophrenia—is significant: "Let the biologists go as far as they can," he said, "and let us [the psychoanalysts] go as far as we can—some day the two will meet." A prophecy which each year appears a trifle nearer fulfillment.

The analysis of dreams was and is regarded as the most reliable road to the understanding of a patient's unconscious. Some questions about the wish-fulfillment element in dreams had already arisen during my analytic sessions with Maeder in Zurich, in 1914, who pictured them as smoke indicating which way the winds of the unconscious were blowing. My own ability to analyze dreams was weak—a weakness in my psychoanalytic approach. I relied then and do now upon unconscious verbalizations or actions that patients report as having impressed them as unintentional and/or contrary to their desires or advantages.

My difficulties and doubts with dream interpretation came to the surface with Freud. Without going into detail, I will say that at the time of the analysis I had been concerned for ten years or more with a definite problem about which I had made no decision. My dreams during analysis were profuse, usually well remembered, and presented for interpretation at the beginning of each session. Many of these dreams were obviously concerned with my immediate problem and whatever their manifest or latent content revealed, Freud said that the affect that accompanied the dream disclosed the true feeling. Basing his interpretation on content and affect of those dreams Freud said that I would act positively; that I would act negatively; and that I would let the matter drift. In other words the dreams indicated that the unconscious also harbored the only three possible solutions. Freud offered me no opinion or advice on the actual problem confronting me and I did not ask him.

Thirty years later the function and interpretation of the dream remains something of an enigma. Attempts are being made to reconstruct the motives that activate the patient's behavior and dreams, the function of the trauma dream to express a need for punishment,[2] the significance of the blank dream.[3]

The presence of so many foreign analysts in Vienna led to the organization of courses. So far as I know they were given for the first time and were among the beginnings of systematic instruction in psychoanalysis, although the Berlin Psychoanalytic Poliklinik, established in 1920, had immediately instituted teaching. The Viennese group spared no pains to make these presentations instructive for the American visitors. The terminology of the vital interplay of instinctive drives and censorship differed from the rather artificial categories of the id, the ego, and superego. Just then such topics as narcissism, "the unconscious," the libido theory's application to neuroses and psychoses, regression, and psychological economics occupied much attention. Among the lecturers were such inspiring teachers as Paul Federn, Ludwig Jekels, Edward Hitschmann, Siegfried Bernfeld, Otto Fenichel—also Otto Rank—all of whom

[2] Wisdom, J. O.: "A Hypothesis to Explain the Trauma Reenactment Dream," *International Journal of Psychoanalysis*, Vol. XX, 1949, p. 15.

[3] Lewin, Bertram D.: "Mania and Sleep," *Psychoanalytic Quarterly*, Vol. XVIII, 1949.

later came to America, and Ferenczi. As a result of these courses the American physicians returned to New York with new ideals for instruction in psychoanalysis.

One idea that all of the analysands took away with them as a result of their analytic experience—perhaps the only one common to them all—was that they would forthwith add a more or less comfortable couch to the fittings in their offices. This piece of furniture has since become emblematic of the psychoanalyst and has found its way into the offices of doctors and laymen whose knowledge of the subject does not go beyond a smattering of terms.

I am not sure that the couch should be used invariably or insisted upon continuously with the same patient. Face to face communication is more realistic when advice, direct suggestions, or orders are introduced into the therapeutic process to supplement free association and interpretation. This is now being admitted by some training analysts who advocate greater flexibility. Protective and convenient as the couch may be for the doctor, it is not the essence of psychoanalytic therapy, and at times far from having the positive value ascribed to it, it may act as a deterrent to the patient's cooperation by indulging his tendencies to submission and retreat.

My own analysis ended after one hundred hours on February 1, 1922. From the experience, I think that there is a disadvantage in having an analysis conducted far from the place where one resides. The impact of the daily occurrences in the habitual environment is missing; the freedom from the daily round of obligations and duties tends to weaken the need for change. Similarly the thrusts of one's usual competitors and critics, in and out of the family, are not brought forcefully into the analytic situation. Furthermore, the ethical values placed upon various attitudes and incidents that are brought up in an analysis differ in Europe and in the United States, especially in what is considered by the analyst as customary, usual, average, and/or normal. These are extremely important factors in a readjustment, which is the aim of therapy.

I presume that this was especially true during my vacation from the responsibilities of active practice in the winter of 1921 in Vienna. As an American visitor I escaped most of the discomforts that the populace of the desolated city endured from a dearth of food and fuel in a cold and penetratingly damp climate. Leisure from the routine of office and hospital work afforded me a perfect chance to loaf and indulge my interest in the theatre where superior performances of classical and modern plays—Shakespeare and Schnitzler particularly—were being given. There was plenty of time, too, for philosophizing in the chilly cafes where energetic little orchestras continued to play gay Strauss waltzes, unaffected by the shabby surroundings.

Possibly because of this complacency, little that was not previously conscious to me came to the surface, even with a profusion of dreams and an abundance of free associations. Nevertheless, the experience of catharsis, of laying one's inner self bare, of allowing the small, still voices of one's conscience to become audible to an impersonal and expert outsider for a critique of one's tendencies and attitudes, is in itself invaluable and unforgettable. Unlike the confessional of the Catholic Church, psychoanalysis offers not an absolution from guilt but rather a dissolution of it. In times of doubt and stress throughout the rest of one's life one is likely to find oneself reverting back to the analysis for reorientation—and in my case with the wondrous figure of Freud to make it vital.

Retrospectively I am unable to say to what extent my personal analysis improved my technique and efficiency, but I think that it definitely increased my tolerance, insight, and patience with the patient. How much more I might have benefited had Freud accepted my suggestion and launched a direct attack on my defense of smugness, or had I continued in analysis with the technique he preferred for another hundred or two hundred hours, I cannot venture to guess. But of this I am sure, neither Freud nor I would have assented to a more prolonged analysis at the time. I think that my restricted imagination and cautious, factual attitude to psychoanalysis, due in part at least to a clinical experience with it for over ten years, and my eagerness for therapeutic results, did not appeal to Freud. When, at the end of the last hour we said good-bye, it was with his analytic reserve, impersonal handshake, and the parting words: "Wir haben keinen Groll"—perhaps best translated: "We harbor no hard feeling."

If my candor has been excessive or attitude critical, neither has vitiated my belief that psychoanalysis nearly always is helpful and only very rarely is harmful to a patient. Nor are they inconsistent with adherence to this method as the first choice in mental disturbances in which continuous communication with the patient is possible.

10. Stormy Years in Psychoanalysis Under New York Leadership, 1920–1930

Upon my return from Vienna in 1922 I found that interest in psychoanalysis was spreading. It was fostered among young physicians by contacts with psychoanalytically oriented psychotherapy at the outpatient clinics of Vanderbilt and Mount Sinai Hospital in New York and at St. Elizabeth's Hospital in Washington. However, Manhattan State Hospital and Cornell, where Dr. Foster Kennedy, a highly gifted neurologist, who was superseding Dr. Dana, and whose scepticism about psychoanalysis had always been intense, had practically ceased to be instruction centers.

Thus during one of my very first contacts with Dr. Dana at Cornell, he told me that during my absence abroad he had proposed my name for an appointment as an Assistant Professor in the Department of Neurology but that it had been rejected by the faculty. When I inquired the reason of Dr. Walter Niles, the Dean of the Medical School, who I think was well disposed toward me as a person, he replied, "Advancement is made not on the basis of what a man has contributed to our teaching in the past, but upon his promise for the future and you are a psychoanalyst. A psychoanalyst has no place in an undergraduate medical school."

The position of the medical faculty, disappointing as it was to me at the time, retrospectively appears to have had back of it considerable validity. The ideology of psychoanalysis, primarily in its sexual emphases, was so far out of line with the cultural, especially the religious, attitudes of most students that they could not possibly accept it. To introduce them abruptly into such an unaccustomed approach, so divergent from the biological concepts prevalent in the rest of their training, could only serve to perplex and bewilder most of them. Indeed there may be something to be said in favor of a moderate degree of "cultural lag" in academic instruction.

To illustrate this state of psychological unpreparedness for psychoanalytic thinking of a large proportion of the student body: On one occasion I mentioned in a lecture that the sight of the genitals of an exhibitionist who suddenly exposed himself was a factor in the development of an hysterical eye symptom in a young woman. Two women students, much offended by this remark, at once submitted a formal complaint to the dean's office, which agreed emphatically with their point of view. And one of my students, now herself an analyst, whom I met at a dinner party some five years after her graduation, scornfully asked me how I could believe such rubbish as I had presented to my classes.

Twenty-five years of dissemination and cultivation of psychoanalysis had to pass before medical schools were ready to include it officially and extensively in their curricula. Today some of the most prominent schools in the East, such as Cornell, Harvard, Johns Hopkins, and Pennsylvania, remain lukewarm to psychoanalysis, although many resident physicians in their psychiatric hospitals have subsequently rounded out their training at psychoanalytic institutes.

The discouragement to my hopes for promotion and university prestige upset me keenly at the time, but like some other disappointments that have come to me, it did not prove to be disadvantageous in the end. Certainly it did not lead to any great professional hardship as might have been the case in a similar situation in Germany, France, or Austria.

Retrospectively it has seemed to me that failure in the fulfillment of consciously cherished goals often is the result of an unconscious desire not to succeed in them in spite of the disappointment and regret at the time. Failures, which a person laments deeply, may allow him to proceed freely in the course nearer his heart's desire. In this instance the apparent setback in my career relieved me from any further allegiance or duty to neurology, to which I would have felt obligated had I been advanced at Cornell. My failure, perhaps unconsciously engineered, permitted me to invest all my endeavor in psychoanalysis, which I found vitally absorbing.

The group of analysts who had been analyzed in Vienna established a pattern that made a personal analysis almost obligatory for professional recognition. The completion of a didactic analysis (as it was then called) rapidly came to be regarded as the essence of training in psychoanalysis, a certificate of efficiency in therapeutic psychoanalysis, a badge of orthodoxy. The student (prospective analyst) made arrangements for such an analysis with an analyst of his choice, and before long certain men who had acquired a reputation for the leniency and speed of their analyses were apt to be sought by candidates looking for an easy way of meeting a still unofficial requirement.

In due course the quality and length of many such analyses began to be questioned when the student presented himself for admission to the New York Psychoanalytic Society or the American Psychoanalytic Association. Nevertheless, a didactic analysis over a regulated period by an officially recognized senior analyst did not become a requisite for admission to the New York Society until about 1929. The fact, however, that the applicant had shown sufficient interest to submit to an analysis at all, redounded to his favor when his name came up for membership, and the qualification assumed increasing professional importance as the years passed.

Marking the inception of educational activities in New York

(and America), lectures and courses, modelled after the series initiated in Vienna in 1921-22 for the New Yorkers studying there, were arranged for younger members of the New York Society and other physicians in the fall of 1922. The first small Educational Committee to direct training was appointed during the following year under my chairmanship.

Meanwhile, the course of psychoanalysis, at that time largely identified with the activity of the New York group, had not been running smoothy. The analyses of the Americans who had gone to Vienna and Berlin instead of creating harmony, in some instances fostered such discord that for a time (1922-24) it threatened the Society's existence. In 1925 I noted: "Dissensions partly of a personal character, partly due to divergence of opinions on questions of theory and technique, early led to the withdrawal from the organization of several physicians earnestly interested in the subject." [1] Particularly acrimonious were the arguments on the Society's policy concerning the scientific requirements for new members, especially the question of compulsory analysis. This proposal to make such analysis a compulsory requirement for membership was rejected on the ground that any student who became sufficiently interested in analysis would appreciate the desirability of didactic analysis and seek it from his own conviction.

When Frink returned to New York in 1923, he conducted himself as though he had been designated the leader of psychoanalysis in the city—perhaps in America. I have no means of knowing whether this was so, but from the unstinted praise with which Freud had spoken to me of Frink, from Freud's aim to direct the destinies of the psychoanalytic world that has since become clear from the disclosure of his formation of the trusted "Ring" circle, and from the open dissatisfaction with which Freud viewed American psychoanalysis, I think it is likely that Frink may have been encouraged in this direction.

---

[1] Oberndorf, C. P.: "History of the Psychoanalytic Movement in America," *Psychoanalytic Review*, Vol. XV, July, 1927, p. 203.

It began with a scathing review of Brill's recently published book *Basic Principles of Psychoanalysis*. At all events, the New York Society, unaccustomed to this type of supervision, was thrown into a rebellious turmoil. Frink's breakdown, which incapacitated him shortly after his return from his second visit to Freud and from which he never completely recovered, removed all immediate possibility of remote control from Vienna. Frink's illness also deprived American psychoanalysis of one of its most gifted and devoted exponents.

The general political uneasiness and theoretical unclarities that confronted the New York Psychoanalytic Society were increased by the appearance in 1923 of a contribution by Freud which has had an enormous bearing on psychoanalytic procedure, namely, *Das Ich und das Es* (*The Ego and the Id*). It marked the development of the third decade of psychoanalysis. Freud adopted the term "id" from Georg Groddeck, who in 1923 had published *The Book of the Id* (*Das Buch vom Es*). In *The Ego and the Id* (*Das Ich und das Es*), Freud defined three categories of the psychic apparatus, called in English the id, the ego, and the superego. The terms and the concepts they represent were almost immediately adopted into psychoanalytic writing and thinking. The id embraces those drives that are instinctual; the ego develops as a result of modifications in the psychic system produced through contact of such primary impulses with the outer world. Gradually, the ego finds itself in a difficult position, attempting to adapt itself to demands thrust upon it by the restless, relentless id and by insistent, inescapable, external impacts. To these threats to the ego are added those patterns of conduct considered exemplary. Such patterns are gradually acquired from parents or parent representatives who continuously demand that the ego perform according to the ethical and moral standards considered appropriate and that these be incorporated and adopted by the person as his own (the superego).

Prior to the introduction of this new nomenclature into the

psychoanalytic vocabulary, the terms conscious and unconscious had been almost synonymous with conscience and instinct. The conscience, a guiding and repressing force analogous to the censor, now became the superego; the unbridled and ruthless instinctive drives and cravings were now called the id. Freud, by this time engrossed in problems of metapsychology and postulating a death instinct, never fully clarified his concept of the function of the ego. The psychology of the ego continues, after twenty-five years, the basis for much controversy among investigative psychoanalysts.

The new terms, for better or for worse, became familiar and popular. Some psychoanalysts seemed to regard these categories as concrete, circumscribed entities confined by definitive borders like a map in geography. The mind became departmentalized like a store: notions and hardware in the basement, general merchandise on the ground floor, promotion and administration above. The existence of a continuous interplay between these divisions became obscured. To some extent the new idea of levels began to weaken the established dynamic concept that the mental apparatus is always in flux.

In one of his last books, *Freud's Contribution to Psychiatry*, based upon the Salmon lectures which he delivered at the New York Academy of Medicine in 1943, A. A. Brill states that when he expressed his admiration to Freud upon reading *Das Ich und das Es* just after it appeared, Freud replied, "I am glad that you like it—one can be a first class analyst without reading it." Ferenczi made almost the identical comment to me at Innsbruck in 1927 and of course all the earliest fundamental contributions to psychoanalysis rest on the study of libidinal factors and their modification by the individual's needs and attitudes.

In the same book Brill ventures the opinion that psychoanalysis was "practically speaking a finished product when I became acquainted with it [in 1907]." Although the latter statement may be tenable for much of the Freudian theory and although Freud's remark is undoubtedly correctly quoted, these basic principles did not include Freud's valuable additions to the structure of psychoanalysis, notably his revision of the concept of anxiety and the defenses against it, which constitute such an important factor in all forms of neurotic illness from simple hysterical conversion symptoms to the most profound type of mental disintegration such as is observed in catatonic schizophrenia.

In Freud's last really important clinical book, *Hemmung, Symptom und Angst* (*Inhibition, Symptom and Anxiety*), which appeared in 1926,[2] he used the terms superego, ego, and id freely in his discussion of the dynamics of symptom formation. Here, instead of regarding anxiety as a manifestation of repressed but free-floating sexual libido, as he did before, Freud thought it to be a signal of danger threatening the individual particularly from within himself but also from the world without. At times it may be difficult to distinguish the latter from a normal fear reaction.

These rapid changes in psychoanalytic theory, which inevitably affected training and opened to question the qualifications of new members, created one critical situation after another in the New York Psychoanalytic Society. From 1911 to 1925 the office of president rotated among the members of the Society. With the appearance of these diverse complexities Brill again assumed control and was president from 1925 to 1936. With the extension of these controversies to national scope, Brill was reelected President of the American Psychoanalytic Association in 1929 and held this office concurrently until 1936.

The agitation in the New York Society was beginning to quiet down a bit when Otto Rank appeared in New York. He had been greatly esteemed by Freud because of his contributions to the structure of psychoanalysis from the study of mythology and folklore. Rank, who was not a doctor of medicine, brought with him a brand new psychobiological theory

---

[2] Freud S.: *Hemmung, Symptom und Angst*. Internationale Psychoanalytische Verlag, Wien, 1926.

and a new idea about technique, of which no one had heard in Vienna only three years before. He advanced the idea that the earliest fears of the child are directly traceable to the traumatic impressions connected with his birth. He stated further, that the setting of a time limit for the ending of the analysis would speed therapeutic progress by spurring the patient to cooperate more helpfully. To advocate such a radical technical change in procedure after a period of observation of its results which could not have exceeded three years struck me as a proposal that a trained clinician would not have ventured to present. Although both these speculations found some appeal when first presented in New York and Philadelphia, Rank never gained any substantial support from experienced analysts. Freud went to considerable length to reject the origin of anxiety in the trauma of birth in *Hemmung, Symptom und Angst*.

In the years that followed, Rank's technical proposals practically disappeared from psychoanalytic procedure. Finally, they were questioned even by their originator, who fluctuated widely in emotional swings before his death at the age of fifty-five, in New York City, in September, 1939. Rank eventually took up residence in Paris, but he made frequent trips to the United States, maintaining a close association with a social work group in Philadelphia. His ideas about limiting therapy have left an imprint on the "functional" approach of the Philadelphia School of Social Work, which is reflected in a limited goal therapy in a few psychiatric and child guidance clinics and is used primarily by some social workers in various social agencies. In these settings, after studying a case for a period of time the therapist decides whether and particularly to what extent the patient should be treated. When this point is reached, help is discontinued and the person is placed on his own responsibility.

No matter which theory of psychotherapy a physician follows or what principles and practices are consistent with that system, his own personal needs and experience unconsciously influence the choice of the school in the first place and how closely he subsequently follows it. When it came to Rank's theory that the trauma of birth is responsible for anxiety that in later life gives rise to neurosis, the circumstance of my own birth argued strongly against it. Because of the great difficulties that my mother had had in labor with her previous children, two of whom died shortly after birth, she came to New York from Alabama to be delivered by a famous obstetrician of the day. In applying the forceps he crushed through the temples on both sides of my skull. The bone necrosed and for many months I lingered between life and death. I have been told that I did not raise my head from the pillow until I was a year old. Here was a most severe birth trauma, and yet the anxieties that I have experienced since childhood seem to have been less than the average as I have noted them up to my present time of life, seventy years.

Such a personal experience prompts the thought that the theory of the trauma of birth is still very questionable and that one of the more important bits of research that should be undertaken is to follow up children born in prolonged labor and to determine to what extent they have subsequently developed anxiety neuroses.

From 1925 onward, other European leaders in psychoanalysis, following the precedent of Rank, decided to visit the United States for longer or shorter stays. When Alfred Adler came in 1925, one of his followers arranged a luncheon at which we discussed the differences in Adler's and Freud's approach. I was astonished at the over-simplification of the concept of the structure and therapy of neuroses that Adler had finally evolved.

Knowing of his long-standing interest in the pedagogical aspects of psychoanalysis, I invited Adler to give a talk before the Pleasantville Cottage School, a specialized, residential institution in which a large proportion of the children are emotionally disturbed. During the long drive to the school, I casually remarked to Adler that Freud had broken with Rank. When he heard this, he dramatically clasped his hands and said: "That is the will of God; the little fellow [Rank] always tried to set the old gentleman [Freud] against me!"—a remark which startled me greatly. Still, it is indicative of the rivalries that existed between Freud's followers for his favor and possibly also of a feeling of real regret on Adler's part that he had terminated his own associations with Freud fifteen years before.

Adler eventually settled in New York, where he attracted a limited following. So also did the brilliant Paul Schilder, who had already distinguished himself as a neuropathologist, neurologist, and psychoanalytic psychiatrist on the staff of Wagner Jauregg in Vienna. Among others who came for brief visits were Sandor Ferenczi, who presented a fascinating interpretation of Swift's *Gulliver's Travels*, entitled "Gulliver Phantasies," before the New York Society for Clinical Psychiatry on December 9, 1926, and finally Wilhelm Stekel who arrived unheralded and without representation by adherents in this country.

A further cause of trouble between the Vienna and New York groups arose when nonmedically trained individuals from this country went to Europe to be trained as therapists without first consulting the education committees that had been organized in the two extant American psychoanalytic societies. The training was done on the basis of individual arrangement between instructor and student. The student would return to the United States with letters or certificates attesting the completion of a personal analysis and on that ground feel entitled to be admitted to the New York Psychoanalytic Society or the American Psychoanalytic Association. This situation embarrassed the Society and incensed the laymen, who had spent much effort and money for training and felt that they had somehow been deceived by the Vienna group, or unjustly discriminated against by the New York Society.

The first opportunity to take up these highly charged issues directly with the Europeans occurred in 1925 at the International Psychoanalytic Congress at Bad Homburg, near Frankfort, before the war a fashionable watering resort. It was the first such congress that Freud did not attend, much to the disappointment of many members who had never seen or heard him speak. It was also the first International Congress at which the two American societies were represented officially and at which an appreciable number of their members attended. Here Dr. Max Eitingon, who had selflessly devoted his time and funds to the establishment of the Berlin Psychoanalytic Institute and Poliklinik, reported on the excellent results of the first five years of its operation. Already at that time fifteen instructional (didactic) analyses had been conducted there. Then Karl Abraham, President of the Association, an alert, pleasant man, with none of the soberness that I had come to associate with German professors, supplemented Eitingon's report with a stirring appeal for the organization of similar institutes by analytic societies in other cities. Abraham's convincing plea led to the formation of the International Training Commission, a committee to consist of not more than seven members, one each from the constituent societies of the International Association. Henceforth, the nature and length of the training given to psychoanalysts would no longer be left to private agreement between teacher and student but subjected to the stipulations and supervision by the educational committees of each society, which in turn would be guided by standards regarded as essential by the International Commission.

Five European Societies and the New York Society were at the time sufficiently well advanced with their training of candidates to participate in the International Commission. These, with their Chairmen, were: Austrian—Helena Deutsch; German—Max Eitingon; Hungarian—S. Ferenczi; British—Edward Glover; American—C. P. Oberndorf; and Dutch—J. H. W. van Ophuijsen.

Brill, who had reassumed the presidency of the New York group in 1925, enjoyed leadership. In addition to his enthusiasm, generosity, and indefatigability, he feared no one.[3] He valued sincerity and integrity of the physician in the practice of psychoanalysis equally with ideological interest, which is so often considered identical with scientific method. He stressed the importance of selecting for training those physicians whose ultimate aim was to become clinical analysts. After I told him of the Homburg deliberations, Brill lost no time in appointing a committee to put the European recommendations into operation by organizing additional courses under the auspices of the Society.

From then on in New York, supervised instruction in psychoanalysis replaced the former indeterminate didactic analyses and self-instruction in which each analyst would adopt from the voluminous psychoanalytic writings those features that appealed most to him from experience and inclination. But the new definitive instruction also tended to prescribe certain attitudes, to regulate reading, to codify approaches. Before long this led to disagreement among the instructors on what in the already vast theory should be considered most fundamental, not only in the ever increasing psychoanalytic literature, but also in the continually developing work of Freud himself.

At the Homburg meeting the American position on lay (nonmedical) analysis came for the first time into an open clash with that of Freud and the European groups, particularly the Austrian and Hungarian Societies, which supported him vigorously. At this time the British Society also accepted a very limited number of lay psychoanalysts into its activities.

The development of psychoanalysis in America had not followed the pattern determined by Freud's attitude in Vienna. There, because of the virtual exclusion by the medical profes-

[3] Perhaps nowhere is Brill's colorful individuality better revealed than in his response at a testimonial dinner given in honor of his 70th birthday on October 12, 1944. See *Bulletin* of the American Psychoanalytic Association, Vol. IV, No. 2, May, 1948.

sion under which Freud had suffered for twenty-five years, he turned for acceptance to extra-medical fields allied to that of his main interest, psychology and the structure of the psychical apparatus. Among the philosophers and sociologists he found a scattered but sympathetic support. In 1922 at the fortnightly meetings of the Vienna Psychoanalytic Society, where the regular attendance rarely exceeded twenty, there were among the influential members: Rank, as pointed out earlier, a doctor of philosophy who specialized in comparative anthropologies; Bernfeld and Aichhorn, pedagogues deeply concerned with the mental disturbances in children; Reik, also a doctor of philosophy, a fluent writer, interested in comparative theology; Hanns Sachs, a lawyer with extraordinary knowledge of poetry and history; H. von Hug-Hellmuth, a physician primarily interested in the psychology of childhood, whose book, *Seelen Leben des Kindes* (1913) furnished basic formulations for pedagogic psychotherapy; and also Freud's brilliant and courageous daughter, Anna Freud, once a schoolteacher.

At one time Freud favored establishing an entirely new preparatory course of study for the therapeutic practice of psychoanalysis—a curriculum combining cultural history, philosophy, psychology, and selected subjects in medicine. Freud's conviction of the desirability of including lay analysts as psychotherapists may have been influenced by the high attainments and valuable contributions of the lay members of the group about him, by his hope of developing an entirely distinct specialty of purely psychological medicine, and also by more personal and possibly unconscious reasons.

In the United States as soon as psychoanalytic literature became popularized, many persons, some of them actual quacks, not by any standards as gifted or well-trained in any scientific field as the nonmedical Viennese, to say nothing of their aptitude or ethics, were drawn to the field of psychoanalytic therapy. As typical of flagrant invasion of psychotherapeutics without preparation one may cite Andre Tridon, a journalist suddenly turned psychoanalyst, who in his book *Psychoanalysis and Love* glibly refers to the patients he is treating. In 1918 Brill, Frink, and I, after investigating one of the most notorious operators of this group, found that nothing could be gained by prosecution of these individuals. Far too many cults, religious or otherwise, were practicing medicine under the inexact laws of New York and other states. The person we investigated protected himself by making his bills to the "patient" for "psychological instruction," although he had not qualified as a psychologist or a teacher.

Unlike the Vienna Psychoanalytic Society, the New York Psychoanalytic Society had begun as and still remains a medical organization regarding psychoanalytic therapy strictly as a branch of the practice of medicine. This position it had decided to sustain even to the point of rupture with the International. The controversy over the question of lay analysis became so acute that in 1927 the *International Journal of Psychoanalysis* published a one-hundred-page discussion on the subject, to which twenty-five analysts from various societies were invited to contribute. Among these was Schilder, whose opening sentence, "It seems to me that unquestionably the treatment of the sick is a matter for the physician," reflected the reservations of most of the contributors about the feasibility of the practice of therapy by lay analysts.

In order to collect funds for the establishment of a teaching institute and outpatient clinic to be staffed by its members, the New York Society authorized the formation of an Educational Trust Fund in 1926 under my chairmanship. When five years later the name of the Fund was changed to the American Psychoanalytic Foundation, over fifty thousand dollars had been subscribed, enough to warrant opening a clinic for ambulatory patients. However, in 1927 at a hearing where Brill, Jelliffe, and I represented the New York Society, the New York State Board of Charities denied the petition of the Society for a charter to establish a treatment center despite the fact that the need for such services to the public had received the endorsement of several influential New York psychiatrists who were not analysts. Among these were Dr. Thomas Salmon, who had so ably headed the Psychiatric Service in World War I, and Doctors Floyd Haviland and George H. Kirby, both on the staff of Manhattan State during the fruitful period when dynamic psychiatry had been almost obligatory there and both of whom later served as presidents of the American Psychiatric Association.

The Board of Charities rejected the application without comment on the merits of psychoanalysis or the need for this form of therapy in the community. It contended that previous experience had shown that independent clinics either lowered their standards or were discontinued after a few years no matter how favorable the circumstances attending their formation. The Board suggested that the clinic be organized under the auspices of an established hospital or medical school. However, the Society thought that such an affiliation would necessarily mean that the direction of the clinic's activities, especially in teaching, would be hampered by unsympathetic or uninformed jurisdiction. On the other hand, it is highly questionable whether any leading hospital or medical school in New York City at that time would have accepted an official affiliation with psychoanalysis. Nevertheless, the Educational Committee informally proposed that some of the teaching be undertaken at the flourishing psychoanalytically attuned outpatient clinic at Mount Sinai to which many of the older members of the Society were attached. But the project lapsed and nearly two decades passed before organized teaching of psychoanalysis in medical schools connected with hospitals was initiated at Columbia University and the New York Medical College.

By 1923 sufficient scientific interest had developed to call for an additional meeting of the American Psychoanalytic during the Christmas week, which was held at the Cornell Club in New York City. A club setting had been chosen because the discussions were to be somewhat informal. However, notice of the meeting got abroad and the attendance, swollen by local psychiatrists now curious about the subject, overflowed the moderate-sized club quarters.

Indicative of the progress of psychoanalysis in the United States, the membership list of the American Psychoanalytic Association in 1925 contained thirty-eight names, fourteen of whom were from the New York group and all actively engaged in the private practice of psychoanalysis. Of the twenty-four living in other localities, there were about half a dozen to whom clinical psychoanalysis represented a major interest; the others circumspectly advocated its principles in the care of the insane and its use in the approach to sociological, criminological, and other problems having psychiatric implications.

The American Psychoanalytic Association followed the principle of the New York Society in identifying itself with the practice of general medicine and psychiatry. With this in mind it arranged that its annual meetings should be held in conjunction with the American Neurological Association or the American Psychiatric Association, which deliberately arranges its meetings in different parts of the country so that the members of these bodies may conveniently attend.

It is not surprising that the first regional psychoanalytic societies and teaching groups after those in New York should have appeared in Washington and Boston. St. Elizabeth's, the United States Government Hospital, under the direction of Dr. White, and Shepard and Enoch Pratt Hospital in nearby Catonville, Maryland, under Dr. Ross Chapman, had encouraged the use of analytic psychology by their staffs and physicians who resided in the vicinity. Gradually group meetings of these physicians were organized and by the fall of 1924 these groups were assuming teaching activities. In Boston a group for the discussion of psychoanalysis had met informally during Putnam's lifetime, but deprived of his competent and stimulating leadership, it practically ceased to exist after his death in

1918. Dr. Isador Coriat, an early member of Putnam's group, may have been conversant with Freud's work before Brill. In 1908, as co-author of the book *Religion and Medicine*,[4] perhaps one of the first collaborations between a psychoanalytic psychiatrist and clergymen in America, he mentions his indebtedness to Freud's *Neurosenlehre*. Coriat gradually assembled New England psychiatrists and two or three laymen who were psychoanalytically disposed; the group later perfected the organization of the Boston Psychoanalytic Society. Soon thereafter (1932) they also began a training institute in Boston.

In an article, "History of the Psychoanalytic Movement in America," written in 1925, I stated that

it must be conceded regretfully that the American investigations which have altered or even supplemented the vast amount of research of European analysts in regard to the theory of the neuroses, or to the functioning of the unconscious, to the science of religion and politics, to interpretation of esthetics, the psychology of the artist and the author, or dream interpretation are relatively meagre.

Retrospectively after twenty-five years I think that this opinion of these earlier contributions need not be revised. It should be added, however, that during this period, quite without design, the Americans were building up a psychoanalytic access to psychiatric theory and social interpretations.

During this era John Dewey recognized that new educational techniques were needed to meet the needs of a democratic society. Influenced by William James' pragmatic philosophy, he was expounding to the future educators the profound effects of the reality of experience, especially on the growing child. So, too, a transient vogue for the Dalcroze method of spontaneous expression to music through rhythmic movement flourished and "progressive" schools encouraged free expression over discipline and assigned tasks far beyond anything suggested by Dewey's philosophy of schools and their function in society.

[4] Worcester, Elwood, D.D., McComb, Samuel, D.D., and Coriat, Isador, M.D.: *Religion and Medicine*. Moffat, Yard & Co., Boston, 1908.

Psychoanalytic concepts had at this point also reached the theater, and New York had already laughed knowingly over Susan Glaspell's successful comedy *Suppressed Desires* (1917), a farce called *Expressing Willie*, and the lyrics of musical comedies with fleeting allusions to Freud and the psychoanalysts. The public relished such cartoons as W. E. Hill's "Have You Been Psyched?"[5] The popularization of the type of problem that psychoanalysis helped led, in time, to an ever widening demand for the services of the analyst, not only in hospitals but also in the schools and courts.

Of course, this interest in Freudian psychology and the experimentation in pedagogy provoked a corresponding opposition and produced a flood of sarcastic comment and ridicule. As typical of this we may cite Frederick Lewis Allen who wrote that after World War I had ended

a fertile ground was ready for the seeds of Freudianism, and one began to hear daily from the lips of flappers that "science taught" new and disturbing things about sex. Sex, it appeared, was the central and pervasive force which moved mankind. . . . New words and phrases began to be bandied about the cocktail tray and Mah Jong table—inferiority complex, sadism, masochism, Oedipus complex. . . . Analysts plied their new trade in American cities, conscientiously transferring the affections of their fair patients to themselves; and clergymen who preached about the virtue of self control were reminded by outspoken critics that their self control was out of date and really dangerous.[6]

At the Tenth International Congress at Innsbruck early in September, 1927 during a turbulent session filled with highly charged argument, the German groups failed in an attempt to impose the acceptance of lay analysis upon the New York society, largely because of the support given to the relatively small American delegation present by Jones of England, van Ophuijsen of Holland, and Anna Freud. However, in the sum-

[5] *Chicago Tribune*, 1924.
[6] Allen, Frederick Lewis: *Only Yesterday*. Harper & Bros., New York, 1931, pp. 98–99.

mer of 1929 before the Eleventh International Congress in Oxford, England, Brill who had not attended the meetings at either Homburg or Innsbruck visited Freud in Vienna and made peace on the subject of lay analysts. So, at Oxford, where for the first time the International Association left the continent, European analysts agreed to accept no American students, physicians or laymen, for training unless they had been cleared by their local American Educational Committee. The representatives of the New York group acquiesced to the principle of admitting nonmedical candidates for training. The New York Society ratified this compromise in the autumn of that year. Because of my opposition to this plan both at the conference in England and later in New York, I ceased to be Chairman of the Educational Committee and Dr. Abram Kardiner succeeded me in 1930. The New York Society soon nullified the agreement by requiring that to qualify for membership one must have completed a full year of training in a recognized psychiatric hospital. This training was impossible for laymen to obtain. A short time thereafter the New York Society restored its medical requirements for full membership and this has continued to be the policy of practically all of the constituent societies of the American Psychoanalytic Association.

Following the Congress at Oxford, in response to my request to Miss Anna Freud, Freud kindly agreed to see me although he had been in failing health for five years or more. Late in August of 1929 I went to Berchtesgaden, where he was spending the summer, with all the anticipation of one to whom a great privilege had been granted. Although the post office address, Professor Sigmund Freud, Berchtesgaden, sufficed for letters, when I arrived at the trim little railway station in the mountains I found the driver of the lone one horse victoria extremely vague about the location of the house of the man who had been acclaimed the world over. "Oh, yes," he said casually, "up there in the hills, such a professor does live. We'll find him somehow." The thrill of anticipation of seeing Freud again made me impatient. The driver wandered slowly and uncertainly around for so long that we arrived at Freud's house nearly a quarter of an hour after the appointed time. Freud, with Mrs. Freud, came walking slowly a little way down a path in the woods near his house to meet me. The first sight of him startled and saddened me. He had aged greatly in the seven years that had passed since I last saw him in Vienna. He was more stooped, far whiter, his face was far thinner, drawn and sunken through suffering, but his deep set eyes still burned brightly.

After a few friendly words of initial greeting, Freud's first question to me was, "And tell me, what do you really have against lay analysis?" in a tone of annoyance and impatience. I tried to explain to him that the laws of New York State forbade it, that the members in America thought a knowledge of the physical manifestations of organic illness necessary so that the physician might compare them with those due to psychological disturbance, that especially in America quacks and impostors, extremely ignorant of the elements of psychoanalysis, presumed to hold themselves out as analysts. Freud waved aside my replies with an abrupt "I know all that," turned, and walked very slowly toward his house.

At luncheon Freud spoke little. He was evidently in great pain, restless, and irritated by a new prosthesis which had just been made for the upper jaw, where a cancerous growth, first operated upon about 1923, continued to destroy the bony structure. Several times during the meal he was compelled to leave the table to remove his dental plate. He seemed greatly relieved when the luncheon had ended. Some of his characteristic quick movement returned, he began to enter the conversation, and he soon asked me, with a gleam in his eye, to come into his workroom to see what he was reading. On his desk lay open Thomas Hardy's *Tess of the D'Urbervilles*. This novel is one of my favorites. When I showed my surprise and pleasure, Freud smiled and said, "He knew psychoanalysis."

One is not at a loss for the reason for Freud's comment on Hardy's deep understanding of human conflict. A passage in *Tess* (published in 1891) is particularly revelatory. After Tess had told her minister husband, Angel Clare, on the day of their marriage of her illegitimate pregnancy in girlhood, he decided to leave her. Nevertheless, they stayed in the same house for three days in estrangement. Then Clare became somnambulistic, as he had previously been on occasions when under the influence of any strongly disturbing emotional force. At midnight, while in a somnambulistic state, he wandered to his wife's room and lifting her body murmured, "My poor Tess—my dearest, darling Tess! So sweet, so good, so true!" "The words of endearment," writes Hardy, "withheld so severely in his waking hours, were inexpressibly sweet to her forlorn and hungry heart."

In the characterization of Angel Clare in another part of the novel Hardy describes strongly conflicting elements in his makeup which correspond to those of neurotics. "Within the remote depths of his constitution, so gentle and affectionate as he was in general, there lay hidden a large logical deposit like a vein of metal in a soft loam which turned the edge of everything which attempted to traverse it." The "vein of metal," the powerful conscience, the rigid superego, is the essence of the repression in most neurotics. It causes an unyielding attachment to some early conceived standard which "turns the edge of all impulses threatening to pass it." The emergence of Angel Clare's repressed feeling in the sleep state is consistent with Freud's demonstration of the appearance of repressed material in the dream.

In the ten years since 1919 when the American doctors went to Vienna for analyses, Freud had come to know with an intimacy seldom found outside of an analyst's office many of the most active members of the American groups. We talked for a while about the personalities, especially Frink, and trends in psychoanalysis in America. I was surprised with what detail

Freud had been kept informed about the presentation of papers at the society's meetings and even their discussion and discussers.

On that bright August afternoon of my visit, Freud appeared greatly fatigued; what he needed most was quiet and rest. At about three o'clock I rode back to the station with Mrs. Dorothy Burlingham's father who had come to visit her. She occupied a house adjacent to Freud's and seemed one of the household. She had begun to interest herself actively in the analysis of children. In collaboration with Anna Freud they subsequently published important observations on the conduct of children whose homes in London were disrupted by the ravages of World War II.

On the train back to Munich nostalgic waves of memories of Vienna in the winter of 1921 came over me. There were images of the dingy shops of Alserstrasse where hungry people in shabby, ill-assorted clothes pressed noses against the frosty windows of food shops, where we, a little group of enthusiastic but floundering American physicians, gathered in our overcoats in chilly cafés to reassure ourselves in repetitious discussions about the progress of our analysis with Freud and psychoanalysis in general; of the Vienna Woods back of Coblenz where the setting October sun threw brilliant shafts of light into the shadows of sturdy fir trees; where in small bars and cabarets an aging actor or actress, who had once bowed to the thunderous applause of huge theater audiences, now went through the performance of an insignificant role with all the meticulous skill and grace that the true artist can never lose.

There came, too, a vision of the aged, frail Freud, a scientist who knew art and an artist who illumined science, continuing his incredibly long routine of work in his study in the unostentatious house in the Berggasse. But two sentences recurred repeatedly in my reverie as the train rolled through the tranquil, verdant landscape of Bavaria. The first was: "Wir wollen alle amtlich punziert sein" (we all wish to be officially stamped sterling), which I had told Freud was one of the reasons for the Americans coming to study in Vienna in 1921. This urge for official certification has continued undiminished as the years have passed but today this type of credential comes in America from institutes of the American Psychoanalytic Association. The second sentence, "And tell me what do you really have against lay analysis?" had been put to me by Freud sharply, almost accusingly. It reflected, I think, Freud's annoyance at the indifference of the leaders of psychoanalysis in America to many of his cherished ideals, a subject that will be considered later.

The dilution of "the pure gold of psychoanalysis," which Freud had earlier predicted would happen in America, he was now regretfully seeing come to pass. Psychoanalysis had remained a cause as well as a science and an art with Freud but its scope and expansion were beginning to pass from his control, directly or even indirectly.

11. Formal Instruction in Psychoanalysis Develops, 1930–1940

A new epoch in the activities of the New York Psychoanalytic Society began in 1930. It had grown rapidly in numbers and the psychoanalytic qualifications of the new members were high. Several had had prolonged personal analyses and had completed courses offered by the psychoanalytic institutes of London, Berlin, and Vienna. A trial period for new members had been inaugurated in the form of an associate membership from which they advanced to full membership. The Society also widened its range by admitting as nonresident members physicians who met the increased requirements but did not live in New York City. This afforded them an association far more vital and continuous than the American Psychoanalytic Association, which met only twice a year. These nonresident members included such men as Doctors Ives Hendrick of Boston, David Slight of Montreal, Smiley Blanton, then of Vassar College in Poughkeepsie, and George Smeltz of Pittsburgh.

The provision for nonmedical applicants stipulated that to be considered eligible for associate membership they must have graduated from an accredited university, give adequate reasons for lacking medical qualifications, and have received three years of training in psychoanalysis "in accordance with the requirements of the International Training Commission."

In November, 1930 Dr. Brill announced that an anonymous donor had made a gift to the Educational Trust Fund toward the foundation of a psychoanalytic institute. With previous smaller contributions from a large number of members of the Society and outsiders, this brought the total fund at the Society's disposal to over $60,000. Dr. Brill at once appointed committees to secure a location and plan for the organization of the institute. This latter proved no easy task; it involved the transfer of the Society's established educational program to a new setting. On September 15, 1931 the new institute was opened at 324 West 86th Street. The site was a large substantial private house, formerly the home of Professor E. R. A. Seligman, Professor of Political Economy at Columbia University.

Thus, twenty years after a small group of men devoted to psychoanalysis had organized the New York Psychoanalytic Society, it had a well-furnished home, a good library, an auditorium, and space for an expanded educational program for the profession and the public. Dr. Brill became President of the new Institute, Dr. Jelliffe its Vice-President, and Dr. Meyer its Executive Director, upon whom the burden of the smooth running of the Institute fell. He continued to serve faithfully in this capacity until he died in February, 1939. (His sudden and premature death, like that of Frink, with whom he had at one time been very intimately associated, removed from the field of psychoanalysis a deeply penetrating and original mind.) A corps of American instructors, most of them trained in Vienna or Berlin, were appointed to meet the needs of an ever growing student body. To facilitate and coordinate training, the Educational Committee decided to engage Dr. Sandor Rado, who had figured prominently as an organizer and teacher at the now seasoned Berlin Psychoanalytic Institute, to direct the scientific activities of the new institute in New York. In the fall of 1931, Dr. Rado assumed charge as the school's first paid Educational Director.

The courses considered essential for the education of the

psychoanalyst were now more fully developed and an ideal that had been in the minds of the leaders of psychoanalysis in New York for a decade at last found its consummation in a teaching organization whose influence and prestige have steadily grown. It has served more or less as a model for similar institutes that have followed rapidly in many other cities in America and that began immediately to affect the teaching of psychiatry and sociological subjects in their particular areas.

An affiliation with the long established Mental Hygiene Clinic at Mount Sinai Hospital was discussed, but it never materialized. This clinic had changed its name to Mental Health Class, a compromise term satisfactory to Dr. Israel Strauss of the Neurological Department, of which it continued to be a part. The tremendous increase in psychiatric activity after World War I had been reflected in this clinic, which operated six mornings a week. Because it had been psychoanalytically oriented from its beginning in 1913, it attracted a large number of a new generation of psychiatrists whose abilities raised its effectiveness, facilitated day in and day out instruction, and widened the scope of therapy.

Although only a few patients were treated by what may be considered classical psychoanalysis practically all received psychoanalytic psychotherapy, which was supplemented by occupational therapy, social work, and recreational therapy. At that time these were innovations in the outpatient treatment of mental illness.[1] These latter were directed by workers familiar with the psychodynamic processes as they affected the individual and his social adaptation. The men who gave or received instruction in psychoanalytic psychotherapy included many who soon became members of the New York Psychoanalytic Society. Among the first chiefs of clinic may be mentioned Doctors Adolph Stern, Dudley Shoenfeld, Monroe A. Meyer, and Sandor Lorand. Although this active psychoan-

---

[1] Oberndorf, C. P.: "Recreation Activities for Outpatient Psychiatric Cases," *Medical Journal and Record*, February 5, 1930.

alytic center was not under the direction of the Educational Committee of the New York Society, because all the chiefs of clinic and many others among the participants were instructors in the Society's educational program, this practical experience added to the effectiveness of their teaching. Also, many candidates for membership in the Society profited by their experience in the clinic.

With the appointment of additional psychoanalysts to positions as psychiatrists at Mount Sinai Hospital in 1927, and as the scope of their consultations on the wards of the hospital broadened, psychodynamic orientation became inevitable for residents of the hospital, especially those on the neurological service. Some of the latter subsequently continued their studies of psychoanalysis and located in other parts of the country: Paul Sloane in Philadelphia, Norman A. Levy in Los Angeles, Norman Reider in San Francisco, Walter Bromberg in Nevada, and Herman Selinsky in Florida, where they participated prominently in the advancement of dynamic psychiatry in their communities.

Actually from the time of its formation, each member of the New York Psychoanalytic Society felt it more or less an obligation to contribute informative—in this sense, instructive—papers and lectures to general practitioners and psychiatrists and to assist young psychiatrists in the study of Freud's works and the writings of other psychoanalysts. Brill gave a series of lectures first in the old Pathological Institute at Ward's Island in 1924 and continued them annually from 1929 to 1943 at the New York State Psychiatric Institute.

Another focus of psychoanalytic teaching has existed under Dr. Philip Lehrman from 1921 to the present at the University Hospital, formerly the New York Post Graduate Medical School and Hospital. Other hospitals, such as the Westchester Division of New York Hospital, Hillside Hospital (1925), and the New York State Psychiatric Institute, have, from time to time, encouraged the intensive use of psychoanalysis in the study of certain cases. About 1932 Dr. George Daniels introduced the psychoanalytic study of several physical disease syndromes at Presbyterian Hospital in New York City, an institution not inclined to accept innovations unless convinced of their potentialities.

Another manifestation of this scientific spurt in New York was the establishment of the new *Psychoanalytic Quarterly* in 1932 with the enterprising Dr. Dorian Feigenbaum, formerly of Vienna, as its editor. Whereas at first it published several translations from the German, the number of original articles, almost entirely from American sources, soon brought its scientific standard to that of the *International Journal of Psychoanalysis*, which had been started in England more than a decade before.

About the same time (1933) the American Psychiatric Association agreed to form a special section on psychoanalysis. Negotiations for gaining this official recognition of psychoanalysis as a part of psychiatry had been in progress for some time by an informal group in which Dr. Brill, Dr. Sullivan and I were active. However, when this intention became generally known, fervid adherents of psychoanalysis in the New York Society fought it bitterly, fearing that its tenets might be weakened by their extension into general psychiatry. The opposite proved to be true; the new Section on Psychoanalysis in the American Psychiatric Association served to introduce psychoanalytic thinking more accurately and fully into general problems of psychiatry.

During the lush years of inflation in the United States (1922-1929) the large trust funds and foundations for the advancement of public welfare increased greatly both in number and in endowment. Some of these, such as the Commonwealth, the Josiah Macy, Jr. and Rosenwald Funds, dedicated to health and medical research, now began to take an interest in psychiatry and even in psychoanalysis as a part of social welfare and have continued to support generously projects in which psychoanalytic thinking is prominent.

FORMAL INSTRUCTION IN PSYCHOANALYSIS DEVELOPS

Thirty years of relatively liberal acceptance of psychoanalysis as a legitimate, medically approved psychotherapeutic procedure and the incorporation of Freud's ideas into studies of a social, cultural, philosophical, religious, and even economic nature had prepared the way for the use of many outstanding minds who found a haven here from political persecution. The philosophy of psychoanalysis, with its high regard for individual needs in contrast to those of the supremacy of the totalitarian state, clashed irreconcilably with the tenets of Fascism under which the individual must sacrifice himself, or be sacrificed, to the will of a dictator or an oligarchy.

There had been ample warning of the wide restrictions on the free expression of thought that were likely to be enforced if the Nazi party ever came to power, as it actually did in 1933. Although the government could not control the thoughts of one hundred million people, it could prevent any overt expression in speech or print of such individualistic thinking as psychoanalysis represented. The few analysts who ventured to stay in Nazi dominated countries either kept discreetly silent or attempted to disguise Freudian ideology with the admixture of a nationalistic coloring. These men were willing to adopt subterfuges rather than face the consequence of opposition. Their Nazi masters, too, were willing to overlook the weak infringements on authoritarianism by such men.

An analogous situation to that in Germany had developed a few years before under the dictatorship of Communist Russia. Psychoanalysis was forbidden as contrary to the state's political policies. The Russian Psychoanalytic Society faded away about 1929, and the Institution for Children in Moscow, directed by Wera Schmidt, where psychoanalytic principles were used in therapy, was closed by the government on grounds of immorality.

About the same time Dr. Frankwood Williams, a psychoanalytic psychiatrist, returned from a visit to the Soviet with enthusiastic accounts of the relative absence of mental disorder in the Soviet Union. He spoke of the extreme sexual freedom permissible there, the easy marriage and even easier divorce (a post card notification of divorce by either party became legal). These factors and the economic security to a ripe old age promised by the state made the future for mental health seem bright indeed to him.

After several conversations with Williams, I became extremely sceptical of his observations, for it seemed to me that the antagonism between individual and communal interest is present in all animal life and is unavoidable among humans. It is inevitable in situations involving the interests of groups of different ages, such as children and adolescents, the middle-aged and the old, to say nothing of the great biological division into male and female. In 1932 I, therefore, spent two weeks in Russia. Fortunately I had a letter of introduction to Professor N. Ossipow, director of the famous Bechterew Institute in Leningrad, formerly a member of the International Psychoanalytic Association, and author of a psychoanalytic study *Tolstoï's Childhood Memories*.[2] Through a happy chance, Ossipow invited me to accompany him on a visit to the state mental hospital of Forel, some twenty miles outside of Leningrad. He had been asked to examine the wife of an official so high in the Soviet Government that one of the precious Army cars had been placed at his disposal.

The hospital, a building of the past century, was overpopulated and meagerly furnished. The patients were dressed in tunics, and the incontinent patients lay in sawdust bunks. I was astonished at the extremely large percentage of young people as compared with the hospital population of similar institutions in America. The director of the hospital explained that these were young people suffering from dementia praecox, a result of their difficulties in adapting to the new order of life. During my visit, a young woman was brought into the admission office. The urgency of her words, her distractibility and

[2] Ossipow, N.: *Tolstoï's Childhood Memories: A Contribution to Freud's Libido Theory*. Internationale Psychoanalytische Verlag, Wien, 1923.

her physical excitement were so characteristic that she would have been considered by any psychiatrist to be in a manic state, whether her language had been Russian, Chinese, or Cherokee. The director of Forel so diagnosed her state immediately and explained that she had had an unhappy love affair. The incident contradicted Williams' report of the absence of manic-depressive cases in Russia.

On the return trip to Leningrad, when I commented to Ossipow on the large number of young people whom I had seen milling about in the crowded courtyard of Forel, he agreed with the director that they were suffering from dementia praecox but naively explained that this was a disease endemic in Russia. When I questioned him about mental conflict and the attitude toward psychoanalysis in Russia, he became extremely wary. Finally he indicated that the use of psychoanalysis for therapy had been forbidden but that psychoanalysis might still be used as an investigative method for diagnostic purposes.

The First International Congress for Mental Hygiene subsidized by the American Foundation for Mental Hygiene met in Washington, D.C. in May, 1930. This represented "the effort to create and carry forward a means effective to the end of promoting and conserving mental health and ameliorating the scourge of mental ill health."[3] Psychiatrists from Germany, Austria, Italy, France, Belgium, and the Netherlands received invitations to attend. Also present were two from Soviet Russia, Dr. Leon Rosenstein and Dr. A. Salkina of Moscow, who greeted the Congress in the name of the Peoples' Commissariat of Public Health and Education and other social organizations. They must have been astonished and perhaps impressed by the liberalism and tolerance shown to psychoanalysis during this five day conference.

Among the psychoanalysts from abroad who contributed to the program we find the names of Otto Rank, Franz Alexander

[3] *Proceedings of the International Congress of Mental Hygiene.* International Committee for Mental Health, Inc., New York, 1932.

from Berlin, and Mary Chadwick from London, a trained nurse whose book *Psychology for Nurses* [4] helped to introduce psychoanalytic thinking into nursing care of medical as well as psychiatric patients. A number of American analysts also participated: Bernard Glueck, William A. White, A. A. Brill, Marion Kenworthy, who had consistently taught the importance of psychoanalytic methods in the management of sociological problems at the New York School for Social Work, and Frankwood Williams, who edited the proceedings of the meeting.

August Aichhorn, whose paper was read in his absence, merits special mention. His book *Wayward Youth*,[5] based upon the application of psychoanalysis to delinquent boys in an institution, had become well known among social workers in the United States. It pointed a way that was soon put into operation at the Pleasantville, New York, Residential Cottage School, where I was asked to establish a psychiatric service in 1925 to assist the teachers in handling severe conduct disorders. It was staffed with physicians and a social worker trained psychoanalytically at the Psychiatric Clinic of Mount Sinai. A great increase in the budget, which followed the introduction of psychiatry into the treatment of the children, did not frighten the trustees of the Pleasantville institution. They had begun to recognize the value of the approach to the emotional disturbances of childhood offered in specific cases by dynamic psychology. And it was from just such separate centers and from the reports of individual social workers and probation officers that psychoanalytic thinking made its influence felt in the programs of schools, the courts, and eventually in many legislatures.

The Thirteenth International Psychoanalytic Congress scheduled for 1931 at the Spa of Wiesbaden was postponed a year

[4] Chadwick, Mary: *Psychology for Nurses*. William Heinemann, London, 1925.
[5] Aichhorn, August: *Wayward Youth*. Viking Press, New York, 1936. Revised and adapted from the German *Verwahrloste Jugend*.

because the monetary chaos in many European countries prohibited travel. The few American members present in 1932 learned firsthand what Nazi regimentation really meant. This meeting, the smallest in attendance since that at the Hague in 1920, was held virtually behind closed doors. The Germans and Austrians present feared, and with good reason, that their public association with psychoanalysis might bring them harm, if not actual persecution when they returned to their homes. The photographs of the Congress, for which not more than fifty members appeared, could not be taken outdoors as had been customary, but secretly in a half-lighted room of the Wiesbaden Kurshaus where the scientific sessions were held.

It was at Wiesbaden that Ferenczi's break with Freud over questions of theory and technique, impending for over seven years, could no longer be concealed. He refused the presidency of the International Association on the ground that his therapeutic methods and goals had drifted far from those of Freud, upon which the Executive Council of the International Association insisted. He felt he could not conscientiously identify himself with the organization to which he had formerly given so firm and warm an allegiance. His defection was of far greater significance than that of Rank, with whom, as far back as 1924, he had written a provocative brochure on the developmental goals of psychoanalysis, in which the authors make a plea for a more active role for the analyst.[6] Ferenczi had been a leading spirit in the development of psychoanalysis, perhaps Freud's most original and productive associate, for nearly a quarter of a century. He was also highly regarded as a training analyst, and several Americans had chosen to receive their preparatory training from the Budapest master. Upon their return to America they clung to Ferenczi's teachings, namely, that the active display of sympathy (love) from the therapist to the patient

[6] Ferenczi, S., and Rank, Otto: *Entwicklungsziele der Psychoanalyse.* Internationale Psychoanalytische Verlag, Leipzig, Wien, Zurich, 1924, p. 6.

provides one of the strongest forces in the relief of anxiety and thereby progress toward recovery.

The choice of sites for the meetings of the International Psychoanalytic Association has always been fortunate—beautiful spots like Homburg, Innsbruck, in the Tyrol, Oxford (England), and Wiesbaden—conducive to group excursions, good fellowship, and close associations. In 1934 Lucerne was selected, not because of its magnificent mountain panorama, its placid lake and faultless hotels, but because in Switzerland the meeting would be free from direct Nazi censorship. Nevertheless, when some speaker incidentally made derogatory comments about the Nazi restrictions, a member from Berlin arose and stomped loudly out of the room, probably fearing not to register an obvious protest. Fifteen minutes later there was a loud knocking at the door. Everyone was startled. "The house is pinched," whispered an American colleague beside me. When the door was opened, it turned out to be merely an overeager messenger with a telegram. Many a German and Austrian participant sighed with relief.

At Lucerne the International Training Commission reconsidered the matter of eligibility for membership in the American Psychoanalytic Association and its flourishing local societies. To ease the situation that had resulted from the Oxford agreement, the International Commission rather reluctantly relinquished its position. Now analysts who had been trained in Europe and were so certified but who in other respects did not meet the requirements of the Society to which they applied could be refused admission.

In an attempt to eliminate the differences on educational policies that had arisen among the American societies themselves, a committee had been appointed which came to the conclusion that the answer lay in converting the American Psychoanalytic Association into a Federation of American Psychoanalytic Societies but retaining the old name. Under the new constitution, influenced to some extent by the idea of states' rights in the United States, each local society had autonomy in its affairs. However, they all agreed that their instruction should be based on the work of Freud and that they be affiliated with the International Association.

Although the Committee on Reorganization of the American Psychoanalytic Association had been holding meetings for over a year, its work was not ratified at Lucerne. Finally, at the thirty-fifth meeting of the Association in Boston, December 28, 1935, it was reported that the constituent societies had ratified a constitution drafted at Chicago the year before. These were in order of their formation, New York (1911), Boston (1930), Washington-Baltimore (1930), and Chicago (1931). Before 1940, Philadelphia and Topeka were added to the list. The new constitution provided that each Society was entitled to one representative on the executive council and three on the influential committee on professional training of the national association.[7] The decisions of this latter group ultimately determined the caliber and preparation of the men to whom workers in the allied sciences necessarily turned for help and clarification.

Brill's long and unprecedented tenure of the highest offices in the New York Society and the American Association, to which he had clung for many years, now came to an end. He gradually withdrew from the activities of the New York Psychoanalytic Society and its Institute, and in the years just prior to his death on March 2, 1948 practically retired from participation in the affairs of the American Psychoanalytic Association. As a tribute to his unflagging enthusiasm and persistence in presenting psychoanalysis to America, the New York Society established a lectureship in his name to be given annually and the American Psychoanalytic Association authorized a gold medal with his likeness to be presented each year to its retiring president.

Possibly because I had been chairman of the Committee on

[7] *International Journal of Psychoanalysis,* Vol. XV, 1934, p. 522.

Reorganization, I was elected as the first president of the new federation. The present practice is that, either through custom or regulation, the presidency of most American psychoanalytic organizations rotates every year or two.

The new American Federation grew and strengthened, and in June, 1937 a sizable *Bulletin of the American Psychoanalytic Association,* a Federation of American Psychoanalytic Societies, was issued. Volume II, June, 1938 to June, 1939 was dedicated to the memory of Sigmund Freud "for the gain in human stature made possible by his life of patient labor."

It so happened that Freud's eightieth birthday fell on May 6, 1936 while the American Psychoanalytic and American Psychiatric Associations were in session in St. Louis. The occasion was observed by a tribute to Freud and his contribution to psychiatry,[8] and his election to honorary membership in the American Psychiatric Association—a distinction utterly inconceivable twenty years before.

So, too, the *American Journal of Sociology* in honor of Freud's eightieth birthday devoted the entire issue of November, 1939 to articles dealing with the influence of psychoanalysis on sociological topics. The titles of these articles and the positions of their authors indicate how in the years from 1920 to 1940 Freud's thinking had permeated American psychology and sociology. It may be stated, fairly I think, that during the following years, the appraisals of the contribution of psychoanalysis to the illumination of vital areas in social and political sciences given in these articles has not essentially altered but its application has been greatly extended.[9]

Among those contributing to the Freud number was Ernest Burgess, Professor of Sociology at the University of Chicago,

---

[8] Oberndorf, C. P.: "Sigmund Freud, His Work and Influence," *American Journal of Psychiatry,* Vol. 93, 1936, p. 21. Address on May 6, 1936 at a joint session of the American Psychoanalytic Association and the American Psychiatric Association, St. Louis.

[9] Schneider, Louis: *The Freudian Psychology and Veblen's Social Theory.* Kings Crown Press, New York, 1948.

who wrote on "The Influence of Sigmund Freud upon Sociology in the United States." He comments that the failure of psychoanalysis to make headway with sociologists in the United States during the first decade after its introduction here may be explained basically by an aversion toward the interpretation of human behavior in terms of sexual motivation, and by the foothold of the simpler and apparently adequate cultural interpretations of behavior, a predisposition against absolute explanations as opposed to relative, the apparently questionable technique of psychoanalysis, its lack of integration with previous studies of instinct, existing sociological conceptual schemes of motivation, a trend away from the theory of instincts, and a preoccupation on the part of sociologists with their own problems. The further working out and integrating of methods for investigating the subjective life of their phenomena were up to that time viewed as the basic methodological problems of the psychological and social sciences.

To Freud, continues Burgess, must go credit for the creation of psychoanalysis as an intellectual discipline and the organization of a unified conceptual system. It was the mutual need in both psychoanalysis and socioanalysis that the two aspects of conduct, psychogenic and cultural, be understood that led students in each field to seek what the other had to offer.

In recent years there have been increasing attempts at integration of viewpoints, concepts, and research methods of psychoanalysis and sociology. A final stage in the combination of psychoanalytic and sociological methods remains to be taken in cooperative research. Freud's most valuable contributions to sociology consist in establishing the role of unconscious factors in human behavior; emphasis on the role of wish-fulfillment; and analysis of the formation of dynamic traits and patterns in personality development independent of cultural influence.

"The Contribution of Freud's Insight Interview to the Social Sciences" is summarized by Harold D. Lasswell, the political scientist, now Professor of Law at Yale University. Lasswell considers that the most abiding contribution of Freud to social science is the observational standpoint that he invented and which is intensive rather than extensive, scientific and therapeutic rather than indoctrinating. It is an interview rather than a participant, spectator, or collector relationship; and it is an interview that aims at simultaneous insight into the person, personality, and culture. From this standpoint the insight interview is a means of acquiring skill in the discovery of culture and hence is important for social scientists, who are mainly concerned with culture. The psychoanalytic approach has prompted the use of more intensive methods in social observation; psychoanalytic findings have stimulated research; and intensive investigation has posed the task of calibrating the observations made from one standpoint with observations made in any other position along the continuum of intensiveness-extensiveness.[10]

In "Totem and Taboo in Retrospect" the anthropologist A. L. Kroeber, Professor of Anthropology at the University of California, reevaluates Freud's explanations of cultural origins and points out that they waver between being historic and psychological in character. As history they remain unfounded, but they may prove to contain elements contributing to understanding the generic human psychology underlying the history of human culture, especially its recurrent or repetitive features. Psychoanalytic intransigeance as to historic interpretation is due partly to an "overdetermination" in Freud's own thinking and partly to rigidity in his followers, as exemplified by Jones and Roheim. Psychoanalysis has maintained an all or none attitude toward general science but nevertheless science has profited by definite absorptions from psychoanalysis.[11]

Havelock Ellis, whose essays over a long period of time illu-

[10] Lasswell, Harold D.: *Power and Personality*. W. W. Norton & Co., New York, 1948.
[11] Kluckhohn, C. and Murray, H. A. (eds.): *Personality: In Nature, Society and Culture*. Alfred A. Knopf, New York, 1948.

minated so many social and sexual problems, writes on "Freud's Influence on the Changed Attitude Toward Sex," an important cultural factor since early in the present century. He points out that the strength of reactions, pro and con, to Freud's theories may be attributed in large part to the traditional sanctity and yet obscenity of the subject of sex and Freud's extravagant presentation of the subject. Freud's art is the poetry of psychic processes which lie in the deepest and most mysterious recesses of the organism, but to emphasize the artist in Freud is not to diminish his significance for science. Thus Freud is to be recognized as one of the greatest masters in thought. By making no allowance for the "sacredness" of sex and by supplying emphasis to the recognition and acceptance of its place in life, Freud has made a powerful contribution to the changing attitude of our time toward sex.

As one of the most recent examples of the ever increasing notice of psychoanalysis in the study of social issues, one may cite the book of Kardiner and Ovesey, practicing psychoanalysts, on the position of the Negro in the American democracy. It is based on the premise that "group characteristics are adapted in nature and therefore not inborn, but acquired." [12] Many sociologists see in the spread of psychoanalytic thinking the possibility of the elimination of religious and social prejudice in groups as well as individuals. By the late twenties laymen and psychiatrists in the Middle West had become familiar with psychoanalysis, especially in Chicago, where Lionel Blitsten had been practicing and advocating psychoanalysis since 1922 but had not organized a group. About the time of the first International Congress for Mental Hygiene in Washington, Franz Alexander of Berlin was asked to become Professor of Psychoanalysis at the University of Chicago, the first such title ever bestowed in America or elsewhere, I think. He spent the next year at the Judge Baker Foundation in Boston and then

---

[12] Kardiner, A. and Ovesey, L.: *The Mark of Oppression.* W. W. Norton & Co., New York, 1951.

established an adequately endowed Institute for Psychoanalysis in Chicago.

Moreover, after the Washington meeting, Karl Menninger, still loyal to the descriptive psychiatry of his great teacher, E. E. Southard of Harvard, decided that psychoanalysis offered a more scientific and productive method and from that time on the Menninger Sanitarium in Topeka, Kansas (now the Menninger Foundation) became a noted teaching center, using psychoanalysis predominantly.

Also from Berlin came the experienced Karen Horney to be Assistant Director to Alexander at the Chicago Institute, which flourished immediately. But when friction developed between Alexander and Horney, perhaps preponderantly on theoretical issues, Horney withdrew and came to New York, where she joined the New York Psychoanalytic Society and Institute. Here, too, differences arose between Horney and the teaching staff of the Institute as to just what was essential and fundamental in Freud's complicated theoretical structure and therefore indispensable in the training of students. Horney again resigned to follow her inclinations independently.

Notwithstanding such sharp dissensions within the ranks of psychoanalysts (and another which forced the withdrawal of the brilliant and prolific Paul Schilder from the New York Society), a general falling in line with psychoanalytic thinking by psychiatrists and social workers became apparent. On the other hand, determined condemnation of psychoanalysis did not disappear. Some highly regarded leaders in "neuro-psychiatry," such as Foster Kennedy of Cornell, Charles W. Burr of the University of Pennsylvania, and Bernard Sachs of New York, seldom missed a chance to launch a tirade against anything Freudian.

In this connection a little anecdote may be related. At a meeting of the American Neurological Association in May, 1936, in connection with the commemoration of Freud's eightieth birthday, Jelliffe read a paper entitled "Sigmund Freud as a

Neurologist." Here he mentioned that four men who were working at Meynert's laboratory in Vienna during the years 1882–1884 were destined to become distinguished in neurology and psychiatry. They were Freud, Bernard Sachs, M. Allen Starr, and Anton. Later at the University at Halle, Germany, these four men were together again at the same laboratory table. Sachs, a formal, dignified man, who was in the audience, thought it proper to comment on the paper. After a few laudatory remarks about Jelliffe's presentation, he said, "How well I remember those student days with Meynert. There were we four men together—my dear friend, the late M. Allen Starr, Professor of Neurology at Columbia University, Anton, myself, and a fourth man. Who was that fourth man?" he said, tapping his forehead in embarrassment. "Somehow I can't remember his name—who was that other fellow?" The audience of scientists, all of whom were thoroughly acquainted with the Freudian interpretation of the psychopathology of everyday life and the meaning of forgetting and of slips of the tongue and pen, shouted, laughing, "Freud!"—much to Sachs' discomfiture.

In 1936 the murky glare of the holocaust at Berlin, where the books of advanced thinkers, including Freud's, were burned in an evil pyre, settled ominously over the European intellectual scene. The harried European Program Committee encountered almost insurmountable obstacles in finding a place where the Fourteenth International Psychoanalytic Congress could meet unmolested. Finally the choice on the continent was narrowed to Czechoslovakia, still a republic where freedom of speech prevailed. The Committee selected Marienbad, which was already trembling at the threat of invasion by the conquest hungry Nazis. And this uncontested conquest soon came to pass.

The American participation in the scientific sessions was comparatively meager. At the business session of the Central Executive it became apparent that the authority of the International Training Commission was rapidly disintegrating. Dr. Jones called for a ratification of the statutes of the new American

Federation, which included one stating that the American Association "will no longer be a Branch Society of the International Association" and that "a main function of the new Federation (Association) is investigation of new societies in the U.S.A." In effect, these statutes recognized the right of the American Association to determine policies affecting its medical and public relations. Pursuing its newly achieved independence, the new Federation, continuously concerned with standards, in 1937 established its own minimal requirements, which were obligatory for the training institutes of its constituent societies.

Although another International Congress (Fifteenth) was held in Paris in 1938, practically no Americans attended because of the hovering war clouds. Here communications sent by the American Association reaffirmed that it had abandoned the administrative and executive bodies of the International. The latter functions today as a congress for scientific purposes. The Federated Societies of the American Psychoanalytic Association also notified the International that it would "no longer recognize memberships in foreign psychoanalytic societies as applicable in the case of any psychoanalyst residing in the United States." This regulation had been established as a result of the mass emigration into this country. America had now disengaged itself from Europe, but not under the same conditions nor in the same spirit that White had called for freedom from Vienna in Atlantic City roughly twenty years before.

Even before the Marienbad Congress the difficulties imposed by the Nazi Government on Jews had sent nearly all psychoanalysts scurrying for safety and shelter to more tolerant lands, some to nearby Holland, France, and Sweden, a number across the channel to England, but by far the largest number to America, especially New York. Here many of them had relatives or professional friends and the opportunities for practice were extremely favorable—thanks to the position that psychoanalysis had achieved for itself in the medical and sociological world.

The American Psychoanalytic Association appointed an energetic committee to aid these exiles financially and professionally. Although a majority of the European analysts remained in New York, many of them spread out to other states, where their competence immeasurably strengthened the pioneer work of local American colleagues. The teaching staffs of all the American Institutes were enriched by psychoanalysts whose reputation had been thoroughly established. To Los Angeles, a fertile territory where psychoanalysis was almost unknown, went two outstanding teachers, Ernst Simmel, versatile clinician, and Otto Fenichel, a veritable encyclopedist of psychoanalytic literature.

Freud was one of the last of the psychoanalysts to leave Vienna. He remained after the Nazis had taken over the city on March 12, 1938 and was held as a hostage. Ransomed by the payment of a cash sum through the efforts of the Princess Marie Bonaparte of France, Mrs. Dorothy Burlingham of New York, and Ernest Jones of England, his devoted disciples and friends, and William C. Bullitt, the American Ambassador to France, he was permitted to go into exile in England, where a pleasant home had been secured for him. Here he continued to work and even to see a few patients until he died on September 23, 1939 in his eighty-third year.

Hanns Sachs, a most loyal and reverent follower who has written so gently of his association with Freud, says: "Although he called me his friend, I did not feel it was so. At the bottom, I was as far removed as at our first meeting." [13] Perhaps this feeling of Sachs was not only a result of psychological differences in their concepts of friendship between two men. After all Freud was the oustanding thinker and genius of his time, delving into the past and brooding over the future of mankind, whereas Sachs remained a revering student and practicing analyst who was seeking something more personal and immediate in the relationship than Freud's constitution may have been ca-

[13] Sachs, Hanns: *Freud, Master and Friend*. Harvard University Press, Cambridge, Mass., 1944.

pable of giving him. Thus, these two superior human beings, on separate levels of thought and cultural striving, did not feel toward each other in the popular conception of friendship. This partially bears out an old adage: the great are always alone.

The war clouds over Europe crashed when Germany invaded Poland on September 1, 1939. It led to a declaration of war by England and France. Freud, a wearied old man, died a few weeks later and was spared the terror of bombs bursting about his new home in London. The war disrupted all activity in science and education in Europe. The *Zeitschrift für Psychoanalyse* was compelled to cease after more than twenty-five years of continuous publication but the *International Journal* in England managed to appear throughout the war, although reduced in size.

The United States did not join in the world strife until more than two years after Warsaw was demolished. The participation of America during the latter years of the war interfered relatively little with educational activity in this country and among the medical specialties psychoanalysis remained almost unaffected. This was due largely to the increment from doctors, no longer young, who had emigrated from enemy countries abroad. Meetings of the American Psychoanalytic Association and the local societies continued regularly and new societies, organized in Detroit and San Francisco just before the United States entered the war, had no difficulty surviving. Incidentally, cis-Atlantic psychoanalysis had extended to several South American countries, and Dr. Angel Garma founded in Buenos Aires the Argentine Psychoanalytic Society in 1943.

All the excitement of World War II, however, had little effect upon the hostilities within the psychoanalytic societies. Thus, as mentioned, Karen Horney, seceding from the American Association about 1941 assembled a group of her own. This group in New York City became known as The American Institute of Psychoanalysis. A very few members of the New

York Society joined her, including Clara Thompson and William V. Silverberg, who had retained membership in the Washington-Baltimore Society but practiced in New York where the demand for psychoanalysis exceeded the supply of doctors. This new coalition did not last long. Friction almost immediately appeared because of differences of opinion about the status of lay members. Then Clara Thompson resigned in 1943. With a few associates she allied herself with the Washington School of Psychiatry, then headed by Harry Stack Sullivan, to form a New York branch. Dr. Sullivan accented the therapeutic importance of interpretation of "interpersonal relationship," in a broad extension of Freud's original analysis of the familial "interpersonal relationships" between parents and children. The potentialities of improving international brotherhood through the investigation of interracial interpersonal relationship is a hope of the World Health Organization, especially the psychiatric division.

A further defection from Horney's Institute by Silverberg in 1944 arose from a difference of opinion over the old question of emphasis on the medical background of therapy. It resulted in the formation of still another teaching center at the New York Medical College. A liaison such as had been recommended by the State Commission when the New York Society originally applied for a clinic charter in 1926 thus became an actuality, and it continues to operate quite apart from the jurisdiction of the American Psychoanalytic Association as an independent institute, subject to the supervision of the Medical College's faculty. Before long similar arrangements for the teaching of psychoanalysis as a part of medical school psychiatry were widely adopted throughout the country. Psychoanalysis had finally become legitimate and respectable, perhaps paying the price in becoming sluggish and smug, hence attractive to an increasing number of minds which find security in conformity and propriety.

12. Post-World War II Deviations in Psychoanalytic Conceptions

The impetus given to the study of psychiatry after World War I was repeated, though on a far greater scale, after World War II. The number of psychiatrists multiplied. Many were physicians in the Armed Forces who had been compelled by emergencies to take charge of the astonishing number of soldiers returning from the battlefront suffering from "combat fatigue" or the "emotional stress of war," terms as variously applied as "shell shock" had been in World War I. Also many young doctors had become impressed with the frequency and gravity of mental illness among draftees at induction centers and army camps, before the men had been sent overseas and faced fire. On their return to civilian duties they decided to become psychiatrists and clamored for further training in general psychiatry and in psychoanalysis. They were impressed with the advantages which the Freudian psychogenic hypotheses offered in grasping psychopathological manifestations and the utility, serviceability, and resourcefulness of psychoanalytic technique. Many sought this training at one of the institutes accredited by the American Psychoanalytic Association, which numbered nearly a dozen in 1945, and these were soon overwhelmed with applications from able doctors.

In May, 1946 the American Psychoanalytic Association changed back from a federation of societies to a direct membership organization. However, through its Executive Council and Board of Professional Standards it exerts considerable control over the activities of the institutes it sponsors and over national issues affecting all affiliated societies. The importance of following the policies of the American Psychoanalytic Association rests in the influence it exerts directly and remotely on all types of professional application of psychoanalysis in America. Hence its decisions will have a great bearing on the position and trends of psychoanalysis (in all its ramifications) for the next decade at least, including those psychoanalytic societies and training schools that operate independently.

The training of analysts has become a major function of institutes sponsored by societies of the American Association. The councils and special committees of the national and local societies give much time to the consideration of criteria for the acceptance of students, the establishment of professional standards, and the qualifications that training institutes and individual members must meet for recognition. These institutes generally admit only doctors of medicine who have served internships in general and psychiatric hospitals. They also require a long course of study of psychoanalysis and a personal analysis, which is usually conducted strictly according to the "classical" technique advocated by Freud.

The requirements for training continue controversial within the American Association and are constantly changing. The latest point of dispute concerns the number of hours necessary for the personal analysis of the prospective analyst. This now consists of a five hour or minimal four hour a week course that continues for two hundred hours at the least. Those who seek to alter this requirement claim that the frequency and length of the training analysis should depend upon the aptitude of the individual. Men with extensive experience as training analysts maintain that in certain instances an analysis adequate for skilled application of therapy is possible with three hours a week, a view with which I concur. Also, as a practical measure shortening of the course would enable an institute to train a larger number of physicians in a given period of time and thereby better meet the current demand for psychoanalytic psychotherapy.

This emphasis on the competence of new members assures the public that a psychoanalyst accredited by the American Psychoanalytic Association has been trained according to prescribed requirements, but the completion of such protracted courses cannot be a substitute for the emotional and judgment factors that enter into psychotherapy to a degree not comparably existent in any other form of medical treatment.

There is something inconsistent in insisting on such a rigorous course for trained physicians and a lenient attitude, sometimes expressed by prominent medical psychoanalysts, toward the admission of psychologists, social workers, and others into the field of private psychotherapeutic, which tends to become psychoanalytic, practice. Curiously enough some training analysts take both of these positions. Recently, too, a new problem has arisen, and the Council of the Association has been called upon to look into bitter schisms over questions of technique and theory within member societies, not only those long and solidly established like New York, but also newly accredited ones in Philadelphia and Los Angeles. In all of these cities two societies exist, both affiliated with the American.

The structure of these new institutes is possibly without precedent in the American scholastic scheme. The societies, which began like other scientific associations for discussion of topics by members already qualified, have undertaken the conduct and control of teaching institutions from which the students graduate to a certification for membership. The motive for this special arrangement is understandable. It originated twenty-five years ago, as has been explained, when a dearth of experienced analysts existed because of the great reluctance of the societies to entrust the teaching program to any but their own members—a caution, even a fear, that the quality and thoroughness of the training might fall short of that which the members regarded as necessary. This type of setup proved unwieldy; the need for a vote by the members of a society on trivial matters, such as minor expenditures, interfered with the smooth operation of the institute. Gradually, about 1945, it became apparent that the societies should function as separate scientific bodies for the presentation and discussion of papers, and the institutes become independent schools devoted to education exclusively.

A significant secession from the parent organization, the New York Psychoanalytic Society, took place in 1946. With the assistance of Dr. Nolan D. C. Lewis, Director of the New York State Psychiatric Institute, Doctors Rado, Kardiner, George E. Daniels, and David M. Levy formed the nucleus of the Association for Psychoanalytic Medicine and the Psychoanalytic Clinic for Training and Research at Columbia University. This move raised the issue of multiple accredited institutes in the same geographic area. It was affirmed by the American Psychoanalytic Association, notwithstanding the fact that to some extent it duplicated training already available in the locality. Its great advantage is that it allows for first-grade psychoanalytic training under university auspices. The Columbia Institute, I think, provided the first residency training in psychoanalytic medicine at a university and afforded the students a rich clinical experience in psychosomatic cases. Some cooperation in training analyses exists between the Columbia group and the New York Psychoanalytic Institute and a number of analysts serve in both organizations. There is really room for two such institutes in a place as large as Manhattan, and both have thrived with little conflict.

Within ten years the activities of the New York Psychoanalytic Institute had outgrown its quarters in West 86th Street. The demand for training and its courses in related disciplines taxed its facilities to the extent that a new physical plant became necessary. The Society, in 1941, purchased and remodelled a large building at 245 East 82nd Street, New York. Soon thereafter it established a much needed treatment center with a paid medical director. It offers courses to dentists, social workers, nurses, schoolteachers, psychologists, and clergymen in its division called The School of Applied Psychoanalysis. This new building has already become inadequate for the many needs it serves. Similar study programs in response to a comparable growth and to multiple requests for psychoanalytic knowledge are to be found at every one of the fifteen odd psychoanalytic institutes within the American Psychoanalytic organization and in others with high standards outside of it.

As the years passed, the personal analysis of the analyst became more and more arduous and prolonged. "By whom were you analyzed?" sometimes has become a weighty criterion for estimating a candidate's fitness for recognition as a member of a constituent society. Some analyses have continued for four hundred hours over a period of three years or more. Among the factors back of this preoccupation with exalted standards of instruction may be doubts and uncertainties of some teaching analysts concerning mooted points in the theory they propound and also in the results that they obtain therapeutically in their daily work with patients.

The rigorous, somewhat conventionalized training program that developed at the various institutes during the fifth decade has not been an unmitigated advantage for the student. It sometimes leads to stereotyped thinking and codified, even mechanized interpretation, which satisfies the analyst's formulas but may not necessarily contribute to the patient's mastering of his difficulties. Furthermore, the long, continuous contact for three hundred hours or more impresses upon the student the ideas and ideals of his analyst, which he may later find difficult to relinquish or modify and often in unconscious duty or devotion perpetuates for years thereafter.

Another anomaly in today's training of the psychoanalyst is the private arrangement he makes with regard to the fee that he pays directly to his supervising analyst. This follows an old

German university custom by which the professor collects the fee for each course from the student. It was adopted in Austria when the idea of training analysis first came into existence, long before the organization of institutes. The fee in this country generally ranges between fifteen and twenty dollars an hour— a considerable sum in a service that is likely to run into three hundred hours.

When such a financial arrangement has operated for fifty hours or more, the analyst is almost sure to feel something of an obligation to continue with the candidate to an eventual certification, and the latter may feel he has an analogous hold on his teacher. This system also at times results in the richer, although not necessarily the most gifted, candidate being able to afford the more expensive and presumably the more competent teacher. At present there is no provision for training analysis at a nominal cost to impecunious students. The pooling of all fees received from students in training, through payment to the institute, and a subsequent prorating among all instructors might rectify some of the economic inequities and psychological implications inherent in the present plan.

A few among the men and women psychoanalysts who had fled from the intolerable political situation abroad carried with them the idea that they had a mission to preserve psychoanalysis in the tradition of Vienna of the 1920's. However, by now most of these Europeans have merged their interests with the American physicians and have come to appreciate the wisdom of the original New York group in allying psychoanalysis closely with psychiatry and general medicine.

The strength of the autonomous American psychoanalytic groups does not mean that they severed their associations with their colleagues in Europe, where with the termination of World War II societies long quiescent began to revive. Eleven years after the Paris Congress in 1938 the International Psychoanalytic Association resumed its meetings at Zurich in August, 1949. There for the first time, an American, Dr. Leo Bartemeier of Detroit, at the time president-elect of the powerful American Psychiatric Association, was elected to head the International. Indeed, the incumbent president, Dr. Jones of London, had made the suggestion that the time had arrived for an American to assume this position. Two years later when the Seventeenth International Congress took place at Amsterdam, an American, Dr. Heinz Hartmann, formerly of Vienna but then the President of the New York Psychoanalytic Society, succeeded Dr. Bartemeier.

Both at Zurich and Amsterdam it was noticeable that a number of the prominent and active psychoanalysts in America, formerly habitually present at such congresses, did not appear. Their absence could be interpreted as reflecting their disinterest in the trends of psychoanalysis that are supported generally by the present leaders in the International Psychoanalytic Association. On the other hand, at both meetings a noticeable increase in the representatives of the South American psychoanalytic societies, notably those of Brazil and Argentina, was apparent.

The closest link between general psychiatry and the specialty of psychoanalysis grew out of the Section on Psychoanalysis of the American Psychiatric Association. The first sparsely attended joint meeting of this Section and the American Psychoanalytic Association took place at the latter's thirty-first meeting at the Waldorf-Astoria in New York on May 30, 1934. In contrast, at the meeting of the American Psychiatric Association in Cincinnati in May, 1951 perhaps five hundred psychiatrists attended the joint session. Such an occurrence would have been considered preposterous in 1930, but it should be noted that during this time the membership of the American Psychiatric Association had more than doubled.

With the integration of psychoanalysis with psychiatry the psychoanalytic approach in the treatment and study of all psychoses, as well as neuroses, continues to spread. Gradually, research in the interrelationship of psychological attitudes and physiological responses has superseded that of other aspects of psychological illness to which psychoanalytic thinking can be so profitably applied. To be sure, if we turn back to some of the very earliest papers in the *Zentralblatt für Psychoanalyse* (1913–1915) we find penetrating articles interpreting the overinvestment of various body organs with libido, cases which were then called conversion hysteria. However, the recent investigations in the United States have followed the pattern of attempting to correlate certain specific emotional conflicts with particular illnesses, such as gastric ulcer, migraine, asthma, diabetes, or a predisposition to common colds or accidents. In several university centers experimentation has been conducted in the production of artificially induced neuroses in animals in the hope of drawing valid inferences of human conduct from animal behavior induced by privation, frustration, stress, and shock.

When the Chicago Psychoanalytic Institute (founded 1932) became firmly established, it began a cooperative program of research. Its members have published a large number of papers upon the psychoanalytic investigation of patients suffering from stubborn disorders of the vegetative nervous system, including the gastrointestinal, respiratory, cardiovascular, and endocrinological systems. They have also published neurophysiological studies. The Chicago investigators have attempted to prove that there is a close relationship between somatic responses and specific emotional disturbances. They distinguish between hysterical conversions and the vegetative neuroses, claiming that in the latter the symptoms do not represent substitute expressions of repressed emotions but are normal concomitant physiological manifestations of emotion. When accompanying emotional tension becomes chronic it may lead to a morbid state in the organ affected.

Similarly, the Institute for Psychoanalytic Medicine at Columbia University and the Psychiatric Service at Mount Sinai Hospital in New York are studying intensively in hospitalized patients the relationship between dysfunction of body organs and emotional disturbances from the interpretative approach of unconscious control.

Also characteristic of the development and practical adaptation of psychoanalysis in America to problems of health is the gradual disappearance of the gaps that separated psychoanalytic training from the medical schools' curricula. The boycott against psychoanalysis by medical men in Europe, which long ago so incensed Freud, never attained any comparable intensity here. As we have seen, the faculties of several outstanding medical schools from 1910 to 1920 permitted presentation of cases with psychoanalytic interpretations to students.

The isolation of psychoanalytic education in institutes operated by psychoanalytic societies was due as much to the psychoanalysts' own zeal as to the opposition of the medical schools. The schism continues to a considerable extent today, partially the outcome of the insistence of many psychoanalysts on a dogmatic course of training, which provokes and nurtures the opposition of the medical school faculties. But undeviating adherence to Freud's original concept and scope of psychoanalysis is weakening among experienced psychoanalysts, including several Europeans, trained in the most orthodox manner.

Some medical schools have established training centers in psychoanalysis, a few of which have met the requirements of the American Psychoanalytic Association. Such graduate departments are now in operation at Columbia University, New York Medical College (Flower Hospital), New York, and the College of Medicine of the recently established State University Medical Center in Brooklyn. Other medical schools, such as Temple in Philadelphia for example, do not have an analogous training center for psychoanalysis although the directing instructors, who are analysts, introduce continually the psychoanalytic contributions to psychiatry. In the psychiatric hospitals controlled by Temple, residents are frequently trained by the Philadelphia Psychoanalytic Institute if they are acceptable.

A further indication of the enormous influence that psychoanalysis is exerting on the psychiatrist of the future in America is revealed in a recent survey of the activities of the members of the American Psychoanalytic Association. Approximately 60 per cent of these were actively engaged in teaching psychiatry in medical schools, university hospitals, and psychoanalytic training centers, often in key positions. In Boston over 90 per cent of the members of the Boston Psychoanalytic Institute had appointments in institutions serving the community at large. In addition a goodly number of students who have not yet completed their training at an institute accredited by the American Psychoanalytic Association held junior appointments in grade A medical schools. A similar participation in teaching of psychoanalytic psychiatry is found among members of societies that are essentially psychoanalytic but are not affiliated with the American Psychoanalytic Association.

Another evidence of this acceptance of psychoanalysis as a branch of psychiatry is an innovation in Chicago, the formation in 1950 of the Associated Psychiatric Faculties, Inc. The psychiatric departments of the University of Chicago, the University of Illinois, the Michael Reese Hospital and the Chicago Psychoanalytic Institute compose the membership of this association. It plans to coordinate the general psychiatric and psychoanalytic training of the residents through a joint responsibility.

In London, the British Society, like some of those in American cities, has separated into two groups but on a basis not mentioned before. One branch continues Freudian in a strict sense. The other follows Melanie Klein, a layman, formerly a member of the Berlin society, who has been associated with the British society for about twenty-five years. She maintains that superego development comes not from the warnings and approbations of the outside world but from feelings of internal frustration in the infant, occurring as early as six months, and from intensely aggressive pregenital drives against the mother for which the child must make reparation (the good breast and the bad breast). The feeling of guilt, so important in all neurotic conflict, does not depend upon the existence or relinquishing of incestuous strivings but from other factors that precede and form them in early infancy. Among these are postulations of unconscious knowledge of the genitalia in infants of both sexes; that anxieties from various sources contribute to Freud's concept of castration fears; and that in the infant girl "the fear of having her body attacked and her loved inner objects destroyed essentially contributes to her anxiety." Such theories are speculative and probably can never be proven. They have found little consideration in America although in Britain Mrs. Klein has an appreciable following.

Obviously, all of these modifications and accentuations by various psychoanalysts, which have led to new "schools," have been developed in the hope of achieving better and/or quicker results, often both. There is no justification in questioning the assertion by the adherents of these various "schools," even the less popular ones, from Stekel to Sullivan, from Rank to Wilhelm Reich, that they each and all at times obtain good, even spectacular results. To be sure, the classical psychoanalysts are inclined to scoff at these methods of innovators and question the permanency and depth of the improvement in patients treated by nonclassical techniques. However, so far as I know, no study has been published by any "classical" or other psychoanalyst of results obtained in a series of consecutive cases followed for a reasonable period of time, let us say for five years, after he has discharged the patients. Hence there is no basis for comparison, questionable as this might be.

That satisfactory outcomes may be achieved by all schools is perhaps a result of the fact that certain elements are constant in all forms of psychotherapy, including classical psychoanalysis, whether it be brief, superficial, or penetrating. Of these constant elements the following are the most important: (1) the personality of the psychotherapist who conducts the treatment; (2) what he says and does, and when; (3) the time at which the treatment is undertaken; (4) how and where it is performed; and finally, (5) the susceptibility of the person upon whom the psychotherapy is practiced. The degree of overlapping of each of these factors and their mutually supportive interaction is inevitable and also highly variable and complex. This will become apparent in the following more detailed consideration of the influence of each one of these elements in attaining results in psychotherapy.

(1) It may be advantageous to consider the qualities of the person administering the treatment. The quality attributed to such agents is usually power, either in the form of authority or of persuasion, ultimately in images of the firm father or the sympathetic mother. At times it is extremely difficult to know whether the patient's positive or negative reaction to the person who conducts the therapy is based upon realistic actualities or reactivation of early childhood attachments. There is much that speaks for the postulate that the comforting influence of encouragement, of almost magical reassurance and tenderness (analogous to that which the young child receives from its mother in the form of stroking and warmth) is a fundamental element in all psychotherapy.

Emotional interaction, later known as transference, was recognized as a force in the cures with hypnotic suggestion practiced by Mesmer and Bernheim. Today, in psychoanalytic therapy when symptoms disappear because the patient's anxieties have been relieved through his confidence in the physician we speak of it as a "transference cure." Such symptomatic relief is theoretically transient because the unconscious factors responsible for the symptom formation have not been thoroughly worked through (analyzed). Nevertheless so-called "transference cures," not only in scientific psychotherapy but in empiric "faith cures," may sometimes be enduring in neuroses in which the infantile roots have not been uncovered. Such a case, the first I treated by psychoanalysis in private practice, is the basis of the story "Christmas Card" which I presented in a fictional setting in *Which Way Out*.[1] I have been able to follow the life course of this woman, now seventy-six years of age, for forty years.

(2) What is said in the course of psychotherapy and its acceptance or denial by the patient is often dependent upon the character, the intelligence, truth, or scientific orientation of the person who advances the idea. Such belief or rejection, and we may call it acceptance, confidence, faith—or disbelief, opposition, distrust—in the practitioner, medical, clerical, or lay, may be influenced by his exalted position, his physique, his age, his brilliance, or at times, oddly enough, his ignorance. A certain amount of identification always exists between the therapist and the patient. Because of this, at times an untrained person may be more effective in changing doubt into acceptance, by scientifically untenable means, in persons of a similar level of intelligence, than the most scientifically trained medical psychotherapist, who may frighten or baffle a simple-minded patient. With patients of meagre intellectual endowment obvious and direct suggestion often is the best psychotherapy.

(3) The time when a person comes for psychotherapy is extremely significant. Often patients have resorted to many forms of physical and drug therapy before they finally decide to accept some type of psychotherapy that involves confession and its transference dynamism. From private psychoanalytic practice it seems to me that when the family or the doctor has induced, sometimes forced, the reluctant patient to come for treatment, the results are far less likely to be favorable than when he comes spontaneously because of his own mounting tension. At such times, when the sufferer feels himself ready to attempt to change the intrapsychic situation he is often overwhelmed by his necessity for support by a person to whom he urgently appeals for aid whether he be physician, pastor, or

---

[1] Oberndorf, C. P.: *Which Way Out*. International Universities Press, New York, 1949.

vendor of nostrums. This great need facilitates transference and transference cures.

During the course of the treatment the element of timing interpretations is also of the utmost importance. The same explanations or interpretations from the same psychotherapist to the same person (patient) may at one time be accepted with apparent or genuine conviction and at another fail to impress. The importance of the time of inception of psychotherapy and of the appropriate timing of interpretations is well recognized, but this latter nuance in the treatment varies widely with competent analysts. It is one of the delicate problems of technique and proper timing is partially intuitive.

(4) How psychotherapy is performed shows great differences even in psychoanalyses in which the "essential principles" of Freud are faithfully followed in the recognized procedure by mature physicians who have completed long preparation. Here again each therapist decides his attitude (in the controversial question of pervading passivity or activity)—to what extent the therapist should avoid even hints at direction or seek to stimulate the patient's power of initiative through encouragement, challenge, surprise, startling, or jarring. Some very active analysts may even "shock" their patients through a deeply unconscious interpretation or threaten them, either of which seems highly questionable to me. However, we must admit that the influence that the therapist's personality exerts upon the patient merely through the contact in therapy, his unconscious tones, his manner, his phraseology, his moods or his attempts to conceal them, his countertransference is subtle and extremely difficult to evaluate. Nevertheless, such powerful intangibles often make for improvement or lack of it in the patient.

(5) The susceptibility of a patient to psychotherapy from purely psychological considerations is dependent upon the plasticity of his superego and his ego integration. From the biological standpoint, future investigations may demonstrate a physio-

logical cellular sensitivity or insensitivity in different patients to the fundamental pain-pleasure principle of Freud. Such suscepibilities are apparent in animal experimentation with different breeds of the same species.

An incident reported by a patient to me recently illustrates some of the points in therapy mentioned above: confidence in the therapist, the latter's age group and his capacity for simple verbalization which the "patient" could clearly comprehend, the timing and setting, and also the difference in susceptibility in two boys born by Caesarean section. The patient originally consulted me because both she and her husband had been driven almost frantic by the fact that their three-year-old son had been interfering with their sleep night after night for over a year, and the husband's efficiency in his work was beginning to suffer. This account of the incident follows closely the description written by the mother and is retold in the first person.

We have two boys who are as different in temperament as two children in almost any family can be. The first child, Tommy, was extremely easy to care for during his infancy, very healthy, and physically comfortable. There was no sleeping problem with him because from birth he was a "thumb sucker." This meant he always had a way to put himself to sleep and consequently voluntarily relinquished the bottle at an early age. He would sleep anywhere and under almost any circumstances.

When Tommy was eighteen and a half months old our second boy, Johnny, was born. Both children were born by Caesarean section. Johnny was smaller at birth than Tommy, and when he was about three weeks old he had colic. He never discovered his thumb.

My husband had planned a business trip to Europe when Johnny was three and a half months and Tommy twenty-two months old and wished me to accompany him. We were to be gone for about seven weeks, leaving the children in our own home with the nurse, the cook, and a married couple who were close friends of ours. The wife of this couple was a trained nurse. This seemed to us the perfect arrangement, and we left without any feeling of anxiety. However, while we were gone, Johnny was quite ill with a respiratory ailment and when we returned from Europe we found he hadn't gained an ounce and his color was that of the sheets he was lying on. We had not been told of Johnny's illness and our shock on seeing this baby was tremendous. Tommy was fine.

Johnny, who seemed to have a will of iron, developed a series of bad habits and I acquired an intense sense of guilt for having left him. His digestive problem didn't straighten itself out until he was about eighteen months old, but this was no reason to assume that I had an invalid to care for.

Johnny wouldn't go to sleep at night without wild screams of pain, which lasted sometimes for over an hour. This meant that I was with him for that period of time and he never went to sleep without me right there. He would then wake up at least once or more often during the night, always crying with what I interpreted to be pain. After several weeks of pacing the floor with him every night I discovered that if I took him into bed with me he would drop off to sleep quietly. My husband and I at least got some sleep.

At the age of three Johnny was still waking up every night, and by this time would get out of his crib, come into Mommy's and Daddy's room, and crawl into bed. If either one of us tried taking him back to his own room he screamed with rage. He was still on a bottle, which seemed the only way of putting him to sleep, and still in diapers, too. There seemed to be no solution to the problem, at least to his father and me, who were becoming worn and terrified because a third child, also to be born by Caesarean, was due in about three months.

It was at this time that we decided that outside help was needed, and I made an appointment to talk to a psychiatrist. From this visit developed a new approach on my part toward both children. The psychiatrist said that I had a therapist right in my own home whom I had overlooked but who might prove useful with Johnny. I was perplexed and sceptical when he said, "Doctor Tommy—he may turn the trick." He suggested that Johnny's bed be moved into Tommy's room and the two boys be put to bed at the same time. I didn't expect quick results, if any.

On the very first night, however, I was happily surprised. The children had been put into their beds. The light was on in their room and they were talking and looking at books. I was in the bathroom cleaning up after their baths when I heard Tommy say to Johnny, "You know, John (not Johnny), if you want to sleep in this room you can't have a bottle." This was the first time I realized that Johnny's bottle was bothering Tommy as well as his father and me. When Johnny asked Tommy why he couldn't have a bottle, Tommy told him simply that his was a grownup boy's room and grownup boys do not take milk from a bottle. He said that Johnny could go back into his own room and have his bottle and come back if he wanted but that he couldn't suck it there. A firm doctor indeed was Tommy, who would consider no compromise. There was a quite a pause after this ultimatum during which Johnny seemed to be thinking the matter over. Then he said, "O.K. I'll have milk and cookies the way you do." Tommy always has a cup of milk and some cookies to take to bed with him. This was the end of the bottle problem—without a word from me.

The children finally went to sleep long after their usual time. Then came the next problem. Would Johnny come into our room that night and follow his custom and pattern? He did come into the room but did not crawl into our bed. Instead he stood quietly beside it and just touched me lightly. I got up and took him back to his bed in Tommy's room. There was no fuss; he asked me only if I would sit in the room. I said I would for just a minute, and I sat in the rocking chair on the other side of the room; within ten minutes he was fast asleep. He slept soundly until 7:30 the next morning. I think that in some way he must have connected the impropriety of taking a bottle in a grownup boy's room with the impropriety of grownup boys seeking to creep into the parents' bed.

My problem with little Johnny was easy from here on. A week later, when Tommy took sick with a bad cold and I felt that Johnny should not sleep in the same room with him, I moved him back into his own room. Now I became fearful about what might happen. But Johnny, back in his own room, went to sleep quickly after a "grownup" boy's night-cap of cookies and milk from a cup.

The captious might quibble about whether Tommy's procedure was psychotherapy or pedagogy. But the element of education and reeducation is inherent in all psychotherapy, including psychoanalysis.

I am inclined to think that no adult psychotherapist could have presented to Johnny, so clearly and effectively, the desirability for a change to conduct appropriate to his age as did his brother, two years older, with whom he could readily identify himself and to whom because of this, in psychoanalytic terms, he could establish a powerful transference.

With the sleeping problem of the child thus rapidly solved, it became possible for me, the psychiatrist, to proceed with the analytic investigation of the mother's essential problems of adjustment in marriage, because of which she had unconsciously indulged and protracted Johnny's infantile habits.

In addition, in our estimate of results we must not overlook favorable or prejudicial external conditions, which may support or thwart the therapist's efforts. Frequently the therapist may not give full credit to propitious happenings in the patient's life situation, but he is seldom reluctant to refer to impossible environmental conditions when the patient does not respond as fully as might be desired.

All of these factors—the personality and competence of the therapist, the content, the timing, the manner of presentation and interpretation of material, and the impressibility and sensibility of the patient—play important roles in achieving success in all psychotherapy including psychoanalysis, no matter which aspect of theory is most favored.

Because one or a combination of these constant elements has operated successfully in various psychopathological situations, an increasingly large number of persons outside the medically dominated groups, associations, and schools have undertaken to treat patients privately and without the supervision inherent in chartered educational organizations. The activities of these lay, nonmedical psychotherapists are largely with children showing conduct disorders, adolescents whose antisocial behavior has brought them into conflict with the law, prisoners already convicted, but they also work with adults suffering from severe neuroses and psychoses. These psychotherapists, many of whom have received the best formal education in their special fields, have all acquired varying degrees of acquaintance with psychoanalysis, through study courses, reading, or personal analyses. The most prominent in this category are clergymen, psychiatric social workers, pedagogues, psychiatrically trained nurses, occasionally occupational therapists and doctors of philosophy in psychology and anthropology.

The curricula of each of these groups have brought them directly in contact either with situations that psychiatrists treat or with theoretical problems to which the psychoanalytic theory offers enlightenment. Strong pressure has been brought to bear by the official organizations in some of these categories, notably the psychologists, for state licensing, which would permit them legally to receive patients for treatment privately. Without licensing, a very considerable number from these academically educated groups are using with private patients the principles and techniques (especially the couch) that psychoanalysis has long approved.

These people, professionally trained, although not in medicine, are not the only ones who presume to cure sick people by psychotherapy. There are also faith healers, persons who have drifted into curing from such mystical systems as palmistry and numerology, and plain frauds who have entered the field of psychological medicine as they always have and still do in other areas of medical practice.

What role the nonmedically trained person can properly assume in the scheme of therapy is an old, tough perennial. The use of these people received a sanction fifty years ago from Freud, as we already know, and he never renounced it although he frequently condemned "wild analysis" by both untrained physicians and laymen. Prior to psychoanalysis the psychotherapy of the priest, the king, or the soothsayer did not greatly concern the doctor of medicine, who ignored or ridiculed it. But through emphasis on the psychological origins of mental illness, beginning with a new use of the old association test by Jung about 1902, psychoanalysis and psychiatry moved closer to academic psychology.

Psychoanalysis, which lifted psychotherapy from an almost entirely intuitive art to a semi-scientific procedure, had its roots in man's total phylogeny and drew heavily upon philosophy, mythology, anthropology, and literature for amplification. However, when Freud founded the first monthly journal of psychoanalysis in 1911, the *Zentralblatt für Psychoanalyse*, he used the subtitle *Medizinische Monatsschrift für Seelenkunde (Medical Monthly for the Understanding of the Mind)*. Oskar Pfister, a Swiss clergyman, and Otto Rank were the only nonmedical men on a large editorial board of collaborators. Some medical analysts twenty-five years ago attributed this divergence of opinion on lay analysis to the fact that psychoanalysis was then still in a transitional state. But, and I think that this indicates the vitality of psychoanalysis, it continues in transition today and has not become stagnant.

Psychoanalysis is such a difficult discipline that the minimum amount of training considered desirable for graduates in medicine has grown to at least one year's residency in a mental hospital in addition to the required three years' instruction at a psychoanalytic institute. It does not seem likely that graduates in other fields could acquire psychotherapeutic proficiency, psychoanalytic or otherwise, in a shorter time. Before long doctors of clinical psychotherapy (if such a category were to be established), as men of science and integrity, would be proposing longer and more diversified training, possibly even making a thorough personal analysis a requirement. The only difference between the length of time needed for the status as practitioner in psychotherapy and that of the psychiatrist would perhaps eventually be only a year of internship in a general hospital.

A solution for the problem of the nonmedical therapist may be found in one or all of several directions. The graduate course in schools of the social sciences may be lengthened by the addition of a year devoted to basic medical subjects and the same might be required for Ph.D.'s in psychology. Also, medical schools may in the future find it desirable to shorten the general medical preparation of the student who decides to specialize in psychotherapy by reducing the amount of time devoted to instruction in some of the specialties, particularly the surgical. In any event, the age for beginning the private practice of psychotherapy with adults should be about thirty, a time when the therapist may be expected to have acquired a perspective on life.

The unity and continuous interaction of mind and body is incontrovertible and hence the necessity for familiarity with both for the maximum effectiveness in diagnosing and treating illness is apparent. Physicians well trained and adept in judging both the mental and physical causes of symptom manifestation will admit that at times they have erred both ways. Perhaps they may have considered and analyzed as hysterical a case that turned out to be brain tumor, with which prompt surgical interference is imperative. Or, on the other hand, as I have seen happen in a very good hospital, a paralysis of one side of the body, thought to be due to a brain tumor, quickly disappeared when the patient was threatened with an operation. When this drastic measure was proposed, the patient nimbly rose from his bed to make a hasty exit from the hospital.

In addition to skill acquired through constant contact with illness in its various forms, doctors of medicine are bound by legal restrictions, both direct and indirect supervision, and ethical standards that have been developed over the centuries. The welfare of the public would therefore seem best guarded if the private practice of psychotherapy and particularly psychoanalysis is left in the hands of specially trained members of this profession.

As I look back on each day's experience, every case under treatment has at some time presented some physical manifestation, as uncertainty in walking, which might have been of organic origin, namely, multiple sclerosis or even Paget's disease. So, too, in cases where the symptoms are obviously mental it is often extremely difficult to decide whether a person is suffering from a mild form of disturbance or from one of many forms of insanity, such as a beginning paresis, in which an entirely different therapy should be instituted. In such instances the occasional consultation by a lay therapist with a psychiatrist cannot replace an appreciation of the manifestations of mental and physical illness that unfold themselves to a physician in his continued contact with a patient.

13. Comments on Current Tendencies

Why is it that America, both scientifically and popularly, has received with so great approval and thereby endorsed the ideas of Freud to an extent that sometimes is puzzling to people in other countries? Many explanations have been proposed, some of them implausible, such as Americans have been piqued because of their unfamiliarity with the devious manifestations of love and sex, or that Americans more than other nationalities are filled with concern about their health. But it is not primarily because of a reaction to the prudery descended from the Puritan conscience that America has welcomed a procedure that deals openly with the generally tabooed subject of sex. It is equally true that in several European countries in which psychoanalysis has made little progress the doctrines of Calvin still linger powerfully in the mores of the people.

Generally greater authority is granted women in America than in most other nations. This may be a factor in the development of neurotic complications that might lead a great number of discontented women seeking an independent career to psychoanalysis, once the method has been accepted as a therapy, and thus add perceptibly to the demand for psychoanalytic treatment. Nevertheless the masculine woman is not indigenous to the United States.

It is equally inadequate as an explanation of American enthusiasm for psychoanalysis to say that problems of the soul and psyche, prominent in European literature, were little known in the United States before Freud, for America has produced the work of Melville and Hawthorne, Poe and Whitman, and Edith Wharton's *Ethan Frome*. Nor does there seem to be much merit in the assertion that America harbors a predilection for systematization and percentages and therefore reaches out eagerly for a theory that offers something approaching a formula in the speculative field of psychology. It is claimed that psychoanalysis flourishes in America because the Americans avidly embrace the newest and latest fad, especially if it comes from abroad, and are the only people sufficiently wealthy to indulge themselves in this expensive procedure. It is also said, perhaps with some justification, that it appeals to them particularly because of the erroneous supposition that psychoanalysis finds palpable excuses (alibis) for those weaknesses and faults of people who have not succeeded in a land where "success" does appear to carry more weight than elsewhere, hence the quip: "have yourself psychoalibied."

There are three main reasons for the substantial place attained by psychoanalysis in this country. The first is the activism and realism of life, perhaps overdeveloped, that prevails in the United States. In this setting of practicality the pragmatism of William James, who influenced psychology more than philosophy, originated and flourishes. It is embodied in the phrase, a popular Americanism, "I'm from Missouri" (and you've got to show me). American psychoanalysts have been able to demonstrate this assessable value to the patient day in and day out, although not always to the degree that their patients or they themselves might wish.

The second reason, dependent in some degree on the first, is the influence of the liberal-minded physician in the United States. Few men were better able to estimate the consideration and esteem bestowed upon respected medical men in America than Henry James. This brother of William James, a novelist who wrote like a psychologist, and at times like a psychoanalyst, had resided for many years in England, France, and Germany. In his penetrating study of the effect of an unconscious, perhaps incestuous, father-daughter relationship, the novel *Washington Square* (1881—half a century later successfully dramatized for the stage and screen), he writes:

> The medical profession in America has constantly been held in honour, and more successfully than elsewhere has put forward a claim to the epithet of "liberal." In a country in which to play a social part, you must either earn your income or make believe that you earn it, the healing art has appeared in a high degree to combine two recognized sources of credit. It belongs to the realm of the practical, which in the United States is a great recommendation; and it is touched by the light of science—a merit appreciated in a community in which the love of knowledge has not always been accompanied by leisure and opportunity.

The third reason for the wide spread of psychoanalysis is due to another philosopher whose theories affected education fundamentally and radically. In all psychotherapy a reeducative factor plays an important, perhaps an indispensable, part. Just at the time when the new form of psychotherapy, psychoanalysis, was slowly but surely affecting American psychiatry a powerful figure advancing a new theory in the educational field was making his bid for recognition in New York City. In 1904 John Dewey became Professor of Philosophy at Columbia University, and for the next twenty-five years his ideas about education dominated the instruction of students at Columbia's Teachers College. Dewey, greatly influenced by James' pragmatic philosophy, regarded James as a pioneer in his perception that experience is "an intimate union of emotion and knowledge." So Dewey in the theory of education insisted that learning is a process of individual experimentation to be opened by those who participate in it. The basis for learning in a child should allow a maximum freedom of initiative rather than the absorption of facts from books or teachers.

The widely scattered alumni of Teachers College have introduced this form of teaching, through experimentation and practice, into schools throughout the land. The psychoanalytic accentuation of the importance of early occurrences in the life of the individual, especially the traumatic ones, were not far removed from the experimental values through which childhood growth could be moulded. The educators in schools, public and private, elementary and collegiate, were ready to welcome and to understand the psychoanalytic psychiatrist as an aid and co-worker in preparing students for adaptation in a democratic society. They found that interpretive psychiatry assisted in solving the problems of both normal and deviant cases.

American psychiatrists, teachers, professors, and sociologists, reared in democracy and less awed by tradition, although not uncritical, were far more ready than their European colleagues to examine and test Freud's ideas in an experimental spirit. Analytic psychiatry has found a place on the college campuses, where perhaps five hundred psychiatrists give full or part time assistance to students in those frequent tensions, depressions, fears and anxieties, associated with love and sex, so prevalent during the stormy transition period from adolescence to adulthood. Although this number is obviously inadequate for therapy, the very presence of this psychiatric service in educational institutions represents an official acknowledgment of students' emotional and mental difficulties, and inferentially of the frequent interference of such troubles with the ability to study, and the possibility of alleviating such difficulties by psychotherapy.[1]

But psychoanalysis, as well as numerous derivatives such as psychoanalytic psychotherapy or dynamic psychiatry, after more than fifty years continues in a state of perennial turmoil. This may be attributable at least partially to a vagueness and ambiguity in the meaning of psychoanalysis itself and the mean-

[1] See symposium, "The Dean and The Psychiatrist," in which the deans of students of Swarthmore and the Massachusetts Institute of Technology, and the medical directors of the University of Chicago and the Massachusetts Institute of Technology participated. *Mental Hygiene*, Vol. XXXV, No. 2, April, 1953.

ing of psychoanalytic terms. A striking example of this dissonance in definition came to light when a committee of the American Psychoanalytic Association, after long discussions and conscientious deliberations lasting over four years (1947 to 1951), made a report that it is "impossible to find a definition of psychoanalysis that is acceptable to even a large group of members of the American Psychoanalytic Association." The committee also records that "this four-year study has shown that a very strong resistance exists among the members of the American Psychoanalytic Association to any investigation on the problem of evaluating results, even on the basis of their own definition." [1a] No decision could be reached as to when and where "true" psychoanalysis (still undefined) merges into psychoanalytic psychotherapy, brief psychoanalysis, or ordinary psychotherapy in which dynamic mechanisms are used superficially.

The above conclusions indicate a confusing state of affairs indeed. They might lead to the erroneous inference that well-trained psychoanalysts do not know what psychoanalysis is or what they are doing. This, of course, is not true, for each psychoanalyst works from a definite theoretical basis, although his might not coincide with that of his most intimate colleague. Indeed, great individualism exists among recognized psychoanalysts, most of whom have definite ideas about which aspects of psychoanalysis they consider most vital and potent in the cure of the patient's illness.

The difficulty of exact definition must be bewildering to the general public, especially in instances (which every consultant encounters) in which a person is suffering from mental disturbances and wishes to avail himself of the best and most appropriate service. Another unfortunate circumstance connected with the inability of the experts to be more specific about psychoanalysis is that it does now, and will in the future,

---

[1a] *Bulletin* of the American Psychoanalytic Association, Vol. VIII, No. 1, March, 1952, p. 49.

serve as a subterfuge for untrained physicians and others to claim that any flimsy and footloose conversational therapy they elect to employ in their practice may be foisted upon patients as psychoanalysis.

The passing years have not remedied this problem, and lack of clarity on terms has often nurtured polemical crossfire in discussions involving such frequent conditions as schizophrenia, psychopathic personality, and neurosis, and even such terms as anxiety, superego, and transference.[2] Analogous difficulties in arriving at an acceptable definition to avoid confusion exist in scientific fields such as physics and to an even greater extent in theology, sociology, and art.

There are indications that some of the interest in the psychoanalytic approach to psychoses and neuroses, which enjoyed ascendency for at least two decades, has been diverted in America, temporarily at least, to pharmacological or physiologically acting agents. The most frequently used methods are insulin relaxation and insulin coma, electric shock, and operations on the brain in the form of topectomy, leucotomy, and gyrectomy. There has also been considerable experimentation in another direction. This includes treatments that permit patients to give way to previously suppressed reactions while they are under the influence of such drugs as sodium amytal or pentothal and hypnosis, which is now used for psychic catharsis in the psychoanalytic framework or reconstructive synthetic suggestion (hypno-analysis). These methods are freely selected for the relief of abnormal mental states such as depressions, mild schizophrenias, and undifferentiated neuroses, which psychoanalysts do not hesitate to include in their therapeutic province and treat with variously modified techniques.

Many of these new procedures have been welcomed by the public and referring physicians because of the costliness and length of time needed in most psychoanalysis, and they are

---

[2] Healy, William and Bronner, Augusta: *The Structure and Meaning of Psychoanalysis*. Alfred A. Knopf, New York, 1930.

sometimes preferred by patients because they do not require the sacrifice of effort and self-revelation inherent in psychoanalytic psychotherapy. Perhaps another reason is the unsatisfactory results of psychoanalysis obtained at times in cases where it is appropriate, even under the aegis of the most competent psychoanalysts. To psychoanalysts who favor, perhaps with unescapable prejudice, the psychological approach, and I number myself among them, some of these new methods seem illogical, repellent, and even barbaric. In psychosurgery the damage to the brain is permanent, and how seriously crippling to the mental functioning of the patient this damage may eventually become only the future can tell. Procedures such as shock, insulin relaxation, pervitin, and sodium amytal are often advocated to render the patient more accessible to subsequent psychotherapy. Sometimes they have been recommended by psychiatrists after the patient has not responded to psychoanalytic treatment or occasionally after his condition reportedly has been aggravated by it. Too little data have been gathered to determine how and when these psychological and physical methods can supplement each other.

Freud, in the summary of his theory, reminds us that "consciousness in general is a highly fugitive condition and the process of a thing becoming conscious is, from a topographical point of view, a phenomenon which occurs in the outermost cortex of the ego." [3] At times Freud uses the word cortex both in this psychological connotation and also in the anatomical sense of the cortex of the brain. His concept was in harmony with the thinking of his time and is not entirely outmoded. It is possible that further experience with psychosurgical procedures may establish that those functions attributed to the superego and ego (so often impossible to separate) are cortical, whereas those belonging to the id are definitely subcortical or midbrain.

[3] Freud, S.: *Outline of Psychoanalysis.* W. W. Norton & Co., New York, 1949, p. 41.

These new physical and pharmaceutical approaches alter quickly and sometimes permanently the functioning of the conscious and weaken, perhaps interrupt, the conflict between conscious and unconscious strivings. In many instances they lessen awareness to both superego demands and instinctual drives and are already shedding some light upon the interrelationship between psychodynamic and brain function. Through the severance of pathways, surgery may diminish the anxiety produced by threats from within the psychic organization as well as those arising from actual dangers from without. It is possible that such a diminution in anxiety induced by pharmaceutical agents, shock, or surgery may render a previously extremely anxious patient more amenable to psychoanalytic therapy, for in a number of cases extraordinary anxiety interferes with transference and continuous cooperation.

It has been suggested that some surgical procedures deprive a person of the capacity of mustering his psychic energy in the interests of recovery, even when he retains a strong desire to get well. At the present time in persons afflicted with this distressing incapacity, some form of psychoanalytic therapy is often advocated to bring about a restoration of function but its efficacy in these cases is not too encouraging.

Group analysis is another ramification of psychoanalysis that has become something of a vogue since World War II—sufficiently great to warrant a periodical devoted to the subject (*International Journal of Group Psychotherapy*). Trigant Burrow, one of the earlier American analysts, made use of the reactions of individuals within a group setting for psychoanalytic interpretation and therapy as early as 1920. This method exposes a large number of participants simultaneously to communal activities and personal interplay that may be viewed in the light of psychoanalytic knowledge. All such groups operate under a leader who may assume a persuasive, authoritarian role. The therapeutic effect generally is attributed to the self-revelation of participants through positive or negative identifications with the leaders or with other members of the group and the unconscious absorption of healthy tendencies within the group.

Although some group psychotherapists invoke what is called the repressive inspirational approach, by far the greater majority aim at the release of repression in their patients and an analysis (explanation-interpretation) of unconscious motives for their manifest behavior. The theories of psychoanalysis are utilized both in the direction of these groups and in the interpretation of their reactions, and most leaders agree that the therapeutic process follows basically that established in individual analyses, although the setting differs fundamentally.

It is difficult enough in individual analysis to establish with reasonable certainty how much the good results in each patient are due to this strictly personal investigation. Just how such group therapy is directly therapeutically effective with the individual can never be gauged. I would be inclined to regard it as quite superficial and evanescent. Indeed, participation in group therapy, like activity in church affairs, may serve to mask revelation of impulses that disturb the individual. When he is disengaged from the group and strong repressed drives are tapped, he is likely to go it alone or align himself with other groups in which the basic standards are different but which assist him to temporary stability and peace.

The increase in what has come to be called "Pastoral Psychiatry," which reflects another growth in the use of psychoanalytic psychology, is also attributable to the experiences of World War II. The soldiers and sailors in the emotional difficulties pointed up by removal from home, deprivation of freedom of action and independent thinking, and the threat of death, either immediately or remotely, usually turned first to the chaplain of their faith. Often he could reassure and console them and relatively seldom felt it necessary to refer them to the psychiatrist, if there happened to be one available. Many of these chaplains were acquainted with psychoanalytic mechanisms either from courses in psychiatry in theological seminaries or from collateral reading.

The interest of the clergy in psychoanalysis is not of recent origin. We find the name of Oskar Pfister, Protestant pastor of Zurich, among the collaborating editors of the first volume of *Zentralblatt für Psychoanalyse* (1911), to which he contributed an article "Concerning the Psychology of the Hysterical Madonna Cult—The Hysteria and Mysticism of Margaret Ebner" (1291 to 1351). When he presented his papers at psychoanalytic meetings, Pfister's delivery retained the characteristics of his calling. In speaking before the New York Psychoanalytic Society in November, 1930, he used that reverential intonation which ministers of all faiths assume most likely to appeal to a deity. Wise clergymen have for centuries used interpretation based on mechanisms that today would be designated Freudian, and of course, the value of confession for the alleviation of the feeling of guilt has been an important part of Catholicism. At the meeting of the International Psychoanalytical Association in Zurich in 1949, a representative of the Dominican Brothers of Montreal applied for the recognition by the Association of a study group in that Order. In April, 1953 Pope Pius XII announced that Roman Catholics might receive psychoanalytic treatment provided the psychiatrist accepts the principle of Christian morality and does not invade the province of the soul—an indeterminate boundary concerning which there may be wide difference of opinion.

For example, about 1915 a young Catholic priest, whom we will call Michael, was referred to me. Father X, head of the theological seminary from which he had been ordained, accompanied him. The young priest made assertions about the sexual life of some of his fellow students that may or may not have been true, for humans are human in khaki or cassock. However, a fantastically embellished, hallucinatory, delusional system of ideas about the Cardinal and leaders of the church left no doubt that he was suffering from dementia praecox, or schizophrenia as it is called today.

Some days later Father X returned to ask my opinion about the situation; upon hearing it he said that he was deeply grieved but that he had suspected Michael's sanity for some time. Then he proceeded, "You see, Doctor, I had a special interest in Micky, as I called him. When I was parish priest in a tenement district on the West Side, I administered the last rites to Micky's mother, a widow. Her dying words to me were 'Father make a priest of Micky,' and I did. I guided him all the way. Then an unusual thing happened. He was trained for the priesthood in the seminary which I now head. Late on the night before Micky was to be ordained I heard a knock on the door of my study, and there stood Micky, anxious, tense, and white. I asked him to come in and sit down, but he entered only a few steps. Finally he muttered, 'Father, I have a great fear that I will not be ordained tomorrow.' And I asked him, 'Micky, what is the reason that you should not be ordained?'" Father X, by his question, apparently made the young priest vaguely aware of his desire not to take certain vows for "he did not reply and walked out of the room."

Here Father X's interpretation of the young priest's phobia corresponded with the theory advanced by Freud—that it represented an unconscious wish on Micky's part to avoid priesthood, for reasons which he may not have acknowledged even to himself. From the content of the seminarian's delusional formation, one would infer that he suffered from strong sexual urges that he would have preferred to indulge rather than to accept vows of chastity.

Of course, Catholic clergymen are not the only ones who listen to confessions or complaints of physical ill-being which they associate with the emotional problems of their parishioners whom they may know very well. The healing quality of faith exists no matter what form the worship may take. It is not entirely lacking as an element in the phenomenon known as transference, and time and again one hears a patient say that he could not go to a certain analyst to whom he was referred, because at the first interview he felt he could never have faith in him, or on the other hand, hears another say that he has implicit faith in his analyst.

The fact is that in recent years clergymen have used psychology, especially psychoanalytic psychology, more and more to clarify the complexities of those who have sought assistance in solving life's struggles, giving them hours of time and often resorting to the practice of free uninterrupted expression. As in group therapy, a special journal (*Pastoral Psychology*) has been launched in America for the consideration of borderline problems, such as anxieties in youth and old age, the role of religion as an aid in healthy living, and the state in which religiosity assumes abnormal proportions. Prominent clergymen, psychiatrists, and sociologists contribute to this periodical devoted to pastoral counseling. Because of his familiarity with dynamic psychology, the progressive pastor is often able to resolve many emotional problems not far removed from those that might be designated psychoneurotic by a psychiatrist.

At least a word should be given to child psychiatry, a field that is growing rapidly and is enormously influenced in this country by the findings of the psychoanalytic school, both in clinics and in private practice.[4] One of the preferred methods in the attempts to adapt these children to an acceptable norm is the cooperative effort of the psychiatrist, psychologist, and the social case worker, many of whom are thoroughly acquainted with the psychoanalytic explanation of the emotional interplay between the child and his parent or parent substitute.

The technique with children, although based on psychoanalysis, is quite special and requires also a special physical equipment of the therapist's room, particularly toys designed to bring

---

[4] A special organization, The American Orthopsychiatric Association, with an excellent journal and regional branches, is the recognized agency that fosters child psychiatry in this country.

out various possibilities of manipulation, running water, and books. Not too many adults retain sufficiently childlike traits to become at home in psychoanalytic psychotherapy with children from the ages of two to ten or twelve. Moreover, as the therapist grows older he or she is apt to lose patience with the difficulties of psychotherapy with children and is likely gradually to change to psychotherapy with adults.

I have referred to the impasse that the Committee on Evaluation of the American Psychoanalytic Association met when it attempted to define just what constituted a psychoanalysis in the therapeutic sense. It resulted in acknowledging the inability to arrive at any description satisfactory to even a majority of the members of the Association. Nevertheless we do have a definition and one to which I personally am content to subscribe. It is Freud's own, as quoted by Ernest Jones, one of the world's most informed and experienced analysts: "Psychoanalysis is simply the study of processes of which we are unaware, of what for the sake of brevity, we call the unconscious, by the free association technique of analyzing observable phenomena of transference and resistance."

Some psychoanalysts in America would not assent to this liberal definition of psychoanalysis but might be inclined to waive a strict definition by merging "classical" theory and practice into a procedure and ideology acceptable to a considerable percentage of their colleagues. Most of them would agree that treatment should be continued until what each regards as the pivotal unconscious factors in the illness are discovered and relived (worked through). Most analysts will also accept the opinion that in cases of stubborn psychoneuroses at least two hundred hours, and often more, are necessary to attain perceptible change and permanent alteration in the personality structures of those patients whom they select as adaptable to the treatment.

Psychoanalysis differs from other forms of therapy in that it attempts a reconstruction of the personality rather than a limited goal of symptom relief. However, as familiarity with the use of psychoanalytic theory in therapy increased, psychotic conditions, if not active psychoses, were also included. This came about inevitably. In many instances it is extremely difficult to draw a boundary between neuroses and situations in which discernible symptoms are pathognomonic of either manic-depressive illness or schizophrenia. In my experience the patient as well as the physician may lose sight of the mood changes and initial symptoms about which the patient came.

Incredible as it may seem, no unison exists among experienced analysts as to which specific type of neurosis, as distinguished from psychosis, according to his own diagnosis of the neuroses (compulsions, phobias, homosexuality, psychopathic personality), is most amenable to psychoanalytic therapy.[5] This therapy attempts to bring about greater harmony between the conflicting nature and aims of instinctual drives (id) and cultural demands (superego) that threaten the disruption of the self (ego). In this connection Freud has said that we have done the best for the patient if as analysts "we raise the mental processes in his ego to a normal level and transform what had become unconscious and repressed into preconscious material and then return it once more to the possession of his ego."[6] There is little doubt that in conditions that might be considered neurotic or psychotic, depending upon the emphasis that the individual psychiatrist might lay upon the particular symptoms, the aim of psychoanalytic therapy is such a reconciliation.

Perhaps because of the extension of the application of the psychoanalytic method results that are completely favorable to both patient and physician are not as frequent as would be theoretically expected. I have pointed out that such cases are often those in which an apparently mild symptomatic front masks more serious and intractable conditions for which the

[5] Oberndorf, C. P.: "Results of Psychoanalytic Therapy," *International Journal of Psychoanalysis*, Vol. XXI, 1943, pp. 107–114.

[6] Freud, Sigmund: "Analysis Terminable and Interminable," *International Journal of Psychoanalysis*, Vol. XVIII, 1937, pp. 373–405.

psychoanalytic method was not originally intended. Among these may be mentioned schizophrenic cases that are early and mildly overt and also those that are deeply latent; manic-depressive reactions; and those borderline allied conditions known as simple depression, schizoid-manic reactions, reactive depressions, or depressions in patients with strong paranoid tendencies. Patients who fall generally into the group of psychopathic personality (which like the spiral it is impossible to define but often easier to recognize) have a weakly developed sense of conscience and obligation (superego), and are unreliable and and shifting. They are particularly unsatisfactory as patients because they usually come for treatment only when they have encountered some serious external difficulty and are unlikely to continue when the immediate danger has passed. It may also be mentioned that among the situations in which psychoanalysis is not likely to give its maximum results are those in which organic illnesses enter into a neurotically constituted person and complicate both symptomatology and the possibility of cure.

The knowledge gained from classically analyzed cases is being used with great benefit to the direction and reorientation of numerous psychotherapeutic situations. Long and continued therapeutic testing of psychoanalysis has brought about the conviction of many American psychiatrists thoroughly versed in Freud's theory that only in a relatively few instances can the method be applied as he recommended it. The position that the psychoanalytic method should be adapted to fit the patient when he cannot be reached by the technique that Freud originated, and that the living through of infantile experiences is necessary only when it helps the patient to meet difficulties with which he is struggling in the present is being accepted by many able psychoanalysts. Such extensions of Freud's methods and hypotheses do not detract from their importance but enlarge and heighten them, in the sense that they become available for the help of a greater number of afflicted persons.

In classical psychoanalytic therapy the analyst seldom sees

the persons involved in the patient's life—husband, wife, parents, or siblings. It has been suggested that it may be therapeutically advantageous, especially in cases of marital discord and those in which the patients are dependent in an immature way upon their families, to draw more frequently into consultation at appropriate instances and times, persons closely concerned so that the patient's values may be compared with those intimate outsiders. A number of analysts have proposed far greater elasticity in manipulating the psychoanalytic method under such names as brief psychoanalytic therapy, directive psychoanalysis, etc. These are not miniature psychoanalyses but an adaptation of psychoanalytic principles to symptomatic relief without the specific objective of inducing major structural changes in the patient's personality. If the latter is appreciably affected, it is incidental to alterations in thinking that the disappearance of crippling symptoms would cause.

If I speak excessively of those cases in which psychoanalysis does not fulfill all its expectations, it is because of a conviction of the inestimable value of psychoanalysis in enabling us to understand humans, individually and in groups, and a desire that its effectiveness be extended. There is no doubt that although psychoanalysis is a method, it cannot be applied identically by any two persons and each case is a case unto itself.

It has been proposed that an extensive statistical study of results with the psychoanalytic method might clarify this question. However, as we have seen, psychoanalysis as a method is indeterminate and is applied to a number of indefinable and illimitable conditions. These facts, no doubt, account for the numerous differences in therapy called psychoanalysis by the therapist. Statistics, as is well known, can be construed to prove almost any aspect that the investigator or tabulator wishes to support, even when the facts are essentially numerical. The statistical approach is particularly vulnerable in psychoanalysis, where variants are so great. A pooling of case records from the work of various physicians would face similar difficulties. A poll of psychoanalysts, in the United States and other countries as well, in active practice for at least fifteen years on their methods, successes, and failures and an open discussion of such polls by the participants, might bring out truths about therapeutic psychoanalysis more clearly since it would be based upon the actual experience of treatment, effort, and choice.

It is true that in all fields a person may repeat the same mistake for innumerable years and call it experience. Nevertheless as one grows more familiar in any art, one should acquire greater proficiency if one is not completely blind to unsatisfactory outcomes. The increased effectiveness in psychotherapy as one practices longer may be the result only of the maturity and wisdom of passing years, or even of an unconscious restriction in the choice of patients whom the psychotherapist selects for treatment. It has seemed in my own case that I have, more or less, chosen unconsciously those individuals irrespective of their psychic problems who would be most likely to respond to the implements and devices of psychoanalysis that I favor. Whatever success has been my fortune may be due partially to this circumstance.

Freud, who thought of his reputation in America as "eines mir vergnügten, übelwohlenden Kritikers" (a self-satisfied malevolent critic),[7] wrote sceptically some thirty years ago that "the popularity of the term psychoanalysis in America is no evidence of a friendly attitude toward the subject or a particularly broad dissemination of, or profound understanding of its teachings." It is possible that Freud might have been displeased with the dilution of his theory and the rough, often crude adaptation of his method in America, or the use of his discoveries in a way now frequently used in outpatient clinics and even in private practice, where thoroughly trained psychoanalysts may see patients only once or twice a week. Freud envisioned something of this sort, for at the Fifth International Psychoanalytic Congress in Budapest in 1918 he said:

[7] Personal letter to the author in 1919.

I will cast a glance at a situation which belongs to the future—one that will seem fantastic to many of you, but which I think, nevertheless, deserves that we should be prepared for it. You know that the therapeutic effects we can achieve are very inconsiderable in number. . . . Now let us assume that by some kind of organization we were able to increase our numbers to an extent sufficient for treating large masses of people. . . . Then clinics and consultation departments will be built, to which analytically oriented physicians will be appointed.

Freud was not a man to cling unreasonably to a method or an idea when convinced that new ones were entitled to succeed them. Thus it is possible, with his appreciation of the vast power that his discovery held for the better understanding of human frailties, that he might have become reconciled to the adaptation of both techniques and goals in the American fashion.

Over a hundred years ago Charles Dickens had written, in the vein of Freud's envious Viennese colleague who slightingly referred to Americans as practical, "It would be well for the American people as a whole, if they loved the Real less and the Ideal somewhat more." But, as I have pointed out, it is precisely because of this utilitarianism that the seat of psychoanalytic practice has been transferred to America, and this country has become a proving ground for its range and feasibility. American psychiatrists refused to be stifled by theoretical dogma or prescribed rules of technique, but instead boldly adapted the powerful implement of psychoanalysis in the advancement of social and medical ideals. They did not feel at all uncomfortable in their neglect of scholarly considerations when as pragmatists they favored that which endures because it is serviceable.

Because of this liberalism the American Psychoanalytic Association has grown to be a strong and powerful, even a formidable force in American psychiatric education. A recent survey shows that the Association's membership has risen to nearly five hundred and that nearly one thousand students are in training at its institutes. Aside from this membership and the students being educated by this Association, other societies and training institutes also bearing the name "psychoanalytic" have a considerable membership and student body. With this large increase of physicians in training by psychoanalysts, the prospect is that the availability of analysts will meet the ever increasing demand for services.

The American Psychoanalytic Association has just added to the list of psychoanalytic periodicals a solid quarterly, *The Journal of the American Psychoanalytic Association*. The title, *American Journal of Psychoanalysis*, had been preëmpted by the Association for the Advancement of Psychoanalysis.

A profuse number of new books based upon psychoanalytic thinking appears uninterruptedly from American publishers, perhaps one a week. Some of these might be classed as actual textbooks; others are highly technical, often on special topics, intended for experienced psychoanalysts. In addition, and perhaps more numerous, are books dealing with the application of psychoanalysis to the disturbances of children. Far more frequent are popular expositions aimed at the general public and varying strikingly in their style and accuracy. In mentioning all this flood of psychoanalytic literature we cannot ignore articles of a psychoanalytic nature that appear in the most conservative general periodicals as well as those in irresponsible, pulp, so-called "health magazines."

It is apparent, then, that psychoanalysis in one form or another has become firmly integrated with psychiatry, general medicine, psychology, and social work. The majority of social workers in America have become familiar with psychoanalysis through teaching or personal analyses and their activity merges with or overlaps that of the psychoanalytically trained psychiatrist. A relatively large number of these social workers, influenced in their ideology by psychoanalysis, are attached to psychiatric clinics and hospitals, courts, correctional institutions, churches, Salvation Army, Travelers Aid Society, schools, and social agencies. They estimate the social situations that they are called upon to investigate from the dynamic standpoint of psychoanalysis.

A social worker who was about to take a particularly aggressive youngster of twelve from the Pleasantville Cottage School for a conference with a psychoanalyst thought it would be best to prepare him for the examination. So she asked him if he knew what a psychoanalyst was. "Sure," replied the boy, "I've been to one." "Well, what is he?" "He's a guy who makes you squeal on yourself."

What more can the psychoanalyst do through the use of free association, transference and counter-transference (active participation), and interpretation than to induce confession or make the patient "squeal on himself," and as a consequence of this technique point out (analyze) how conflicts arose, the troubles that resulted from them within the mind, and their possible solutions?

In nearly all instances the psychoanalyst begins his therapy with an examination of the patient's difficulties as exposed in the current situation and works back to the earlier determining conditions and combinations. He attempts to weaken the manifold and variegated resistances.

What can the psychoanalyst do for those who are sick because they are miserably enmeshed in a strong but loose and confining net of conflict and are mentally miserable because they are sick? The analyst, like the priest, through faith can invoke confession but unlike the priest he cannot allay the suffering through absolution to be repeated at each new crisis.[8] The analyst can and does effect a dissolution of guilt arising from conflict through revaluations of early standards. At times

---

[8] See Charcot, J. M.: *Le Foi Qui Guerit*. Felix Alcan, Paris, 1897. This little treatise written after the work of Breuer and Freud does not deny faith cure. Charcot ends with this quotation from Shakespeare, perhaps still valid notwithstanding all the accretions to mental life gained through psychoanalysis: "There are more things in heaven and earth, than are dreamt in our philosophy."

through introjection the patient becomes his own judge with a new point of view. Because of this his symptoms frequently become permanently attenuated or disappear.

No one can honestly doubt that psychoanalysis, since its introduction into America fifty years ago, has added each year to its credit a very great number of cures that prior to its advent would have resisted less understanding and intensive individual therapies. A woman whose 24-year-old niece had been cured of a longstanding dismenorrhea once remarked to me, quite generously I think, "You psychiatrists at times seem to perform miracles. But that is no reason why we should expect you to do so always." Also, it is certain that psychoanalysis has revolutionized the teaching and scope of psychiatry and the philosophy of individual treatment and social medicine.

What is psychoanalysis likely to produce in the future to make the method surer and less circumstantial? Can psychoanalysis ever be applied as a science and if so, as Hocking [9] has asked, will the psychoanalyst find that more science is not enough? A glance at the latest articles by the most thoughtful and experienced psychoanalysts does not supply an answer to these questions.

Thus although psychoanalysis has established the psychological mechanisms that produce symptoms, we are still in the dark about what type of physical structure affects a person's impressionability and fosters the quick and permanent formation of tensions when confronted with inner conflict or realistic threats. Nor have we discovered how these innate predispositions can be changed. Such discoveries will not replace psychoanalysis but may place at the disposition of psychological medicine biological and chemical agents that may lessen tensions in neurotic sufferers. They may also provide agents to supplement the psychoanalytic truths that have proven so valuable in restoring neurotic and psychotic sufferers to health, efficiency, and happiness.

---

[9] Hocking, William E.: *What Man Can Make of Man.* Harper & Bros., New York, 1952.

APPENDIX

Chronological Outline
of Psychoanalysis in America

1832   Amariah Brigham, M.D. published *Remarks on the Influence of Mental Cultivation and Mental Excitement upon Health* —psychosomatic studies of dyspepsia and cardiac illness.

1850   Nathaniel Hawthorne described a psychoanalytic technique for the investigation and cure of a somatic condition associated with the feeling of guilt in a minister—*The Scarlet Letter*.

1870   Oliver Wendell Holmes, M.D. in *Mechanism in Thought and Morals* called attention to the enormous influence of the unconscious on conscious thinking and illness.

1877   Andrew J. Ingersoll, M.D. ascribed hysteria to the voluntary suppression of sexuality—*In Health*, 2nd Edition, 1892.

* * * * *

1856   On May 6, Sigmund Freud born in Freiberg, Moravia, Austria.

1884   Freud discovered the application of cocaine to the eye, which Carl Koller, ophthalmologist of New York, developed further.

1893   Freud and Josef Breuer published their *Preliminary Communication Concerning the Psychic Mechanism of Hysterical Phenomena*.

1895   Robert Edes, M.D. accepted Breuer and Freud's hypothesis about hysteria (Shattuck Lecture, Boston).

1896   William James pointed out the therapeutic potentiality of Freud's theories in appropriate cases (Lowell Lecture).

1900   August Hoch began to use psychodynamic psychiatry with cases at McLean Hospital, Waverly, Massachusetts.

1903   At Frederick Peterson's suggestion, Hoch became first Assistant Physician and Special Pathologist at Bloomingdale Hospital.

1907 Around this time Adolf Meyer introduced dynamic (psychoanalytic) psychiatry at Manhattan State Hospital, Ward's Island.

1907 Peterson advised A. A. Brill to continue postgraduate studies at Burghölzli Hospital in Zurich where Freud's theories were being tested with psychotic patients.

1909 Freud delivered five lectures at Clark University, Worcester, Massachusetts. C. G. Jung and S. Ferenczi also attended.

1910 James J. Putnam presented a paper on "Personal Experience with Freud's Psychoanalytic Method" before the American Neurological Association.

1911 In February Brill organized New York Psychoanalytic Society (Horace W. Frink, Secretary).

1911 In May Ernest Jones organized the American Psychoanalytic Association (James J. Putnam, President).

1914 Boston Psychoanalytic Society organized (Putnam, President; Coriat, Secretary). Gradually ceased to function for lack of support.

1914 Communication between American analysts and Austria interrupted by World War I.

1919 First American psychoanalyst visited Vienna for didactic analysis (Adolph Stern).

1922 First didactic analyses of physicians wishing to become analysts begun in New York.

1925 Friction developed between the American Psychoanalytic Association and New York Psychoanalytic Society on the one hand and the Educational Training Commission (European) over question of training laymen as analysts.

1927 The Educational Trust Fund of New York Psychoanalytic Society, later American Psychoanalytic Foundation, founded (C. P. Oberndorf, Chairman).

1927 In February Brill appointed New York Psychoanalytic Society's first comprehensive Educational Committee (Oberndorf, Chairman).

1930 First International Congress for Mental Hygiene in Washington brought many European psychoanalysts as participants.

1931 Franz Alexander became Visiting Professor of Psychoanalysis, University of Chicago.

1931 In September New York Psychoanalytic Institute was established (Sandor Rado, Educational Director).

1932 Around this time political persecution in Central Europe compelled large emigration of psychoanalysts, especially to America.

1935 In December American Psychoanalytic Association became a federation of four psychoanalytic societies (New York, Chicago, Washington, and Boston).

1939-1945 World War II further separated European and American psychoanalytic contacts.

1940 Independent institutes directed by members or former members of the American Psychoanalytic Association were being formed (Karen Horney, William Silverberg, Clara Thompson).

1941 First training institute in psychoanalysis under auspices of medical school established at New York Medical College (Stephen Jewett, Director).

1945 Second psychoanalytic institute in New York associated with American Psychoanalytic Association established as a postgraduate service of the College of Physicians and Surgeons, Columbia University (Sandor Rado and David M. Levy, Directors).

1949 Brill Memorial Lecture established in March by New York Psychoanalytic Society.

1949 Meetings of the International Psychoanalytic Association resumed after lapse of 11 years (Leo Bartemeier, Detroit, President).

1950 Anna Freud, at the invitation of Clark University, visits America, presenting papers in several cities.

1953 *Journal of the American Psychoanalytic Association* begins publication in January (John Frosch, editor).

Brief Biographical Notes

Abraham, Karl (1877–1925). Berlin psychoanalyst. Member of Burghölzli group, 1904–1907. "The first true psychoanalyst in Germany."

Adler, Alfred (1870–1937). Vienna psychiatrist. Member of Freud's earliest group. Later the founder of individual psychology. Author, *The Neurotic Constitution*, 1909.

Aichhorn, August (1878–1949). Vienna educator. Introduced psychoanalytic methods into the study of delinquency. Author, *Wayward Youth*, 1925.

Bernheim, Hippolyte-Marie (1840–1919). French (Nancy) psychotherapist who contributed especially to the study of hypnotism. Author, *L'Hysterie*, 1913.

Bleuler, Eugen (1857–1939). Swiss (Zurich) psychiatrist who first applied Freud's theories to the interpretation of psychoses, especially dementia praecox (schizophrenia).

Boas, Franz (1858–1942). Anthropologist. Professor of Anthropology, Columbia University, 1899–1937. Author, *The Mind of Primitive Man*, 1911.

Breuer, Josef (1842–1925). Vienna physician whose observations on hysteria formed the basis for Freud's subsequent elaboration of psychoanalysis.

Brigham, Amariah (1798–1849). New England psychiatrist. Author, *Observations on The Influence of Religion on The Health and Physical Welfare*, 1835.

Brill, Abraham A. (1874–1948). New York psychiatrist. Leading early exponent of psychoanalysis in America. Author, *Freud's Contribution to Psychiatry*, 1944.

Burgerstein, Leo. Austrian educator. Royal Professor in the Oberrealschule, Vienna.

Burrow, Trigant (1875–1950). American psychiatrist. First applied psychoanalytic concepts in group therapy. Author, *The Neuroses of Man: An Introduction to The Science of Human Behavior*, 1949.

Campbell, C. Macfie (1876–1941). Scottish-born psychiatrist. Professor of Psychiatry, Harvard Medical School, 1920–1941.

Charcot, Jean-Martin (1825–1893). French (Paris) neurologist and psychiatrist. Head of noted clinic at the Salpêtrière where Freud began his studies of functional mental disorders.

Clark, L. Pierce (1870–1933). New York neurologist and psychiatrist. Wrote profusely on psychoanalytic topics, especially the psychodynamics of epilepsy.

Coriat, Isador H. (1875–1943). Boston psychiatrist. Early active practitioner of psychoanalysis in New England. Author, *The Meaning of Dreams*, 1915.

Dana, Charles L. (1852–1935). New York neurologist. Favorably disposed to the concept that "clinical psychiatry is in fact only morbid psychology" (1904).

Dix, Dorothea L. (1802–1887). New England crusader for improvement of the treatment of the insane.

Dubois, Paul-Charles (1848–1918). Swiss (Berne) psychiatrist. Originator of the persuasive method of psychotherapy. Author, *The Psychoneuroses and Their Moral Treatment*, 1909.

Edes, Robert (1838–1923). New England physician. Professor of Materia Medica and Clinical Professor of Medicine, Harvard Medical School.

Eitingon, Max (1881–1943). Berlin psychoanalyst. Founded Berlin Psychoanalytic Institute, 1920.

Federn, Paul (1872–1950). Vienna psychoanalyst. Settled in New York. Wrote extensively on the psychology of the ego.

Feigenbaum, Dorian (1887–1937). Vienna psychoanalyst. Settled in New York, 1924. Cofounder of *Psychoanalytic Quarterly*.

Fenichel, Otto (1897–1946). European psychoanalyst. Settled in Los Angeles. Author, *The Psychoanalytic Theory of Neuroses*, 1945.

Ferenczi, Sandor (1873–1933). Hungarian (Budapest) psychiatrist. Prolific and original writer, especially on clinical psychoanalysis.

Fliess, Wilhelm (1858–1928). Berlin physician (laryngologist).

Freud, Sigmund (1856–1939).

Frink, Horace W. (1883–1936). New York psychoanalyst. Charter member, New York Psychoanalytic Society. Author, *Morbid Fears and Compulsions*, 1918.

Gregory, Menas S. (circa 1872–1941). New York psychiatrist. Director, Bellevue Hospital, Psychiatric Division, 1904–1934.

Groddeck, Georg (1866-1934). German physician, essayist, and novelist. Author, *Das Buch des Es.*

Hall, G. Stanley (1846-1924). New England psychologist and educator. Author, *Adolescence,* 1904.

Hartmann, Eduard von (1842-1906). German philosopher. Noted for his emphasis on the power of the unconscious.

Hoch, August (1868-1919). Swiss born psychiatrist who first actively applied dynamic psychiatry in America. Professor of Psychiatry, Cornell University, 1909-1917.

Horney, Karen (1885-1953). Berlin psychoanalyst. Later resided in Chicago and New York. Author, *The Neurotic Personality of Our Time,* 1937.

Hug-Hellmuth, Hermine von (died 1924). Vienna psychoanalyst. Pioneer in child analysis. Author, *Aus dem Seelenleben des Kindes,* 1913.

Jackson, James (1777-1867). Professor of Medicine, Harvard Medical School, 1812-1836. Author, *Letters to a Young Physician,* 1855.

James, William (1842-1910). American psychologist. Professor of Philosophy, Harvard University, 1897-1907.

Janet, Pierre (1859-1947). French physician and psychologist. Author, *Obsessions and Psychasthenia,* 1904.

Jastrow, Joseph (1863-1944). Psychologist. Professor of Psychology, University of Wisconsin, 1888-1927. Author, *The House That Freud Built,* 1922.

Jelliffe, Smith Ely (1866-1945). American neurologist and psychiatrist. Editor with W. A. White, *The Modern Treatment of Nervous and Mental Diseases.*

Jennings, Herbert S. (1868-1947). Naturalist, geneticist. Professor of Zoology, Johns Hopkins University, 1910-1947. Author, *The Universe and Life,* 1933.

Karpas, Morris J. (1889-1918). Died in military service. American psychiatrist. Active in establishing psychoanalysis in New York City.

Kirby, George H. (1875-1935). New York psychiatrist. Director, New York Psychiatric Institute, 1917-1931.

MacCurdy, John T. (1886-1947). American physician and psychoanalyst. Later taught psychology at Oxford University, England.

Mesmer, Franz Anton (1733-1815). Vienna physician. Migrated to France. Discoverer of "mesmerism" which later became hypnosis.

Meyer, Adolf (1866-1950). Swiss-born psychiatrist. Professor of Psychiatry, Johns Hopkins University, 1910-1941.
Meyer, Monroe A. (1892-1939). New York psychoanalyst. First Executive Director, New York Psychoanalytic Institute.
Mitchell, S. Weir (1829-1914). Philadelphia neurologist and novelist. Author, *Dr. North and His Friends*, 1900.
Peterson, Frederick (1859-1938). New York psychiatrist and poet. Clinical Professor of Psychiatry, Columbia University, 1903-1917.
Prince, Morton (1854-1929). Boston psychopathologist. Professor of Nervous Diseases, Tufts Medical School, 1902-1912. Author, *Dissociation of a Personality*, 1906.
Putnam, James J. (1846-1918). Boston neurologist. Past President, American Neurologist Association. Professor of Neurology, Harvard Medical School.
Rank, Otto (1884-1939). Vienna Doctor of Philosophy. Later practiced psychoanalysis in Paris and America. Author, *Das Inzestmotiv in Dichtung und Sage*.
Rickman, John (1891-1951). British psychiatrist. Editor, *International Journal of Psycho-Analysis*. Author, *The Peoples of Greater Russia*, 1949.
Sachs, Bernard (1858-1944). Attending neurologist, Mount Sinai Hospital. Opponent of psychoanalysis.
Sachs, Hanns (1881-1947). Vienna lawyer, psychoanalyst. Settled in Boston. Author, *Freud, Master and Friend*, 1944.
Salmon, Thomas W. (1876-1927). New York psychiatrist. Senior Consultant in Neuropsychiatry, A.E.F. during World War I.
Schilder, Paul (1886-1946). Vienna neurologist, neuropathologist, and psychiatrist. Settled in New York. Author, *Introduction to Psychoanalytic Psychiatry*, 1928.
Sidis, Boris (1868-1923). New England psychologist. Author, *Psychology of Suggestion*, 1902.
Simmel, Ernst (1882-1947). Berlin psychoanalyst. A founder, Berlin Psychoanalytic Institute. Settled in Los Angeles. Notable studies of war neuroses, World War I.
Southard, Elmer E. (1876-1920). New England psychiatrist and neuropathologist. Director, Boston Psychopathic Hospital, 1912-1920.
Stekel, Wilhelm (1868-1942). Vienna psychoanalyst. Author, *Compulsion and Doubt*, 1927.
Stern, William. Pedagogist. Extraordinary Professor of Philosophy,

University of Breslau. Author, *Beiträge zur Psychologie der Aussage.*

Sullivan, Harry Stack (1892–1949). Washington psychiatrist. Founder of William Alanson White Psychiatric Foundation.

Titchener, Edward B. (1867–1927). Psychologist, philosopher. Professor of Psychology, Cornell University, 1895–1927. Author, *Experimental Psychology of Thought-Processes,* 1909.

Van Ophuijsen, J. H. W. (1882–1950). Dutch psychoanalyst. Active in establishing Dutch Psychoanalytic Society. Later settled in New York.

White, William Alanson (1870–1937). Psychiatrist. Superintendent, St. Elizabeth's Hospital, Washington, D. C., 1903–1937.

Williams, Frankwood (1883–1936). American psychiatrist. Director, National Committee for Mental Hygiene, 1922–1931.

Wittels, Fritz (1880–1951). Vienna psychiatrist and novelist. Settled in New York. Author, *Freud and His Time,* 1931.

Woodward, Samuel B. (1787–1850). New England psychiatrist. First President of the American Psychiatric Association.

Former Officers and Meetings of the American Psychoanalytic Association

Year	Spring Meeting	President	Secretary	Midwinter Meeting
1911	Washington	James J. Putnam (Boston)	Ernest Jones	
1912	Boston	James J. Putnam	Ernest Jones	
1913	Washington	August Hoch (New York)	Ernest Jones	
1914	Albany	August Hoch	John MacCurdy	
1915	New York	Joint Meeting with the American Psychopathological Association		
1916	Washington	William A. White (Washington)	John MacCurdy	
1917	(No meeting—World War I)			
1918	(No meeting)			
1919	Atlantic City	William A. White	John MacCurdy	
1920	New York	A. A. Brill (New York)	Adolph Stern	
	Movement to dissolve Association defeated.			
1921	Atlantic City	G. L. Taneyhill (Baltimore)	Adolph Stern	
1922	Washington	G. L. Taneyhill	C. P. Oberndorf	
1923	Boston	C. C. Wholey (Pittsburgh)	C. P. Oberndorf	
1924	Atlantic City	C. P. Oberndorf (New York)	Adolph Stern	New York

Practice begins of holding meetings at same time as American Psychiatric Association.

262 A HISTORY OF PSYCHOANALYSIS IN AMERICA

Year	Spring Meeting	President	Secretary	Midwinter Meeting
1925	Richmond	Isador H. Coriat (Boston)	Adolph Stern	New York
1926	New York	Trigant Burrow (Baltimore)	Adolph Stern	New York
1927	Cincinnati	Adolph Stern (New York)	C. P. Oberndorf	New York
1928	Minneapolis	William A. White	C. P. Oberndorf	New York
1929	Atlanta	A. A. Brill	C. P. Oberndorf	New York
1930	Washington	A. A. Brill	C. P. Oberndorf	New York
1931	Toronto	A. A. Brill	Ernest E. Hadley	New York
1932	Philadelphia	A. A. Brill	Ernest E. Hadley	New York
1933	Boston	A. A. Brill	Ernest E. Hadley	Washington
1934	New York	A. A. Brill	Ernest E. Hadley	Chicago
1935	Washington	A. A. Brill	Ernest E. Hadley	Boston

Becomes a Federation of American Societies.

1936	St. Louis	C. P. Oberndorf	Ernest E. Hadley	New York
1937	Pittsburgh	Isador H. Coriat	Lewis B. Hill	Washington
1938	Chicago	Franz Alexander (Chicago)	L. S. Kubie	

Most papers presented at Chicago again read at American Psychiatric meeting at San Francisco.

1939	Chicago	Franz Alexander	L. S. Kubie	
1940	Cincinnati	Lewis B. Hill (Baltimore)	L. S. Kubie	
1941	Richmond	David M. Levy (New York)	John M. Murray	
1942	Boston	K. A. Menninger (Topeka)	L. H. Bartemeier	
1943	Detroit	K. A. Menninger	L. H. Bartemeier	
1944	Philadelphia	L. H. Bartemeier (Detroit)	Robert P. Knight	
1945	(No meeting. United States fully mobilized in World War II.)			
1946	Chicago	B. D. Lewin (New York)	Robert P. Knight	

Year	Spring Meeting	President	Secretary	Midwinter Meeting
1947	New York	W. C. Menninger (Topeka)	George J. Mohr	New York
1948	Washington	W. C. Menninger	George J. Mohr	New York
1949	Montreal	M. Ralph Kaufman (New York)	LeRoy M. A. Maeder	New York
1950	Detroit	M. Ralph Kaufman	LeRoy M. A. Maeder	New York
1951	Cincinnati	Robert P. Knight (Stockbridge, Mass.)	LeRoy M. A. Maeder	New York
1952	Atlantic City	Robert P. Knight	LeRoy M. A. Maeder	New York
1953	Los Angeles	Ives Hendrick (Boston)	Richard Frank	New York

The American Psychoanalytic Association, Inc.: Approved Affiliate Societies and Institutes

Society Name	Date Society Organized	Date Institute Accepted
1. New York Psychoanalytic Society	1911	1932
2. Washington-Baltimore Psychoanalytic Society *	1930	1932
3. Chicago Psychoanalytic Society	1931	1932
4. Boston Psychoanalytic Society (reorganized)	1933	1933
5. Philadelphia Psychoanalytic Society	1937	1939
6. Topeka Psychoanalytic Society	1938	1938
7. Detroit Psychoanalytic Society	1940	1940
8. San Francisco Psychoanalytic Society	1941	1942
9. Association for Psychoanalytic Medicine sponsors Columbia University Psychoanalytic Clinic	1945	1946
10. Los Angeles Psychoanalytic Society	1946	1946
11. Baltimore Psychoanalytic Society	1946	1952
12. Philadelphia Association for Psychoanalysis	1949	1950
13. Society for Psychoanalytic Medicine of Southern California	1950	1950

* Because of the separation of the Washington-Baltimore Psychoanalytic Society, the Washington Society became a separate entity in 1947 and was admitted as a separate institute in 1952.

Society Name	Date Society Organized	Date Institute Accepted
14. Psychoanalytic Institute of the State University Medical Center at New York		1951
15. Western New England Psychoanalytic Society	1951	1953

By changes in constitution and by-laws in April, 1946, societies have become affiliates, and membership in a local society does not automatically confer membership in the Association. New by-laws provide for more than one society and institute in one city or geographical area.

In addition to the above institutes, the following training centers are sponsored by the American Psychoanalytic Institute:

Seattle Training Center, Northwest Clinic, Seattle, Washington. Sponsored by the San Francisco Psychoanalytic Society.

New Orleans Psychoanalytic Study Group, New Orleans, Louisiana. Sponsored by the Washington Psychoanalytic Institute.

Approved training is also carried on in Cleveland, Ohio under the auspices of the Detroit Psychoanalytic Institute.

The following institutes not connected with the American Psychoanalytic Association should be mentioned:

American Institute for Psychoanalysis, Inc., chartered by the State of New York in 1946.

William Alanson White Institute for Psychiatry, Inc., chartered by the State of New York in 1951.

Comprehensive Course in Psychoanalysis, administered by the New York Medical College-Flower and Fifth Avenue Hospitals since 1942.

Several other independent schools and societies exist, some definitely designated as psychoanalytic and others not but all strongly influenced by psychoanalytic thinking.

Congresses of International Psychoanalytic Association

1st Congress: 1908—spring—Salzburg, Austria. Informal meeting.

2nd Congress: 1910—spring—Nuremburg, Germany. The foundation of International Psychoanalytic Association is credited to Ferenczi (Internat. J. Psycho-Analysis, Vol. 15, p. 485). Jung elected first president.

3rd Congress: 1911 (Sept. 21–22)—Weimar, Germany. Jung re-elected president, although cleavage between Freud and Jung was imminent. Putnam delivered opening address: "The Significance of Philosophy for the Further Development of Psychoanalysis."

4th Congress: 1913 (Sept.)—Munich, Germany. Jung continues as president.
April, 1914: Jung's resignation from Executive Committee of the International Psychoanalytic Association accepted. Karl Abraham selected interim president.
(1914–1918: World War I.)

5th Congress: 1918—autumn—Budapest, Hungary.

6th Congress: 1920 (Sept. 8–10)—The Hague, Holland.

7th Congress: 1922 (Sept. 25–27)—Berlin, Germany. Ernest Jones presiding.

8th Congress: 1924 (April 21–23)—Salzburg, Austria. Ernest Jones presiding.

9th Congress: 1925 (Sept. 3–5)—Bad Homburg, Germany. Karl Abraham presiding. First sizeable participation by American members.

10th Congress: 1927 (Sept. 1–3)—Innsbruck, Austria.

APPENDIX

11th Congress: 1929 (July 27–31)—Oxford, England. Max Eitingon presiding. First Congress outside Continental Europe. Perhaps largest attendance from America of any Congress.
(In 1930, the Nazi Party made itself felt in Central Europe. Meeting scheduled to be held at Interlaken Sept. 7–11 postponed.)

12th Congress: 1932 (Sept. 4–7)—Wiesbaden, Germany. Max Eitingon presiding. (Held under surveillance of German police.)

13th Congress: 1934 (Aug. 26–31)—Lucerne, Switzerland. Ernest Jones presiding. Program had grown to eight scientific sessions.

14th Congress: 1936 (Aug. 2–7)—Marienbad, Czechoslovakia. Ernest Jones presiding. (All Central European societies on the verge of collapse.)

15th Congress: 1938 (Aug. 1–5)—Paris, France. Ernest Jones presiding.
(1939–1945: World War II. During these years all the European societies and institutes were weakened or closed. Meanwhile psychoanalysis flourished in America.)

16th Congress: 1949 (Aug. 15–19)—Zurich, Switzerland. Ernest Jones presiding. First postwar meeting. In the interim twenty new societies or groups, mostly in North and South America, had become sufficiently established to apply for acceptance into the Association.

17th Congress: 1951 (Aug. 7–10)—Amsterdam, Holland. Leo Bartemeier of Detroit, U. S. A., presiding.

18th Congress: 1953 (July 26–30)—London, England. Heinz Hartmann of New York, presiding.

Index

Abnormal psychology, 53
Abraham, Karl, 49, 116, 173, 266; note *re*, 256
Adam Bede (Eliot), 101
Adler, Alfred, 48, 50; in America, 171 f.; deviation from Freud's postulates, 130 f.; *re* Freud and Rank, 172; *The Neurotic Constitution*, 131; note *re*, 256; *Study of Organic Inferiority and Its Psychical Compensation*, 131
Agoraphobia, case of, 119
Aichhorn, August, 175, 194; note *re*, 256
Alexander, Franz, 193, 201 f., 254
Allen, Frederick Lewis, *Only Yesterday*, 180
Alzheimer, Alois, 77
American Institute of Psychoanalysis, 206
American Journal of Insanity, see American Journal of Psychiatry
American Journal of Psychiatry, 129
American Journal of Psychoanalysis, 248
American Journal of Psychology, 129
American Journal of Sociology, 129; issue in honor of Freud, 198
American literature, anticipations of Freud's thinking, 23-39, 231; psychoanalytic, 155
American Medico-Psychological Association, 37; *see also* American Psychiatric Association
American Orthopsychiatric Association, 241
American Psychiatric Association, 125; Freud's election to honorary membership, 198; Section on Psychoanalysis, 190, 214
American Psychoanalytic Association, 125, 165; aid to émigré analysts, 205; argument *re* proposed dissolution of, 136; change in relation with International Association, 204; constituent societies, qualification for membership, 181; federation, 255; independent institutes directed by members, 255; membership and activities, 177 f., 217, 247 f.; officers and meetings, 261-263; origin and membership, 126; reorganization, 196 ff.; requirements for training, 209 ff.; reversion from federation to a direct membership organization, 208; search for definition of psychoanalysis, 234; in World War II, 206
American Psychoanalytic Association, Inc., approved affiliate societies and institutes, 264-265
American Psychoanalytic Foundation, denied charter for treatment center, 176 f.
American Therapeutic Congress, 112
Ames, Thaddeus, 117 f.
Analysand, fee to personal analyst, 212 f.; number of hours necessary for the personal analysis of, 209, 212
Anger, 29
Anthropology, psychoanalysis and, 200
Anton, Gabriel, 203
Anxiety, 237; associated with a sense of guilt, 23 ff.; Freud *re*, 148, 169; function in mental disorder, 13
Argentine Psychoanalytic Society, 206

INDEX

Associated Psychiatric Faculties, Inc., Chicago, 217
Association for the Advancement of Psychoanalysis, 248
Association of Medical Superintendents of American Institutions for the Insane, see American Medico-Psychological Association
Association test, 53

Bartemeier, Leo, 125, 213, 255, 267
Beard, Charles A., 2
Beard, George M., 50
Bechterew Institute, Leningrad, 192 f.
Beer, effects of, 77
Belden, L. W., *An Account of Jane C. Rider*, 18 f.
Bellevue Hospital, at the turn of the century, 63 ff.; New York City Psychopathic Service, 80; types of patient and treatment, 64
Berlin Psychoanalytic Poliklinik, 159
Bernays, Ely, 58
Bernfeld, Siegfried, 150, 159, 175
Bernheim, Hippolyte-Marie, 42, 219; note *re*, 256
Birth trauma, Rank's theory of, 170 f.
Bjerre, Poul, *History and Practice of Psychoanalysis*, 76
Blanton, Smiley, 186
Bleuler, Eugen, 1, 48 f.; note *re*, 256
Blitsten, Lionel, 201
Bloomingdale Hospital, 82 f.
Blumgart, Leonard, 138
Boas, Franz, note *re*, 256
Body and mind, see Mind and body
Boerhaave, Hermann, 12 f.
Boerhaave, Kaau, 12 f.
Bonnell, J. S., *Pastoral Psychiatry*, 118
Bookhammer, Robert, 5
Boston, 178 f.
Boston Psychoanalytic Institute, 217
Boston Psychoanalytic Society, 179, 254

Brand bath, 65
Breuer, Josef, 44 f., 256
— and Sigmund Freud, *Über den psychischen Mechanismus Hysterischer Phänomene*, 45, 253
Brigham, Amariah, *Remarks on the Influence of Mental Cultivation and Mental Excitement upon Health*, 19 f., 253; note *re*, 256
Brill, Abraham A., 3, 60, 135, 187, 194; contributions of, 112 f.; disagreement with Freud, 148; friendship with Jones, 109 f.; lectures, 189; note *re*, 256; organized New York Psychoanalytic Society, 254; personality, 107, 111 f., 174; postgraduate studies, 54; retirement from the New York Society and the American Association, 197; translations, 128; visit to Freud *re* lay analysis, 181
— Writings: "A Fragment of the Analysis of a Compulsion Neurosis," 114; *Basic Principles of Psychoanalysis*, 167; *Freud's Contribution to Psychiatry*, 168 f.; *Fundamental Conceptions of Psychoanalysis*, 132
Brill, Edmund, 5
Brill Memorial Lectures established, 255
British Psychoanalytic Society, 113, 217
Bromberg, Walter, 189
Brother and sister, sexual stimulation between, 94 ff.
Bulletin of the American Psychoanalytic Association, Vol. II dedicated to Freud, 198
Bullitt, William C., 205
Bunker, H. A., note *re*, 37
Burgerstein, Leo, note *re*, 256
Burgess, Ernest, "The Influence of Sigmund Freud upon Sociology in the United States," 198 f.
Burghölzli Hospital, Zurich, 54, 109, 253
Burlingham, Dorothy, 184, 205
Burr, Charles W., 130, 202
Burrow, Trigant, 86, 88, 126, 133, 237; note *re*, 256

INDEX

Campbell, Macfie, 85; "Psychological Mechanisms with Special Regard to Wish-Fulfillment, 103; note *re*, 257
Canada, lack of interest in psychoanalytic thinking, 113
Casamajor, Louis, *re* Freud, 78
Catharsis, 161
Catholic Church, confessional of, 161; *re* psychoanalytic treatment, 239 ff.
Catholic priest, case history, 239 f.
Cautery, *see* Paquelin cautery
Chadwick, Mary, *Psychology for Nurses*, 194
Chapman, Ross, 178
Character analysis, 145
Charcot, Jean-Martin, 42; *Le Foi Qui Guerit*, 249; note *re*, 257
Charité Hospital, Berlin, 73 ff.
Cheney, Clarence, 86
Chicago, psychoanalysis in, 201
Chicago, University of, 217
Chicago Psychoanalytic Institute, program of research, 215, 217
Childhood experiences: memories of, as determining influences, 4; as factor in a case of suicidal flight, 90 ff.; value of, 233; value of close contact with Nature, 55
Child psychiatry, 241 f.
Children, analysis of, 184
Christian Science, 35
Clark, L. Pierce, 133; note *re*, 257
Clarke, Edward H., *Visions: A Study of False Sight*, 33
Clark University, 55, 254
Classical analysis, 148; meaning of, 144; occupational therapy, social work, and recreational therapy, 188
Clergymen, development of pastoral psychiatry, 238 ff.
Cocaine, first use as an anesthetic in eye operations, 44, 253
Columbia University, Association for Psychoanalytic Medicine and the Psychoanalytic Clinic for Training and Research, 211; Institute for Psychoanalytic Medicine, research, 215 f., 255
Commonwealth Fund, 190

Confession, 161, 249
Conner, Lewis A., 70
Conscience, 168; and mental illness, 17, 22; *see also* New England conscience
Consciousness, Freud *re*, 236
Conversion hysteria, 215
Cooper, Anne, 5
Coriat, Isador, 125; co-author of *Religion and Medicine*, 179; note *re*, 257
Cornell Clinic, 107, 118
Cornell Medical School, 163; psychoanalytic concepts in classroom instruction, 122 f.
Cortex, Freud's use of term, 236
Couch, introduction of, in analytic procedure, 123; use of, 141, 160
Countertransference, 117

Dalcroze method, self-expression, 179
Dana, Charles L., 4, 63 f., 163; note *re*, 257
Daniels, George E., 190, 211
Davis, Andrew Jackson, 35
Dejerine, Joseph Jules, 119
Deleuze, 43
Delinquent boys, application of psychoanalysis to, 194
Dementia praecox, 1, 83; case of, 87; in Soviet Union, 192 f.; *see also* Schizophrenia
Demoniacal possession, 18
Denver (Colorado) *Medical Times*, 129
Depression, 154
Dercum, Francis X., 130
Destruction of personal property, in a case of suicidal flight, 96 ff.
Deutsch, Helena, 173
Dewey, John, 178; Freud *re*, 143; theory of education, 232 f.
Disease, disparity between textbook description and reality, 66
Dix, Dorothea L., 7, 35 f.; note *re*, 257
Dogs, Freud's anecdote *re*, 157
Dominican Brothers (Montreal), 239
Dream interpretation, 158; value of psychodynamics for the understanding of, 1

INDEX

Dreams, 15, 19; appearance of repressed material in, 183; Holmes' knowledge of the importance of, 32 f.
Drugs, use of, in psychotherapy, 13, 235 f.
Dubois, Paul-Charles, 78 f., 119; note *re*, 257
Dynamic psychiatry, 54; growth in application of, 188 f.
Dynamic psychology, 48; use at Bloomingdale, 60; at Ward's Island, 81
Dyspepsia, 19, 21

Earnest, Ernest, 52
Eastman, Max, 143
Eating, compulsive, 155
Eddy, Mary Baker, 35
Edes, Robert, 41, 253; note *re*, 257
Educational Training Commission, European, 254
Ego, 13, 167 ff.
Eitingon, Max, 173, 267; note *re*, 257
Eliot, George, *Silas Marner*, 4
Elliotson, John, use of hypnosis, 33 f.
Ellis, Havelock, *re* Freud's theories, 200 f.
Emerson, L. E., 125
Escape, *see* Flight
Esquirol, J. E. D., 7

Failure, often the result of unconscious desire not to succeed, 165
Faith, healing quality of, 240 f.
Family, patient's, advantage of consultation with, 245
Fay, James Wharton, *American Psychology before William James*, 18 f.
Federation of American Psychoanalytic Societies, 196 ff.; minimal requirements established by, 204
Federn, Paul, 116, 118 f., 145, 159; note *re*, 257
Fee, analysand's to personal analyst, 212 f.
Feigenbaum, Dorian, 190; note *re*, 257
Fenichel, Otto, 159; note *re*, 257

Ferenczi, Sandor, 27, 48, 116, 160, 173; break with Freud, 195 f.; interpretation of Swift's *Gulliver's Travels*, 172; note *re*, 257; president of International Psychoanalytic Association, 128 f.; *Versuch eine Genitaltheorie*, 143
— and Otto Rank, *Entwicklungsziele der Psychoanalyse*, 195
Fisher, Charles, and Edward Joseph, "Fugue with Awareness of Loss of Personal Identity," 102
Flexner, Abraham, 114
Fliess, Wilhelm, 46; letters of Freud to, 150; note *re*, 257
Flight, Fisher and Joseph *re*, 102; suicidal, study of, 89–102
Fordham University, 117
Forel, state mental hospital, 192 f.
Forgetting, incident of Sachs *re* Freud, 203
France, care of the insane, 10
Franklin, Benjamin, 42
Free association, 53; Holmes' understanding of, 32
French Academy of Medicine, investigation of Mesmer, 42
Freud, Anna, 58, 180; collaboration with Dorothy Burlingham, 184; lectures in America, 255
Freud, Sigmund: achievements in other fields, 44; additions to the structure of psychoanalysis, 169; American professional analysands, 138–151; *re* Americans, 139, 147 ff.; analytic method, 144 ff.; annoyance at the defection of American leadership, 185; appearance and personality, in 1921–22, 141 f.; attitude toward Adler's work, 131; attitude toward lay analysis, 175, 227; attitude toward therapeutic results of analysis, 158; biographies of, 150; concepts of, 3, 8 f.; *re* consciousness, 236; correspondence with Fliess, 46 f.; criterion of successful analysis, 243; definition of psychoanalysis, 242; desire to control psychoanalytic field, 166; *re* Dewey, 143; disagreement with Brill, 148; early antagonism to

theories of, 43 ff.; early nineteenth century precursors, 6-22; eightieth birthday honored, 198 f., 202 f.; exile and death in England, 205 f.; re Ferenczi, 144; first followers of, 48 ff.; re Frink, 166; re future of psychoanalysis, 246 f.; growth of support, 110 ff.; home and office in Vienna, 140 f.; impersonal technique, 27, 146; in 1929, 181; later works, 135; lectures at Clark University, 55, 254; neglect of, in German clinics, 77; Nemon's statue of, 150 f.; note re, 253, 257; psychic difficulties of, 46 f., 146; re psychoanalysis in America, 246; reaction to American visit, 59; reaction to Vienna riot, 146 f.; reception in America, 56; re the rest cure, 51 f.; sharp wit, 147; status and influence, 148 f.; terminology adopted, 130; use of term "resistance," 115; winner of Goethe prize in literature, 149; writings reviewed in American scientific journals, 52 f.

— Writings: *Analysis Terminable and Interminable*, 4; *Future Prospects of Psychoanalytic Therapy*, 116; *Hemmung, Symptom und Angst (Inhibition, Symptom and Anxiety)*, 169 f.; *Das Ich und das Es (The Ego and the Id)*, 167 ff.; *Jenseits des Lust Prinzips*, 131; *Massenpsychologie und Ich Analyse*, 12 n.; *Selbstdarstellung*, 56; "Selected Papers on Hysteria and Other Psychoneuroses," 128; *Three Contributions to the Theory of Sex*, 1, 78; *Zur Geschichte der psycho-analytischen Bewegung*, 110

— and Joseph Breuer, *Studies on Hysteria*, 40 f.

Freud-Bernays families, 58

Frink, H. W., 114, 135; "Analysis of a Mixed Neurosis," 115; "Die Amerikanische Psychoanalytische Literatur," 155 n.; Freud's opinion of, 148; *Morbid Fears and Compulsions*, 132; note re, 257; self-appraisal of leadership status, 166 f.

Fugue, see Flight

Functional psychology, James re, 57

Functional psychoses, Kraepelin's contribution re, 77

Garma, Angel, 206
Germany, Nazism vs. psychoanalytic ideology, 191, 196
Glaspell, Susan, *Suppressed Desires*, 180
Glover, Edward, 173
Glueck, Bernard, 125, 194
Goodman, Nathan G., *Benjamin Rush*, 18 f.
Goolker, Paul, 5
Greenacre, Phyllis, 125
Gregory, Menas S., 64, 80; note re, 257
Griesinger, Wilhelm, 7
Grinker, Roy R., re Freud, 149
Groddeck, Georg, *The Book of the Id (Das Buch vom Es)*, 167; note re, 258
Group psychotherapy, 88, 237
Guilt, sense of, 23

Hall, G. Stanley, 55, 132; *Adolescence*, 56; note re, 258
Hallucinosis, induced by repression, 106
Hamill, Ralph C., 126
Harris, Thomas Lake, 35
Hartmann, Eduard, note re, 258; *Philosophy of the Unconscious*, 16
Hartmann, Heinz, 214, 267
Haviland, Floyd, 177
Hawthorne, Nathaniel, *The Scarlet Letter*, 23 ff., 253
Healy, William and Augusta Bronner, *The Structure and Meaning of Psychoanalysis*, 235
Heart disease, pace of living and, 20
Henderson, Sir David, 86
Hendrick, Ives, 186

INDEX

Heredity, influence of, 91 ff.
Hillside Hospital, 189
Hinkle, Beatrice M., "Jung's Libido Theory and the Bergsonian Philosophy," 117
Hitschmann, Edward, 159
Hoch, August, 60, 81 f.; "Constitutional Features in the Dementia Precox Group," 103; at McLean Hospital, 82, 253; note re, 258; *Psychogenic Factors in Some Paranoiac Conditions, with Suggestions for Prophylaxis and Treatment*, 85
Hocking, William E., *What Man Can Make of Man*, 250
Holmes, Oliver Wendell, 50; *Pages from an Old Volume of Life: Mechanism in Thought and Morals*, 31 n., 253; pre-Freudian concepts in, 30–33
Holt, Edwin B., *The Freudian Wish and Its Place in Ethics*, 132
Homosexuality, unconscious, 154
Horney, Karen, 202, 206 f., 255; note re, 258
Hospital, general, psychiatric clinics, 124
Hug-Hellmuth, Hermine von, note re, 258; *Seelen Leben des Kindes*, 175
Hunt, J. Ramsey, 70
Hypnosis: as fact-finding technique, 93 ff.; Oberndorf re, 152 f.; and origin of psychoanalysis, 42; use as psychic catharsis, 235; use as therapy, 33 ff., 219
Hysteria, 41; early shock treatment of, 12
Hysterical tympanites, shock therapy, 66 f.

Id, 167 ff.
Identification, between therapist and the patient, 220; and mass hysteria, 12
Illinois, University of, 217
Inferiority complex, 50
Ingersoll, Andrew J., 20, 253
Inner Circle of the Seven Rings, 142 f., 166

Institute for Psychoanalysis, Chicago, 202
Institution for Children, Moscow, 191
Instruction, psychoanalytic, development of, 113, 186–207; see also under Medical education
International Congress for Mental Hygiene, First, 193 f., 254
Internationale Zeitschrift für Psychoanalyse, 128
International Journal of Psychoanalysis, 129, 190, 206; discussion of lay analysis, 176
International Psychoanalytic Association, choice of sites for the meetings of, 196; Congresses of: 266–267; 1918, 246; 1925, 173 f.; 1927, 180; 1929, 181; 1932, 194 f.; 1936, 203 f.; 1938, 204; 1949, 213 f.; encouragement of analysis of analysts, 117; formation of, 109; founding of official organ, 128 f.; meetings resumed after World War II, 255
International Training Commission, 186, 196, 203; constituent societies of, and their chairmen, 173
Interpersonal relationships, 207
Intoxication, cases of, 68 f.

Jackson, James, 23; *Letters to a Young Physician*, 21; note re, 258
Jahrbuch für psychoanalytische und psychopathologische Forschungen, 109, 128
James, Henry, *Washington Square*, 231 f.
James, William, 231; and Freud, 56 ff.; note re, 258; on psychopathology, 41, 253
Janet, Pierre, note re, 258; theories, 120 f.
Jastrow, Joseph, note re, 258
Jauregg, Wagner von, 48
Jefferson Medical College, 130
Jekels, Ludwig, 159
Jelliffe, Smith Ely, 3, 60, 187; evaluation of organic diseases according to Freudian principles, 133; "Glimpses of a Freudian

Odyssey," 117; note *re*, 258; "Sigmund Freud as a Neurologist," 44, 202 f.; at Ziehen's clinic, 74; *see also* White and Jelliffe
Jennings, Herbert S., note *re*, 258
Jews, and dogs, Freud's anecdote *re*, 157; emigration from Nazi Germany, 204; Freud *re*, 146
Joan of Arc, 6
Joffroy, A., and R. Dupouy, *Fugues et Vagabondage*, 90 *n*.
Johns Hopkins Medical School, 125
Jones, Ernest, 116, 180, 205; and the American Psychoanalytic Association, 126, 254; and Brill, 109 f.; and the International Psychoanalytic Association, 203 f., 214, 267; leadership, 60; paper at the American Therapeutic Congress, 1909, 112; "Rationalization in Everyday Life," 53; at the University of Toronto, 60, 113
Josiah Macy, Jr., Fund, 190
Journal of Abnormal Psychology, 52, 127
Journal of the American Psychoanalytic Association, 248, 255
Journal of Nervous and Mental Disease, 74
Jung, Carl G., 117; *re* dementia praecox, 89; and International Psychoanalytic Association, 266; *The Psychology of Dementia Praecox*, 49, 112, 128; *The Psychology of the Unconscious*, 131; reformulations of psychoanalytic theory, 131 f.; theories of, 118

Kardiner, Abram, 123, 138, 181, 211
— and L. Ovesey, *The Mark of Oppression*, 201
Karpas, Morris J., 86, 135; "Contribution to the Etiology of Dementia Praecox," 89; note *re*, 258
Kempf, E. J., *Physiology of Attitude and Emergence of Ego-Organization*, 125
Kennedy, Foster, 135, 163, 202
Kenworthy, Marion, 194
Kirby, George H., 85, 177; note *re*, 258

Klein, Melanie, theories of, 217 f.
Kluckhohn, C., and H. A. Murray, eds., *Personality: In Nature, Society and Culture*, 200
Koller, Carl, 44, 253
Kraepelin, Emil, 7, 54, 76 f.; descriptive psychiatry and nomenclature, 83 f.
Kroeber, A. L., "Totem and Taboo in Retrospect," 200

Lasswell, Harold D., "The Contribution of Freud's Insight Interview to the Social Sciences," 199 f.
Lay, Wilfrid, *The Child's Unconscious Mind*, 134
Lay analysis, 48; American vs. European attitude toward, 174 ff.; Freud *re*, 182, 185; friction over training, 254
Lay psychotherapists, 210 ff., 226–229; area of special effectiveness, 220; suggested courses for training, 228
Lecky, William, *Rationalism in Europe*, 15 f.
Lehrman, Philip, 189
Levy, David M., 211, 255
Levy, Norman A., 189
Lewin, Bertram D., 125
Lewis, Nolan D. C., 125, 128, 211
Liébault, H., 42
Literature, use of Freudian concepts in, 111
Lorand, Sandor, 188
Lucerne, 196
Ludwig, Emil, *Doctor Freud*, 150
Lunatic asylums, *see* Mental hospitals

MacCurdy, John T., 126, 133; note *re*, 258
McLean Hospital, Massachusetts, 82
Maeder, Alphons, 119
Magic, failure as cure, 67 f.
Magnetism, 43
Maloney, J. W., 117
Manhattan State Hospital, 1, 60 ff., 163; attitude of older physicians toward interpretative psychiatry,

103 f.; growth of psychoanalytic psychiatry, 80–108; program of training, 113; staff, 86
Manic-depressive insanity, 83
Marie Bonaparte, Princess, 205
Marienbad, 203
Masculine protest, 50
Masturbation, dire non-professional predictions *re*, 95; as factor in a case of suicidal flight, 92 *ff.*
Mather, Cotton, 17
Matthiessen, F. O., 41
Maturity, delayed, effects of, 71 f.
Medical education, Impact of psychoanalysis on, 122–137; psychotherapeutic training in, 186–207, 216, 228
Medical Record, 129
Medical Schools, 114; reluctance to include psychoanalysis in curricula, 62, 163 *ff.*, 177; psychoanalytic training in, 186–207, 216
Melville, Herman, 30
Menninger, Karl, 202
Mental hospitals, amenability of patients to psychoanalytic therapy, 104; inadequacies of, 36 f.; suggestions for improvement of, 105; types of therapy in, 14 f.; work of Dorothea Dix, 35
Mental hygiene, as a phase of public health, 38
Mental illness, 188; change in concept of, 7 *ff.*; chronic, failure of psychotherapy for, 104 f.; due to organic changes in the central nervous system, 86; early methods of treatment, 10 *ff.*; modern problem of, 36–39; procedures for the treatment of, 37; spiritual conflict in, 18 *ff.*, 29 f.; use of drugs as treatment, 13, 235 f.
Mesmer, Franz Anton, 42, 219; note *re*, 258
Mesmerism, *see* Hypnosis
Meyer, Adolf, 3, 56, 60, 62, 81 f., 106, 126, 187; attitude toward psychoanalysis as therapy, 84; as disciple of Freud, introduces dynamic psychiatry at Manhattan State Hospital, 62, 253; note *re*, 259

Meyer, Monroe A., 123, 188; analysis with Freud, 138; note *re*, 259
Meynert's laboratory, Vienna, 203
Michael Reese Hospital, 217
Mills, Charles K., 130
Mind and body, interdependence of, 11 *ff.*, 24 *ff.*, 214; Rush *re*, 18
Mitchell, S. Weir, 50; note *re*, 259; opinions about Freud, 52
Moore, George, *Power of the Soul over the Body, Considered in Relation to Health and Morals,* 34
Moore, Joseph, 86
Mother, son's attachment to, 94
Mount Sinai Hospital, 163; Mental Hygiene Clinic, 188; Outpatient Department, 124; Psychiatric Service, research, 215 f.
Muller, Friedrich, 76
Murray, Henry A., *Introduction to Pierre*, 30 *n.*

National Mental Health Act, 38
Naudeau, Franciscus, 10 *ff.*; definition of insanity, 11
Negro, 201
Nemon, Olen, statue of Freud, 150 f.
Neurasthenia, 50
Neurological Institute, staff, 107
Neurosis, 243; artificially induced in animals, 215; Freud vs. Federn *re*, 144
New England conscience, 17, 23
New Orleans Psychoanalytic Study Group, 265
New York Hospital, Westchester Division, 189; *see also* Bloomingdale
New York Medical College, 207, 216; first training institute in psychoanalysis, 255
New York Medical College–Flower and Fifth Avenue Hospitals, comprehensive course in psychoanalysis, 265
New York Medical Journal, 129
New York Post Graduate Medical School and Hospital, *see* University Hospital

INDEX

New York Psychoanalytic Institute, 211 f., 254

New York Psychoanalytic Society, 151, 178; *re* didactic analysis of members, 165; disharmony in, 167, 169; Educational Committee, 166, 174, 254; Educational Trust Fund, 176, 254; founding and work of psychoanalytic institute, 187 ff.; members analyzed by Freud, 138; membership and activities, 113 ff.; position *re* psychoanalytic therapy, 176; qualification for membership, 181, 186; secession from parent organization, 211; support of Jung and Adler, 118

New York State Board of Charities, 176 f.

New York State Psychiatric Institute, 81, 86

New York State University Medical Center, Brooklyn, 216

New York University, 123

Niles, Walter, 163

Noguchi, Hideyo, 86

Oberndorf, Clarence P., 48, 173; advancement denied at Cornell, 163 ff.; analysis with Freud, 118 f., 138 ff., 152–162, 160, 161 f.; at Bellevue Hospital, 63–71; boyhood experience of the failure of magic as cure, 67 f.; choice of patients, 246; clinical use of theory, 2; at Cornell, 135; debt to Freud, 3; education and early career, 61–78; first trip to Europe, 71; impressions of Freud, 140 ff.; introduction to Freud's work, 78; at Manhattan State Hospital, 103 ff.; at Mount Sinai Hospital, 124; personal view *re* birth trauma, 171; and Pleasantville Residential Cottage School, 194; postgraduate study in Europe, 73 ff.; private practice, 152 ff.; reasons for choice of career, 62, 70 ff.; start of private practice, 105 f.; study of suicidal flight, 89–102; visit to Freud, 1929, 181–185; visit to Russia, 192 ff.

— *Writings:* "Cases Allied to Manic-Depressive Insanity," 106; "Demonstration of a Case," 115; "History of the Psychoanalytic Movement," 179; *Psychiatric Novels of Oliver Wendell Holmes,* 30 n.; "Recreation Activities for Outpatient Psychiatric Cases," 188; "Sigmund Freud, His Work and Influence," 198; "Substitution Reactions," 124; *Treatment of Mental Disease in France at the End of the Eighteenth Century,* 10 n.; *Which Way Out,* 106, 220

Obsession, associated with fantasied abdominal growth, 65 f.

Oneida Community, 20 f.

Onuf, B., 114

Ophuijsen, J. H. W. van, 173, 180; note *re,* 260

Organic diseases, complicating factor in analysis, 244; evaluation of, according to Freudian principles, 133

Ossipow, N., 192 f.

Page, Charles W., note *re,* 37

Paquelin cautery, 12, 65

Paralysis agitans, 70

Paresis, 86 f.

Pastoral psychiatry, 238 ff.

Pastoral Psychology, 241

Patient, analyst and family of, 245; attitude toward his illness, 25; causes of misunderstanding and mistreatment of, 68 ff.; expression of anger against physician, 29; importance of life history to therapist, 84; importance of readiness for treatment, 220; number of visits to analyst, 156; positive or negative reaction to therapist, 219; susceptibility to psychotherapy, 221 f.

Patient and physician, relation between, 13, 195 f.; in works of Hawthorne and others, 24 ff.

Personality, structural changes as goal of psychoanalysis, 153, 242

INDEX

Peterson, Frederick, 53 f., 81; *Credulity and Cures*, 54; note *re*, 259
Pfister, Oskar, Protestant pastor of Zurich, 227, 239
Philadelphia Psychoanalytic Institute, 216
Philadelphia School of Social Work, 170
Phipps Clinic, Baltimore, 85
Physician, 231; Hawthorne *re* attitude of, 26; *see also* Patient and Physician; Psychoanalyst; Psychotherapist
Pinel, Philippe, 7, 10
Pius XII, 239
Plaut, Felix, 77
Pleasantville (New York) Residential Cottage School, 194
Poate, Ernest, 88 f.
Polon, Albert, 138
Pregnancy fantasy, 65; in a male, 66 f.
Presbyterian Hospital, New York, 190
Prince, Morton, 53, 127; note *re*, 259
Projection, mechanism of, 77 f.
Psychasthenia, term, 120
Psyche, 20 *n*.
Psychiatric Clinic, Munich, 76
Psychiatry, change in concept of mental illness, 7 ff.; first recognition in medical curricula, 62 f.; French school, 120; psychoanalytic contributions to, 216 f.
Psychoanalysis, achievements of, 250; American contributions to theory of, 132 ff.; American investigations, 179; causes of unsatisfactory results, 29 f.; the contribution of Freud, 8; current developments in, 230–250; difficulty of medical students in accepting ideology of, 164; early history, 6; establishment of special journals, 127 ff.; expansion of clinical practice and organization, 109–121; first reference to at Bloomingdale, 82 f.; first regular catalogued courses in, 125, 159; as integral part of medical practice, 127; integration of, with psychiatry, 214; integration with other fields, 248; introduction in America, 40–60; limitations in application of, 153 ff.; method adapted to fit the patient, 244 f.; national movements, 126; a new era in sociological appraisals of, 83; passive technique in, 26; popularization of, in various media, 180; prejudice against, 76; prominent contributors to application of, 116; provocation as therapeutic technique, 28; reasons for early neglect of, in social sciences, 199; rooted in man's total phylogeny, 227; sexual connotation of, among laymen, 134 f.; unfamiliar terminology, 127; use of, 8; use of pharmacological or physiologically acting agents, 235 ff.; *see also* Lay analysis
Psychoanalysis (term), 40; confusion over definition of, 234 f.; first used by Freud, 42; Freud's definition, 242 f.
Psychoanalyst: American analysands, 166; dissensions among, 202; European, in the U.S., 204, 213; function of, 108; "a guy who makes you squeal on yourself," 249; individualism among, 234; personal analysis as professional requirement, 165; popular idea of relations with patients, 135; possible connotation of use of shock treatment, 12; problems in analysis of, 155 f.; submission to analysis, 116 ff.; *see also* Lay analyst; Physician; Psychotherapist
Psychoanalytic journals, withholding of publication of unsatisfactory results, 154
Psychoanalytic Quarterly, establishment of, 190
Psychoanalytic Review, 128
Psychoanalytische Bewegung, 111
Psychocatharsis, Breuer's development of, 44 f.
Psychology, Freud's influence on, 198

Psychopathic personality, 244
Psychoses, functional, 49
Psychosomatic, introduction of the term, 20 n.
Psychosomatic medicine, theory, 26
Psychosurgery, 236 f.
Psychotherapist, personality and qualities, 219 ff.; question of active or passive role in therapeutic procedure, 221
Psychotherapy, disorders amenable to, 243 f.; elements constant in all forms of, 218; incident of small boy as therapist for younger brother, 222–225; invasion of field by untrained practitioners, 175; lay practice of, 226 ff.; qualities of the person administering the treatment, 219
Public, impact of psychoanalysis on, 122–137
Publicity, problem of psychiatrists and psychoanalysts, 19
Puner, Helen W., *Freud & His Mind*, 150
Punishment, need for, 159
Putnam, James J., 125; application of Freud's theories, 56 f.; "Concerning the Significance of Philosophy for the Further Development of Psychoanalysis," 110, 266; endorsement of Freud, 59 f.; note *re*, 259; "Personal Experience with Freud's Psychoanalytic Method," 254; "Recent Experiences in the Study and Treatment of Hysteria at the Massachusetts General Hospital," 57 n.
Puységur, Marquis de, 43

Quimby, Phineas, 35

Rado, Sandor, 211, 255
Rank, Otto, 143, 159, 193, 227; collaboration with Ferenczi, 195; contributions of, 169; note *re*, 259
Read, Stanford, "Bibliography and Review of Recent Psychoanalytic Literature," 132

Reich, Valerie, 5
Reider, Norman, 189
Reik, 175
Rein, David N., 50
Repression, 238
Resistance, an integral part of the psychoanalytic process, 28 ff.
Resistance (term), 115
Rest cure, 50 f.
Rickman, John, 139; note *re*, 259
Ricksher, and Jung, *Investigation of Galvanic Phenomena*, 53
Rosenstein, Leon, 193
Rosenwald Fund, 190
Rush, Benjamin, *Medical Inquiries and Observations on Diseases of the Mind*, 17 f.
Russell, William L., 82
Russia, *see* Union of Soviet Socialist Republics
Russian Psychoanalytic Society, 191

Sachs, Bernard, 202; note *re*, 259; vs. psychoanalysis, 138; revealing lapse of memory *re* Freud, 203
Sachs, Hanns, 175; *Freud, Master and Friend*, 142; *re* his association with Freud, 205 f.; note *re*, 259
Sadger, I., 48
St. Elizabeth's Hospital, Washington, 125, 163, 178
Salkina, A., 193
Salmon, Thomas W., 177; note *re*, 259
Scarlet Letter (Hawthorne), pre-Freudian concepts and techniques in, 24–30, 253
Schilder, Paul, 155, 172, 202; *re* analysis, 176; note *re*, 259
Schizophrenia, 49; treatment, 11; *see also* Dementia praecox
Schmidt, Wera, 191
Schneider, Louis, *The Freudian Psychology and Veblen's Social Theory*, 198
Schoenfeld, Dudley, 188
Schonow Haus, Zehlendorf, 75
Scripture, E. W., "Freud's Theory of Sex," 115 f.

INDEX

Seattle Training Center, 265
Self-expression, therapeutic effect of, 23; *see also* Suppression
Seligman, E. R. A., 187
Selinsky, Herman, 189
Sex, Ellis on Freud's theories *re*, 201; popular identification of Freudian concepts with, 180
Sexual drives, 16, 49; fulfillment of, Freud's emphasis on, as an essential to happiness, 148; repression of, and neurotic symptoms, 20 f.; subject ignored in early medico-psychiatric curricula, 63
Shepard and Enoch Pratt Hospital, 178
Shock therapy, 11 f., 221; for hysteria, 66 f.
Sidis, Boris, *Psychopathology of Everyday Life*, 52; note *re*, 259
Silberer, 116
Silverberg, William V., 207, 255
Simmel, Ernst, 205; note *re*, 259
Sleep, function of, 15
Slight, David, 113, 186
Sloane, Paul, 189
Smeltz, George, 186
Smith, George, 3 f.
Social welfare, interest in psychiatry and psychoanalysis as part of, 190
Social work, psychoanalysis and, 248 f.
Sociology, Freud's influence on, 198 ff.
Soma, 20 *n*.
Somnambulism, 18 f., 33, 183
South America, 206, 214
Southard, Elmer E., 202; note *re*, 259
Spas, European, 72
Spiegel, Frances, 5
Spiller, William G., 130
Stainbrook, Edward, 41
Starr, 203
Stekel, Wilhelm, 48, 116, 172; note *re*, 259
Stern, Adolph, 115, 188; analysis with Freud, 138, 254
Stern, William, note *re*, 259

Sterne, Laurence, *Tristram Shandy*, 14
Strachey, James, 139
Strauss, Israel, 188
Students, college, psychiatric service to, 233
Sublimation, 24
Suicide, 17; desire for, attributed by patient to inability to overcome habit of masturbation, 93; legislation *re*, 64; *see also* Flight, suicidal
Sullivan, Harry Stack, 125, 207; note *re*, 260
Superego, 22, 102, 167 ff.; *see also* New England conscience
Suppression, effect of, 17, 19
Symbolism, Freudian, 97 f.
Symptoms, diagnostic problems presented by, 68 ff., 228 f., 243
Syphilis, arsenical preparations for the cure of initial, 87

Taneyhill, G. Lane, 123, 126; at Johns Hopkins Medical School, 125
Teachers College, Columbia University, 232
Temple Medical School, 216
Terminology, psychoanalytic, 83 f., 115, 130, 235
Tess of the D'Urbervilles, 182 f.
Theater, 180
Thompson, Clara, 125, 207, 255
Thompson, Gilman, 63
Thomsen's disease, misinterpretation of symptoms, 74 f.
Timing, of therapy and interpretations, 220 f.
Titchener, Edward B., 56; note *re*, 260
Toronto, University of, 60, 112 f.
Traditional analysis, *see* Classical analysis
Training, psychoanalytic, *see* Instruction, psychoanalytic; Medical education
Transference, 27; positive, 45
Transference cure, 219 f.
Tridon, Andre, *Psychoanalysis and Love*, 175 f.
Tukes, 7

Tumor, phantom, cases of, 65 f.
Twain, Mark, *Huckleberry Finn*, 111

Unconscious, 15, 16, 49; dreams as factor in understanding of, 158
Unconscious mentation, 149
Union of Soviet Socialist Republics, official attitude toward psychoanalytic principles, 191–193
University Hospital, 189

Vanderbilt Clinic, 123
Vanderbilt Hospital, 163
Venereal diseases, 63
Vienna, in 1921–22, 184; psychoanalysis in, 138–151; riot of 1921, 146
Vienna Psychoanalytic Society, Freud presiding, 142; members, 175

Ward's Island, *see* Manhattan State Hospital
Washington, D. C., 178
Washington-Baltimore Psychoanalytic Society, 264 n.
Washington School of Psychiatry, 207
Wassermann test, 127; in diagnosis of mental disease, 77, 86 f.
Wharton, Edith, *Ethan Frome*, 231
White, Samuel, *Annual Address on Insanity*, 1844, 22
White, William A., 60, 74, 136, 194; *Forty Years of Psychiatry*, 61; note *re*, 260; *Outline of Psychiatry and Mental Mechanisms*, 125
— and S. E. Jelliffe, joint publications, 128
Wilcox, Walter, 3

William Alanson White Institute for Psychiatry, Inc., 265
Williams, Frankwood, *re* mental health in Soviet Union, 191 f.; note *re*, 260
Wilson, Woodrow, 147
Wish fulfillment, function of the dream, 33
Witchcraft, 6 f., 17
Wittel, Fritz, *Freud and His Time*, 150; note *re*, 260
Woman's Medical Journal, 129
Women, American, authority of, as factor in neurotic complications, 230
Woodward, Samuel B., 19; note *re*, 260
Worcester State Hospital, Massachusetts, 82
Word association test, 93
World War I, 188; effect on interest in psychoanalysis, 135
World War II, expansion of psychoanalysis at end of, 206, 208; effect on European psychoanalytic societies and institutes, 267
Wortis, Joseph, *re* Freud, 149

Yale Psychological Laboratory, 115
Young, S. Alexander, 126

Zeitschrift für Psychoanalyse, cessation of, 206
Zentralblatt für Psychoanalyse, 111, 114, 127 f., 227, 239; articles interpreting the overinvestment of various body organs with libido, 215
Ziehen, Theodor, 73 f.

Revised August, 1964

harper ⚜ torchbooks

HUMANITIES AND SOCIAL SCIENCES

American Studies

JOHN R. ALDEN: The American Revolution, 1775-1783.† *Illus.* TB/3011

RAY STANNARD BAKER: Following the Color Line: *American Negro Citizenship in the Progressive Era.*‡ *Illus. Edited by Dewey W. Grantham, Jr.* TB/3053

RAY A. BILLINGTON: The Far Western Frontier, 1830-1860.† *Illus.* TB/3012

JOSEPH L. BLAU, Ed.: Cornerstones of Religious Freedom in America. *Selected Basic Documents, Court Decisions and Public Statements. Enlarged and revised edition with new Intro. by Editor* TB/118

RANDOLPH S. BOURNE: War and the Intellectuals: *Collected Essays, 1915-1919.*‡ *Edited by Carl Resek* TB/3043

A. RUSSELL BUCHANAN: The United States and World War II. † *Illus.* Volume I TB/3044
Volume II TB/3045

ABRAHAM CAHAN: The Rise of David Levinsky: *a novel. Introduction by John Higham* TB/1028

JOSEPH CHARLES: The Origins of the American Party System TB/1049

THOMAS C. COCHRAN: The Inner Revolution: *Essays on the Social Sciences in History* TB/1140

T. C. COCHRAN & WILLIAM MILLER: The Age of Enterprise: *A Social History of Industrial America* TB/1054

EDWARD S. CORWIN: American Constitutional History: *Essays edited by Alpheus T. Mason and Gerald Garvey* TB/1136

FOSTER RHEA DULLES: America's Rise to World Power, 1898-1954.† *Illus.* TB/3021

W. A. DUNNING: Reconstruction, Political and Economic, 1865-1877 TB/1073

A. HUNTER DUPREE: Science in the Federal Government: *A History of Policies and Activities to 1940* TB/573

CLEMENT EATON: The Growth of Southern Civilization, 1790-1860.† *Illus.* TB/3040

HAROLD U. FAULKNER: Politics, Reform and Expansion, 1890-1900.† *Illus.* TB/3020

LOUIS FILLER: The Crusade against Slavery, 1830-1860.† *Illus.* TB/3029

EDITORS OF FORTUNE: America in the Sixties: *the Economy and the Society. Two-color charts* TB/1015

LAWRENCE HENRY GIPSON: The Coming of the Revolution, 1763-1775.† *Illus.* TB/3007

FRANCIS J. GRUND: Aristocracy in America: *Jacksonian Democracy* TB/1001

ALEXANDER HAMILTON: The Reports of Alexander Hamilton.‡ *Edited by Jacob E. Cooke* TB/3060

OSCAR HANDLIN, Editor: This Was America: *As Recorded by European Travelers to the Western Shore in the Eighteenth, Nineteenth, and Twentieth Centuries. Illus.* TB/1119

MARCUS LEE HANSEN: The Atlantic Migration: 1607-1860. *Edited by Arthur M. Schlesinger; Introduction by Oscar Handlin* TB/1052

MARCUS LEE HANSEN: The Immigrant in American History. *Edited with a Foreword by Arthur Schlesinger, Sr.* TB/1120

JOHN D. HICKS: Republican Ascendancy, 1921-1933.† *Illus.* TB/3041

JOHN HIGHAM, Ed.: The Reconstruction of American History TB/1068

DANIEL R. HUNDLEY: Social Relations in our Southern States.‡ *Edited by William R. Taylor* TB/3058

ROBERT H. JACKSON: The Supreme Court in the American System of Government TB/1106

THOMAS JEFFERSON: Notes on the State of Virginia.‡ *Edited by Thomas Perkins Abernethy* TB/3052

WILLIAM L. LANGER & S. EVERETT GLEASON: The Challenge to Isolation: *The World Crisis of 1937-1940 and American Foreign Policy* Volume I TB/3054
Volume II TB/3055

WILLIAM E. LEUCHTENBURG: Franklin D. Roosevelt and the New Deal, 1932-1940.† *Illus.* TB/3025

LEONARD W. LEVY: Freedom of Speech and Press in Early American History: *Legacy of Suppression* TB/1109

ARTHUR S. LINK: Woodrow Wilson and the Progressive Era, 1910-1917.† *Illus.* TB/3023

ROBERT GREEN McCLOSKEY: American Conservatism in the Age of Enterprise, 1865-1910 TB/1137

BERNARD MAYO: Myths and Men: *Patrick Henry, George Washington, Thomas Jefferson* TB/1108

JOHN C. MILLER: Alexander Hamilton and the Growth of the New Nation TB/3057

JOHN C. MILLER: The Federalist Era, 1789-1801.† *Illus.* TB/3027

---

† The New American Nation Series, edited by Henry Steele Commager and Richard B. Morris.

‡ American Perspectives series, edited by Bernard Wishy and William E. Leuchtenburg.

* The Rise of Modern Europe series, edited by William L. Langer.

❙ Researches in the Social, Cultural, and Behavioral Sciences, edited by Benjamin Nelson.

§ The Library of Religion and Culture, edited by Benjamin Nelson.

Σ Harper Modern Science Series, edited by James R. Newman.

⁰ Not for sale in Canada.

PERRY MILLER: Errand into the Wilderness　TB/1139
PERRY MILLER & T. H. JOHNSON, Editors: The Puritans: A Sourcebook of Their Writings
　　　　　Volume I　TB/1093
　　　　　Volume II　TB/1094
GEORGE E. MOWRY: The Era of Theodore Roosevelt and the Birth of Modern America, 1900-1912.† Illus.　TB/3022
WALLACE NOTESTEIN: The English People on the Eve of Colonization, 1603-1630.† Illus.　TB/3006
RUSSEL BLAINE NYE: The Cultural Life of the New Nation, 1776-1801.† Illus.　TB/3026
RALPH BARTON PERRY: Puritanism and Democracy　TB/1138
GEORGE E. PROBST, Ed.: The Happy Republic: A Reader in Tocqueville's America　TB/1060
WALTER RAUSCHENBUSCH: Christianity and the Social Crisis.‡ Edited by Robert D. Cross　TB/3059
FRANK THISTLETHWAITE: America and the Atlantic Community: Anglo-American Aspects, 1790-1850　TB/1107
TWELVE SOUTHERNERS: I'll Take My Stand: The South and the Agrarian Tradition. Introduction by Louis D. Rubin, Jr.; Biographical Essays by Virginia Rock　TB/1072
A. F. TYLER: Freedom's Ferment: Phases of American Social History from the Revolution to the Outbreak of the Civil War. Illus.　TB/1074
GLYNDON G. VAN DEUSEN: The Jacksonian Era, 1828-1848.† Illus.　TB/3028
WALTER E. WEYL: The New Democracy: An Essay on Certain Political and Economic Tendencies in the United States.‡ Edited by Charles Forcey　TB/3042
LOUIS B. WRIGHT: The Cultural Life of the American Colonies, 1607-1763.† Illus.　TB/3005
LOUIS B. WRIGHT: Culture on the Moving Frontier　TB/1053

Anthropology & Sociology

BERNARD BERELSON, Ed.: The Behavioral Sciences Today　TB/1127
JOSEPH B. CASAGRANDE, Ed.: In the Company of Man: 20 Portraits of Anthropological Informants. Illus.　TB/3047
W. E. LE GROS CLARK: The Antecedents of Man: An Introduction to the Evolution of the Primates.º Illus.　TB/559
THOMAS C. COCHRAN: The Inner Revolution: Essays on the Social Sciences in History　TB/1140
ALLISON DAVIS & JOHN DOLLARD: Children of Bondage: The Personality Development of Negro Youth in the Urban South∥　TB/3049
ST. CLAIR DRAKE & HORACE R. CAYTON: Black Metropolis: A Study of Negro Life in a Northern City. Introduction by Everett C. Hughes. Tables, maps, charts and graphs　Volume I　TB/1086
　　　　　Volume II　TB/1087
CORA DU BOIS: The People of Alor. New Preface by the author. Illus.　Volume I　TB/1042
　　　　　Volume II　TB/1043
LEON FESTINGER, HENRY W. RIECKEN & STANLEY SCHACHTER: When Prophecy Fails: A Social and Psychological Account of a Modern Group, that Predicted the Destruction of the World∥　TB/1132
RAYMOND FIRTH, Ed.: Man and Culture: An Evaluation of the Work of Bronislaw Malinowski ∥º　TB/1133

L. S. B. LEAKEY: Adam's Ancestors: The Evolution of Man and his Culture. Illus.　TB/1019
KURT LEWIN: Field Theory in Social Science: Selected Theoretical Papers.∥ Edited with a Foreword by Dorwin Cartwright　TB/1135
ROBERT H. LOWIE: Primitive Society. Introduction by Fred Eggan　TB/1056
BENJAMIN NELSON: Religious Traditions and the Spirit of Capitalism: From the Church Fathers to Jeremy Bentham　TB/1130
TALCOTT PARSONS & EDWARD A. SHILS, Editors: Toward a General Theory of Action: Theoretical Foundations for the Social Sciences　TB/1083
JOHN H. ROHRER & MUNRO S. EDMONSON, Eds.: The Eighth Generation Grows Up: Cultures and Personalities of New Orleans Negroes∥　TB/3050
ARNOLD ROSE: The Negro in America: The Condensed Version of Gunnar Myrdal's An American Dilemma. New Introduction by the Author; Foreword by Gunnar Myrdal　TB/3048
KURT SAMUELSSON: Religion and Economic Action: A Critique of Max Weber's The Protestant Ethic and the Spirit of Capitalism.∥º Trans. by E. G. French; Ed. with Intro. by D. C. Coleman　TB/1131
PITIRIM SOROKIN: Contemporary Sociological Theories: Through the First Quarter of the Twentieth Century　TB/3046
MAURICE R. STEIN: The Eclipse of Community: An Interpretation of American Studies. New Introduction by the Author　TB/1128
SIR EDWARD TYLOR: The Origins of Culture. Part I of "Primitive Culture."§ Introduction by Paul Radin　TB/33
SIR EDWARD TYLOR: Religion in Primitive Culture. Part II of "Primitive Culture."§ Introduction by Paul Radin　TB/34
W. LLOYD WARNER & Associates: Democracy in Jonesville: A Study in Quality and Inequality**　TB/1129
W. LLOYD WARNER: A Black Civilization: A Study of an Australian Tribe.∥ Illus.　TB/3056
W. LLOYD WARNER: Social Class in America: The Evaluation of Status　TB/1013

Art and Art History

EMILE MÂLE: The Gothic Image: Religious Art in France of the Thirteenth Century.§ 190 illus.　TB/44
MILLARD MEISS: Painting in Florence and Siena after the Black Death. 169 illus.　TB/1148
ERWIN PANOFSKY: Studies in Iconology: Humanistic Themes in the Art of the Renaissance. 180 illustrations　TB/1077
ALEXANDRE PIANKOFF: The Shrines of Tut-Ankh-Amon. Edited by N. Rambova. 117 illus.　TB/2011
JEAN SEZNEC: The Survival of the Pagan Gods: The Mythological Tradition and Its Place in Renaissance Humanism and Art. 108 illustrations　TB/2004
OTTO VON SIMSON: The Gothic Cathedral: Origins of Gothic Architecture and the Medieval Concept of Order. 58 illus.　TB/2018
HEINRICH ZIMMER: Myths and Symbols in Indian Art and Civilization. 70 illustrations　TB/2005

Business, Economics & Economic History

REINHARD BENDIX: Work and Authority in Industry: Ideologies of Management in the Course of Industrialization　TB/3035

THOMAS C. COCHRAN: The American Business System: *A Historical Perspective, 1900-1955* TB/1080

ROBERT DAHL & CHARLES E. LINDBLOM: Politics, Economics, and Welfare: *Planning and Politico-Economic Systems Resolved into Basic Social Processes* TB/3037

PETER F. DRUCKER: The New Society: *The Anatomy of Industrial Order* TB/1082

ROBERT L. HEILBRONER: The Great Ascent: *The Struggle for Economic Development in Our Time* TB/3030

ABBA P. LERNER: Everybody's Business: *A Re-examination of Current Assumptions in Economics and Public Policy* TB/3051

ROBERT GREEN McCLOSKEY: American Conservatism in the Age of Enterprise, 1865-1910 TB/1137

PAUL MANTOUX: The Industrial Revolution in the Eighteenth Century: *The Beginnings of the Modern Factory System in England*[o] TB/1079

WILLIAM MILLER, Ed.: Men in Business: *Essays on the Historical Role of the Entrepreneur* TB/1081

PERRIN STRYKER: The Character of the Executive: *Eleven Studies in Managerial Qualities* TB/1041

PIERRE URI: Partnership for Progress: *A Program for Transatlantic Action* TB/3036

Contemporary Culture

JACQUES BARZUN: The House of Intellect TB/1051

JOHN U. NEF: Cultural Foundations of Industrial Civilization TB/1024

PAUL VALÉRY: The Outlook for Intelligence TB/2016

History: General

L. CARRINGTON GOODRICH: A Short History of the Chinese People. *Illus.* TB/3015

BERNARD LEWIS: The Arabs in History TB/1029

SIR PERCY SYKES: A History of Exploration.[o] *Introduction by John K. Wright* TB/1046

History: Ancient and Medieval

A. ANDREWES: The Greek Tyrants TB/1103

P. BOISSONNADE: Life and Work in Medieval Europe.[o] *Preface by Lynn White, Jr.* TB/1141

HELEN CAM: England before Elizabeth TB/1026

NORMAN COHN: The Pursuit of the Millennium: *Revolutionary Messianism in medieval and Reformation Europe and its bearing on modern Leftist and Rightist totalitarian movements* TB/1037

G. G. COULTON: Medieval Village, Manor, and Monastery TB/1022

HEINRICH FICHTENAU: The Carolingian Empire: *The Age of Charlemagne* TB/1142

F. L. GANSHOF: Feudalism TB/1058

J. M. HUSSEY: The Byzantine World TB/1057

SAMUEL NOAH KRAMER: Sumerian Mythology TB/1055

FERDINAND LOT: The End of the Ancient World and the Beginnings of the Middle Ages. *Introduction by Glanville Downey* TB/1044

STEVEN RUNCIMAN: A History of the Crusades. Volume I: *The First Crusade and the Foundation of the Kingdom of Jerusalem. Illus.* TB/1143

HENRY OSBORN TAYLOR: The Classical Heritage of the Middle Ages. *Foreword and Biblio. by Kenneth M. Setton* [Formerly listed as TB/48 under the title *The Emergence of Christian Culture in the West*] TB/1117

J. M. WALLACE-HADRILL: The Barbarian West: *The Early Middle Ages, A.D. 400-1000* TB/1061

History: Renaissance & Reformation

R. R. BOLGAR: The Classical Heritage and Its Beneficiaries: *From the Carolingian Age to the End of the Renaissance* TB/1125

JACOB BURCKHARDT: The Civilization of the Renaissance in Italy. *Introduction by Benjamin Nelson and Charles Trinkaus. Illus.* Volume I TB/40 Volume II TB/41

ERNST CASSIRER: The Individual and the Cosmos in Renaissance Philosophy. *Translated with an Introduction by Mario Domandi* TB/1097

EDWARD P. CHEYNEY: The Dawn of a New Era, 1250-1453.* *Illus.* TB/3002

WALLACE K. FERGUSON, et al.: Facets of the Renaissance TB/1098

WALLACE K. FERGUSON, et al.: The Renaissance: *Six Essays. Illus.* TB/1084

MYRON P. GILMORE: The World of Humanism, 1453-1517.* *Illus.* TB/3003

JOHAN HUIZINGA: Erasmus and the Age of Reformation. *Illus.* TB/19

ULRICH VON HUTTEN, et al.: On the Eve of the Reformation: *"Letters of Obscure Men." Introduction by Hajo Holborn* TB/1124

PAUL O. KRISTELLER: Renaissance Thought: *The Classic, Scholastic, and Humanist Strains* TB/1048

NICCOLÒ MACHIAVELLI: History of Florence and of the Affairs of Italy: *from the earliest times to the death of Lorenzo the Magnificent. Introduction by Felix Gilbert* TB/1027

ALFRED VON MARTIN: Sociology of the Renaissance. *Introduction by Wallace K. Ferguson* TB/1099

MILLARD MEISS: Painting in Florence and Siena after the Black Death. *169 illus.* TB/1148

J. E. NEALE: The Age of Catherine de Medici[o] TB/1085

ERWIN PANOFSKY: Studies in Iconology: *Humanistic Themes in the Art of the Renaissance. 180 illustrations* TB/1077

J. H. PARRY: The Establishment of the European Hegemony: 1415-1715: *Trade and Exploration in the Age of the Renaissance* TB/1045

HENRI PIRENNE: Early Democracies in the Low Countries: *Urban Society and Political Conflict in the Middle Ages and the Renaissance. Introduction by John Mundy* TB/1110

FERDINAND SCHEVILL: The Medici. *Illus.* TB/1010

FERDINAND SCHEVILL: Medieval and Renaissance Florence. *Illus.* Volume I: *Medieval Florence* TB/1090 Volume II: *The Coming of Humanism and the Age of the Medici* TB/1091

G. M. TREVELYAN: England in the Age of Wycliffe, 1368-1520[o] TB/1112

VESPASIANO: Renaissance Princes, Popes, and Prelates: *The Vespasiano Memoirs: Lives of Illustrious Men of the XVth Century. Introduction by Myron P. Gilmore* TB/1111

3

History: Modern European

FREDERICK B. ARTZ: Reaction and Revolution, 1815-1832.* Illus. TB/3034
MAX BELOFF: The Age of Absolutism, 1660-1815 TB/1062
ROBERT C. BINKLEY: Realism and Nationalism, 1852-1871.* Illus. TB/3038
CRANE BRINTON: A Decade of Revolution, 1789-1799.* Illus. TB/3018
J. BRONOWSKI & BRUCE MAZLISH: The Western Intellectual Tradition: From Leonardo to Hegel TB/3001
GEOFFREY BRUUN: Europe and the French Imperium, 1799-1814.* Illus. TB/3033
ALAN BULLOCK: Hitler, A Study in Tyranny.º Illus. TB/1123
E. H. CARR: The Twenty Years' Crisis, 1919-1939: An Introduction to the Study of International Relationsº TB/1122
WALTER L. DORN: Competition for Empire, 1740-1763.* Illus. TB/3032
CARL J. FRIEDRICH: The Age of the Baroque, 1610-1660.* Illus. TB/3004
LEO GERSHOY: From Despotism to Revolution, 1763-1789.* Illus. TB/3017
ALBERT GOODWIN: The French Revolution TB/1064
CARLTON J. H. HAYES: A Generation of Materialism, 1871-1900.* Illus. TB/3039
J. H. HEXTER: Reappraisals in History: New Views on History and Society in Early Modern Europe TB/1100
A. R. HUMPHREYS: The Augustan World: Society, Thought, and Letters in Eighteenth Century England TB/1105
HANS KOHN, Ed.: The Mind of Modern Russia: Historical and Political Thought of Russia's Great Age TB/1065
SIR LEWIS NAMIER: Vanished Supremacies: Essays on European History, 1812-1918º TB/1088
JOHN U. NEF: Western Civilization Since the Renaissance: Peace, War, Industry, and the Arts TB/1113
FREDERICK L. NUSSBAUM: The Triumph of Science and Reason, 1660-1685.* Illus. TB/3009
RAYMOND W. POSTGATE, Ed.: Revolution from 1789 to 1906: Selected Documents TB/1063
PENFIELD ROBERTS: The Quest for Security, 1715-1740.* Illus. TB/3016
PRISCILLA ROBERTSON: Revolutions of 1848: A Social History TB/1025
ALBERT SOREL: Europe Under the Old Regime. Translated by Francis H. Herrick TB/1121
N. N. SUKHANOV: The Russian Revolution, 1917: Eyewitness Account. Edited by Joel Carmichael
Volume I TB/1066
Volume II TB/1067
JOHN B. WOLF: The Emergence of the Great Powers, 1685-1715.* Illus. TB/3010
JOHN B. WOLF: France: 1814-1919: The Rise of a Liberal-Democratic Society TB/3019

Intellectual History

HERSCHEL BAKER: The Image of Man: A Study of the Idea of Human Dignity in Classical Antiquity, the Middle Ages, and the Renaissance TB/1047
J. BRONOWSKI & BRUCE MAZLISH: The Western Intellectual Tradition: From Leonardo to Hegel TB/3001

ERNST CASSIRER: The Individual and the Cosmos in Renaissance Philosophy. Translated with an Introduction by Mario Domandi TB/1097
NORMAN COHN: The Pursuit of the Millennium: Revolutionary Messianism in medieval and Reformation Europe and its bearing on modern Leftist and Rightist totalitarian movements TB/1037
ARTHUR O. LOVEJOY: The Great Chain of Being: A Study of the History of an Idea TB/1009
ROBERT PAYNE: Hubris: A Study of Pride. Foreword by Sir Herbert Read TB/1031
BRUNO SNELL: The Discovery of the Mind: The Greek Origins of European Thought TB/1018
ERNEST LEE TUVESON: Millennium and Utopia: A Study in the Background of the Idea of Progress. ¶ New Preface by Author TB/1134

Literature, Poetry, The Novel & Criticism

JAMES BAIRD: Ishmael: The Art of Melville in the Contexts of International Primitivism TB/1023
JACQUES BARZUN: The House of Intellect TB/1051
W. J. BATE: From Classic to Romantic: Premises of Taste in Eighteenth Century England TB/1036
RACHEL BESPALOFF: On the Iliad TB/2006
R. P. BLACKMUR, et al.: Lectures in Criticism. Introduction by Huntington Cairns TB/2003
ABRAHAM CAHAN: The Rise of David Levinsky: a novel. Introduction by John Higham TB/1028
ERNST R. CURTIUS: European Literature and the Latin Middle Ages TB/2015
GEORGE ELIOT: Daniel Deronda: a novel. Introduction by F. R. Leavis TB/1039
ETIENNE GILSON: Dante and Philosophy TB/1089
ALFRED HARBAGE: As They Liked It: A Study of Shakespeare's Moral Artistry TB/1035
STANLEY R. HOPPER, Ed.: Spiritual Problems in Contemporary Literature§ TB/21
A. R. HUMPHREYS: The Augustan World: Society, Thought, and Letters in Eighteenth Century Englandº TB/1105
ALDOUS HUXLEY: Antic Hay & The Gioconda Smile.º Introduction by Martin Green TB/3503
ALDOUS HUXLEY: Brave New World & Brave New World Revisited.º Introduction by C. P. Snow TB/3501
ALDOUS HUXLEY: Point Counter Point.º Introduction by C. P. Snow TB/3502
HENRY JAMES: The Princess Casamassima: a novel. Introduction by Clinton F. Oliver TB/1005
HENRY JAMES: Roderick Hudson: a novel. Introduction by Leon Edel TB/1016
HENRY JAMES: The Tragic Muse: a novel. Introduction by Leon Edel TB/1017
ARNOLD KETTLE: An Introduction to the English Novel. Volume I: Defoe to George Eliot TB/1011
Volume II: Henry James to the Present TB/1012
JOHN STUART MILL: On Bentham and Coleridge. Introduction by F. R. Leavis TB/1070
PERRY MILLER & T. H. JOHNSON, Editors: The Puritans: A Sourcebook of Their Writings
Volume I TB/1093
Volume II TB/1094
KENNETH B. MURDOCK: Literature and Theology in Colonial New England TB/99
SAMUEL PEPYS: The Diary of Samuel Pepys.º Edited by O. F. Morshead. Illustrations by Ernest Shepard TB/1007

ST.-JOHN PERSE: Seamarks TB/2002
O. E. RÖLVAAG: Giants in the Earth. *Introduction by Einar Haugen* TB/3504
GEORGE SANTAYANA: Interpretations of Poetry and Religion§ TB/9
C. P. SNOW: Time of Hope: *a novel* TB/1040
DOROTHY VAN GHENT: The English Novel: *Form and Function* TB/1050
E. B. WHITE: One Man's Meat. *Introduction by Walter Blair* TB/3505
MORTON DAUWEN ZABEL, Editor: Literary Opinion in America Volume I TB/3013
Volume II TB/3014

Myth, Symbol & Folklore

JOSEPH CAMPBELL, Editor: Pagan and Christian Mysteries. *Illus.* TB/2013
MIRCEA ELIADE: Cosmos and History: *The Myth of the Eternal Return*§ TB/2050
C. G. JUNG & C. KERÉNYI: Essays on a Science of Mythology: *The Myths of the Divine Child and the Divine Maiden* TB/2014
ERWIN PANOFSKY: Studies in Iconology: *Humanistic Themes in the Art of the Renaissance*. 180 illustrations TB/1077
JEAN SEZNEC: The Survival of the Pagan Gods: *The Mythological Tradition and its Place in Renaissance Humanism and Art*. 108 illustrations TB/2004
HELLMUT WILHELM: Change: *Eight Lectures on the I Ching* TB/2019
HEINRICH ZIMMER: Myths and Symbols in Indian Art and Civilization. *70 illustrations* TB/2005

Philosophy

HENRI BERGSON: Time and Free Will: *An Essay on the Immediate Data of Consciousness*° TB/1021
H. J. BLACKHAM: Six Existentialist Thinkers: *Kierkegaard, Nietzsche, Jaspers, Marcel, Heidegger, Sartre*° TB/1002
ERNST CASSIRER: Rousseau, Kant and Goethe. *Introduction by Peter Gay* TB/1092
FREDERICK COPLESTON: Medieval Philosophy° TB/76
F. M. CORNFORD: From Religion to Philosophy: *A Study in the Origins of Western Speculation*§ TB/20
WILFRID DESAN: The Tragic Finale: *An Essay on the Philosophy of Jean-Paul Sartre* TB/1030
PAUL FRIEDLÄNDER: Plato: *An Introduction* TB/2017
ETIENNE GILSON: Dante and Philosophy TB/1089
WILLIAM CHASE GREENE: Moira: *Fate, Good, and Evil in Greek Thought* TB/1104
W. K. C. GUTHRIE: The Greek Philosophers: *From Thales to Aristotle*° TB/1008
F. H. HEINEMANN: Existentialism and the Modern Predicament TB/28
IMMANUEL KANT: The Doctrine of Virtue, *being Part II of The Metaphysic of Morals. Translated with Notes and Introduction by Mary J. Gregor. Foreword by H. J. Paton* TB/110
IMMANUEL KANT: Lectures on Ethics.§ *Introduction by Lewis W. Beck* TB/105
WILLARD VAN ORMAN QUINE: From a Logical Point of View: *Logico-Philosophical Essays* TB/566

BERTRAND RUSSELL et al.: The Philosophy of Bertrand Russell. *Edited by Paul Arthur Schilpp*
Volume I TB/1095
Volume II TB/1096
L. S. STEBBING: A Modern Introduction to Logic TB/538
ALFRED NORTH WHITEHEAD: Process and Reality: *An Essay in Cosmology* TB/1033
WILHELM WINDELBAND: A History of Philosophy I: *Greek, Roman, Medieval* TB/38
WILHELM WINDELBAND: A History of Philosophy II: *Renaissance, Enlightenment, Modern* TB/39

Philosophy of History

NICOLAS BERDYAEV: The Beginning and the End§ TB/14
NICOLAS BERDYAEV: The Destiny of Man TB/61
WILHELM DILTHEY: Pattern and Meaning in History: *Thoughts on History and Society.*° *Edited with an Introduction by H. P. Rickman* TB/1075
RAYMOND KLIBANSKY & H. J. PATON, Eds.: Philosophy and History: *The Ernst Cassirer Festschrift. Illus.* TB/1115
JOSE ORTEGA Y GASSET: The Modern Theme. *Introduction by Jose Ferrater Mora* TB/1038
KARL R. POPPER: The Poverty of Historicism° TB/1126
W. H. WALSH: Philosophy of History: *An Introduction* TB/1020

Political Science & Government

JEREMY BENTHAM: The Handbook of Political Fallacies: *Introduction by Crane Brinton* TB/1069
KENNETH E. BOULDING: Conflict and Defense: *A General Theory* TB/3024
CRANE BRINTON: English Political Thought in the Nineteenth Century TB/1071
EDWARD S. CORWIN: American Constitutional History: *Essays edited by Alpheus T. Mason and Gerald Garvey* TB/1136
ROBERT DAHL & CHARLES E. LINDBLOM: Politics, Economics, and Welfare: *Planning and Politico-Economic Systems Resolved into Basic Social Processes* TB/3037
JOHN NEVILLE FIGGIS: Political Thought from Gerson to Grotius: 1414-1625: *Seven Studies. Introduction by Garrett Mattingly* TB/1032
F. L. GANSHOF: Feudalism TB/1058
G. P. GOOCH: English Democratic Ideas in the Seventeenth Century TB/1006
ROBERT H. JACKSON: The Supreme Court in the American System of Government TB/1106
DAN N. JACOBS, Ed.: The New Communist Manifesto and Related Documents TB/1078
DAN N. JACOBS & HANS BAERWALD, Eds.: Chinese Communism: *Selected Documents* TB/3031
ROBERT GREEN McCLOSKEY: American Conservatism in the Age of Enterprise, 1865-1910 TB/1137
KINGSLEY MARTIN: French Liberal Thought in the Eighteenth Century: *A Study of Political Ideas from Bayle to Condorcet* TB/1114
JOHN STUART MILL: On Bentham and Coleridge. *Introduction by F. R. Leavis* TB/1070
JOHN B. MORRALL: Political Thought in Medieval Times TB/1076

KARL R. POPPER: The Open Society and Its Enemies
Volume I: *The Spell of Plato* TB/1101
Volume II: *The High Tide of Prophecy: Hegel, Marx, and the Aftermath* TB/1102
JOSEPH A. SCHUMPETER: Capitalism, Socialism and Democracy TB/3008

G. RACHEL LEVY: Religious Conceptions of the Stone Age and their Influence upon European Thought. Illus. Introduction by Henri Frankfort TB/106
MARTIN P. NILSSON: Greek Folk Religion. *Foreword by Arthur Darby Nock* TB/78
ALEXANDRE PIANKOFF: The Shrines of Tut-Ankh-Amon. *Edited by N. Rambova.* 117 illus. TB/2011
H. J. ROSE: Religion in Greece and Rome TB/55

Psychology

ALFRED ADLER: Problems of Neurosis. *Introduction by Heinz L. Ansbacher* TB/1145
ANTON T. BOISEN: The Exploration of the Inner World: *A Study of Mental Disorder and Religious Experience* TB/87
LEON FESTINGER, HENRY W. RIECKEN, STANLEY SCHACHTER: When Prophecy Fails: *A Social and Psychological Study of a Modern Group that Predicted the Destruction of the World* TB/1132
SIGMUND FREUD: On Creativity and the Unconscious: *Papers on the Psychology of Art, Literature, Love, Religion.*§ *Intro. by Benjamin Nelson* TB/45
C. JUDSON HERRICK: The Evolution of Human Nature TB/545
ALDOUS HUXLEY: The Devils of Loudun: *A Study in the Psychology of Power Politics and Mystical Religion in the France of Cardinal Richelieu*§° TB/60
WILLIAM JAMES: Psychology: *The Briefer Course. Edited with an Intro. by Gordon Allport* TB/1034
C. G. JUNG: Psychological Reflections. *Edited by Jolande Jacobi* TB/2001
C. G. JUNG: Symbols of Transformation: *An Analysis of the Prelude to a Case of Schizophrenia.* Illus.
Volume I TB/2009
Volume II TB/2010
C. G. JUNG & C. KERÉNYI: Essays on a Science of Mythology: *The Myths of the Divine Child and the Divine Maiden* TB/2014
SOREN KIERKEGAARD: Repetition: *An Essay in Experimental Psychology. Translated with Introduction & Notes by Walter Lowrie* TB/117
KARL MENNINGER: Theory of Psychoanalytic Technique TB/1144
ERICH NEUMANN: Amor and Psyche: *The Psychic Development of the Feminine* TB/2012
ERICH NEUMANN: The Origins and History of Consciousness Volume I *Illus.* TB/2007
Volume II TB/2008
C. P. OBERNDORF: A History of Psychoanalysis in America TB/1147
JEAN PIAGET, BÄRBEL INHELDER, & ALINA SZEMINSKA: The Child's Conception of Geometry TB/1146

Biblical Thought & Literature

W. F. ALBRIGHT: The Biblical Period from Abraham to Ezra TB/102
C. K. BARRETT, Ed.: The New Testament Background: *Selected Documents* TB/86
C. H. DODD: The Authority of the Bible TB/43
M. S. ENSLIN: Christian Beginnings TB/5
M. S. ENSLIN: The Literature of the Christian Movement TB/6
H. E. FOSDICK: A Guide to Understanding the Bible TB/2
H. H. ROWLEY: The Growth of the Old Testament TB/107
D. WINTON THOMAS, Ed.: Documents from Old Testament Times TB/85

Christianity: Origins & Early Development

ADOLF DEISSMANN: Paul: *A Study in Social and Religious History* TB/15
EDWARD GIBBON: The Triumph of Christendom in the Roman Empire *(Chaps. XV-XX of "Decline and Fall," J. B. Bury edition).*§ *Illus.* TB/46
MAURICE GOGUEL: Jesus and the Origins of Christianity.° *Introduction by C. Leslie Mitton*
Volume I: *Prolegomena to the Life of Jesus* TB/65
Volume II: *The Life of Jesus* TB/66
EDGAR J. GOODSPEED: A Life of Jesus TB/1
ADOLF HARNACK: The Mission and Expansion of Christianity in the First Three Centuries. *Introduction by Jaroslav Pelikan* TB/92
R. K. HARRISON: The Dead Sea Scrolls: *An Introduction*° TB/84
EDWIN HATCH: The Influence of Greek Ideas on Christianity.§ *Introduction and Bibliography by Frederick C. Grant* TB /18
ARTHUR DARBY NOCK: Early Gentile Christianity and Its Hellenistic Background TB/111
ARTHUR DARBY NOCK: St. Paul° TB/104
JOHANNES WEISS: Earliest Christianity: *A History of the Period A.D. 30-150. Introduction and Bibilography by Frederick C. Grant* Volume I TB/53
Volume II TB/54

RELIGION

Ancient & Classical

J. H. BREASTED: Development of Religion and Thought in Ancient Egypt. *Introduction by John A. Wilson* TB/57
HENRI FRANKFORT: Ancient Egyptian Religion: *An Interpretation* TB/77
WILLIAM CHASE GREENE: Moira: *Fate, Good and Evil in Greek Thought* TB/1104

Christianity: The Middle Ages, The Reformation, and After

G. P. FEDOTOV: The Russian Religious Mind: *Kievan Christianity, the tenth to the thirteenth centuries* TB/70
ÉTIENNE GILSON: Dante and Philosophy TB/1089
WILLIAM HALLER: The Rise of Puritanism TB/22
JOHAN HUIZINGA: Erasmus and the Age of Reformation. *Illus.* TB/19

JOHN T. McNEILL: Makers of Christianity: *From Alfred the Great to Schleiermacher* TB/121
A. C. McGIFFERT: Protestant Thought Before Kant. Preface by Jaroslav Pelikan TB/93
KENNETH B. MURDOCK: Literature and Theology in Colonial New England TB/99
GORDON RUPP: Luther's Progress to the Diet of Worms° TB/120

Judaic Thought & Literature

MARTIN BUBER: Eclipse of God: *Studies in the Relation Between Religion and Philosophy* TB/12
MARTIN BUBER: Moses: *The Revelation and the Covenant* TB/27
MARTIN BUBER: Pointing the Way. Introduction by Maurice S. Friedman TB/103
MARTIN BUBER: The Prophetic Faith TB/73
MARTIN BUBER: Two Types of Faith: *the interpenetration of Judaism and Christianity*° TB/75
MAURICE S. FRIEDMAN: Martin Buber: *The Life of Dialogue* TB/64
FLAVIUS JOSEPHUS: The Great Roman-Jewish War, with The Life of Josephus. Introduction by William R. Farmer TB/74
T. J. MEEK: Hebrew Origins TB/69

Oriental Religions: Far Eastern, Near Eastern

TOR ANDRAE: Mohammed: *The Man and His Faith* TB/62
EDWARD CONZE: Buddhism: *Its Essence and Development.*° Foreword by Arthur Waley TB/58
EDWARD CONZE, et al., Editors: Buddhist Texts Through the Ages TB/113
ANANDA COOMARASWAMY: Buddha and the Gospel of Buddhism TB/119
H. G. CREEL: Confucius and the Chinese Way TB/63
FRANKLIN EDGERTON, Trans. & Ed.: The Bhagavad Gita TB/115
SWAMI NIKHILANANDA, Trans. & Ed.: The Upanishads: *A One-Volume Abridgment* TB/114
HELLMUT WILHELM: Change: *Eight Lectures on the I Ching* TB/2019

Philosophy of Religion

RUDOLF BULTMANN: History and Eschatology: *The Presence of Eternity* TB/91
RUDOLF BULTMANN AND FIVE CRITICS: Kerygma and Myth: *A Theological Debate* TB/80
RUDOLF BULTMANN and KARL KUNDSIN: Form Criticism: *Two Essays on New Testament Research.* Translated by Frederick C. Grant TB/96
MIRCEA ELIADE: The Sacred and the Profane TB/81
LUDWIG FEUERBACH: The Essence of Christianity.§ Introduction by Karl Barth. Foreword by H. Richard Niebuhr TB/11
ADOLF HARNACK: What is Christianity?§ Introduction by Rudolf Bultmann TB/17
FRIEDRICH HEGEL: On Christianity: *Early Theological Writings.* Edited by Richard Kroner and T. M. Knox TB/79
KARL HEIM: Christian Faith and Natural Science TB/16
IMMANUEL KANT: Religion Within the Limits of Reason Alone.§ Introduction by Theodore M. Greene and John Silber TB/67

PIERRE TEILHARD DE CHARDIN: The Phenomenon of Man° TB/83

Religion, Culture & Society

JOSEPH L. BLAU, Ed.: Cornerstones of Religious Freedom in America: *Selected Basic Documents, Court Decisions and Public Statements.* Enlarged and revised edition, with new Introduction by the Editor TB/118
C. C. GILLISPIE: Genesis and Geology: *The Decades before Darwin*§ TB/51
BENJAMIN NELSON: Religious Traditions and the Spirit of Capitalism: *From the Church Fathers to Jeremy Bentham* TB/1130
H. RICHARD NIEBUHR: Christ and Culture TB/3
H. RICHARD NIEBUHR: The Kingdom of God in America TB/49
RALPH BARTON PERRY: Puritanism and Democracy TB/1138
WALTER RAUSCHENBUSCH: Christianity and the Social Crisis.‡ Edited by Robert D. Cross TB/3059
KURT SAMUELSSON: Religion and Economic Action: *A Critique of Max Weber's The Protestant Ethic and the Spirit of Capitalism.*|° Trans. by E. G. French; Ed. with Intro. by D. C. Coleman TB/1131
ERNST TROELTSCH: The Social Teaching of the Christian Churches.° Introduction by H. Richard Niebuhr
Volume I TB/71
Volume II TB/72

Religious Thinkers & Traditions

AUGUSTINE: An Augustine Synthesis. Edited by Erich Przywara TB/35
KARL BARTH: Church Dogmatics: *A Selection.* Introduction by H. Gollwitzer; Edited by G. W. Bromiley TB/95
KARL BARTH: Dogmatics in Outline TB/56
KARL BARTH: The Word of God and the Word of Man TB/13
THOMAS CORBISHLEY, S. J.: Roman Catholicism TB/112
ADOLF DEISSMANN: Paul: *A Study in Social and Religious History* TB/15
JOHANNES ECKHART: Meister Eckhart: *A Modern Translation* by R. B. Blakney TB/8
WINTHROP HUDSON: The Great Tradition of the American Churches TB/98
SOREN KIERKEGAARD: Edifying Discourses. Edited with an Introduction by Paul Holmer TB/32
SOREN KIERKEGAARD: The Journals of Kierkegaard.° Edited with an Introduction by Alexander Dru TB/52
SOREN KIERKEGAARD: The Point of View for My Work as an Author: *A Report to History.*§ Preface by Benjamin Nelson TB/88
SOREN KIERKEGAARD: The Present Age.§ Translated and edited by Alexander Dru. Introduction by Walter Kaufmann TB/94
SOREN KIERKEGAARD: Purity of Heart. Translated by Douglas Steere TB/4
SOREN KIERKEGAARD: Repetition: *An Essay in Experimental Psychology.* Translated with Introduction & Notes by Walter Lowrie TB/117
SOREN KIERKEGAARD: Works of Love: *Some Christian Reflections in the Form of Discourses* TB/122

WALTER LOWRIE: Kierkegaard: *A Life*
    Volume I   TB/89
    Volume II   TB/90
GABRIEL MARCEL: Homo Viator: *Introduction to a Metaphysic of Hope*   TB/97
PERRY MILLER: Errand into the Wilderness   TB/1139
PERRY MILLER & T. H. JOHNSON, Editors: The Puritans: *A Sourcebook of Their Writings*
    Volume I   TB/1093
    Volume II   TB/1094
PAUL PFUETZE: Self, Society, Existence: *Human Nature and Dialogue in the Thought of George Herbert Mead and Martin Buber*   TB/1059
F. SCHLEIERMACHER: The Christian Faith. *Introduction by Richard R. Niebuhr*   Volume I   TB/108
    Volume II   TB/109
F. SCHLEIERMACHER: On Religion: *Speeches to Its Cultured Despisers. Intro. by Rudolf Otto*   TB/36
PAUL TILLICH: Dynamics of Faith   TB/42
EVELYN UNDERHILL: Worship   TB/10
G. VAN DER LEEUW: Religion in Essence and Manifestation: *A Study in Phenomenology. Appendices by Hans H. Penner*   Volume I   TB/100
    Volume II   TB/101

NATURAL SCIENCES AND MATHEMATICS

Biological Sciences

CHARLOTTE AUERBACH: The Science of GeneticsΣ TB/568
A. BELLAIRS: Reptiles: *Life History, Evolution, and Structure. Illus.*   TB/520
LUDWIG VON BERTALANFFY: Modern Theories of Development: *An Introduction to Theoretical Biology*   TB/554
LUDWIG VON BERTALANFFY: Problems of Life: *An Evaluation of Modern Biological and Scientific Thought*   TB/521
JOHN TYLER BONNER: The Ideas of Biology.Σ *Illus.*   TB/570
HAROLD F. BLUM: Time's Arrow and Evolution   TB/555
A. J. CAIN: Animal Species and their Evolution. *Illus.*   TB/519
WALTER B. CANNON: Bodily Changes in Pain, Hunger, Fear and Rage. *Illus.*   TB/562
W. E. LE GROS CLARK: The Antecedents of Man: *An Introduction to the Evolution of the Primates.*° *Illus.*   TB/559
W. H. DOWDESWELL: Animal Ecology. *Illus.* TB/543
W. H. DOWDESWELL: The Mechanism of Evolution. *Illus.*   TB/527
R. W. GERARD: Unresting Cells. *Illus.*   TB/541
DAVID LACK: Darwin's Finches. *Illus.*   TB/544
J. E. MORTON: Molluscs: *An Introduction to their Form and Functions. Illus.*   TB/529
ADOLF PORTMANN: Animals as Social Beings.° *Illus.*   TB/572
O. W. RICHARDS: The Social Insects. *Illus.*   TB/542
P. M. SHEPPARD: Natural Selection and Heredity. *Illus.*   TB/528
EDMUND W. SINNOTT: Cell and Psyche: *The Biology of Purpose*   TB/546
C. H. WADDINGTON: How Animals Develop. *Illus.*   TB/553

Chemistry

J. R. PARTINGTON: A Short History of Chemistry. *Illus.*   TB/522
J. READ: A Direct Entry to Organic Chemistry. *Illus.*   TB/523
J. READ: Through Alchemy to Chemistry. *Illus.* TB/561

Geography

R. E. COKER: This Great and Wide Sea: *An Introduction to Oceanography and Marine Biology. Illus.*   TB/551
F. K. HARE: The Restless Atmosphere   TB/560

History of Science

W. DAMPIER, Ed.: Readings in the Literature of Science. *Illus.*   TB/512
A. HUNTER DUPREE: Science in the Federal Government: *A History of Policies and Activities to 1940*   TB/573
ALEXANDRE KOYRÉ: From the Closed World to the Infinite Universe: *Copernicus, Kepler, Galileo, Newton, etc.*   TB/31
A. G. VAN MELSEN: From Atomos to Atom: *A History of the Concept Atom*   TB/517
O. NEUGEBAUER: The Exact Sciences in Antiquity   TB/552
H. T. PLEDGE: Science Since 1500: *A Short History of Mathematics, Physics, Chemistry and Biology. Illus.*   TB/506
GEORGE SARTON: Ancient Science and Modern Civilization   TB/501
HANS THIRRING: Energy for Man: *From Windmills to Nuclear Power*   TB/556
WILLIAM LAW WHYTE: Essay on Atomism: *From Democritus to 1960*   TB/565
A. WOLF: A History of Science, Technology and Philosophy in the 16th and 17th Centuries.° *Illus.*
    Volume I   TB/508
    Volume II   TB/509
A. WOLF: A History of Science, Technology, and Philosophy in the Eighteenth Century.° *Illus.*
    Volume I   TB/539
    Volume II   TB/540

Mathematics

H. DAVENPORT: The Higher Arithmetic: *An Introduction to the Theory of Numbers*   TB/526
H. G. FORDER: Geometry: *An Introduction*   TB/548
GOTTLOB FREGE: The Foundations of Arithmetic: *A Logico-Mathematical Enquiry into the Concept of Number*   TB/534
S. KÖRNER: The Philosophy of Mathematics: *An Introduction*   TB/547
D. E. LITTLEWOOD: Skeleton Key of Mathematics: *A Simple Account of Complex Algebraic Problems*   TB/525
GEORGE E. OWEN: Fundamentals of Scientific Mathematics   TB/569
WILLARD VAN ORMAN QUINE: Mathematical Logic   TB/558
O. G. SUTTON: Mathematics in Action.° *Foreword by James R. Newman. Illus.*   TB/518
FREDERICK WAISMANN: Introduction to Mathematical Thinking. *Foreword by Karl Menger*   TB/511

Philosophy of Science

R. B. BRAITHWAITE: Scientific Explanation TB/515

J. BRONOWSKI: Science and Human Values. *Illus.* TB/505

ALBERT EINSTEIN: Philosopher-Scientist. *Edited by Paul A. Schilpp* Volume I TB/502
Volume II TB/503

WERNER HEISENBERG: Physics and Philosophy: *The Revolution in Modern Science. Introduction by F. S. C. Northrop* TB/549

JOHN MAYNARD KEYNES: A Treatise on Probability.º *Introduction by N. R. Hanson* TB/557

STEPHEN TOULMIN: Foresight and Understanding: *An Enquiry into the Aims of Science. Foreword by Jacques Barzun* TB/564

STEPHEN TOULMIN: The Philosophy of Science: *An Introduction* TB/513

G. J. WHITROW: The Natural Philosophy of Timeº TB/563

Physics and Cosmology

DAVID BOHM: Causality and Chance in Modern Physics. *Foreword by Louis de Broglie* TB/536

P. W. BRIDGMAN: The Nature of Thermodynamics TB/537

A. C. CROMBIE, Ed.: Turning Point in Physics TB/535

C. V. DURELL: Readable Relativity. *Foreword by Freeman J. Dyson* TB/530

ARTHUR EDDINGTON: Space, Time and Gravitation: *An outline of the General Relativity Theory* TB/510

GEORGE GAMOW: Biography of PhysicsΣ TB/567

MAX JAMMER: Concepts of Force: *A Study in the Foundation of Dynamics* TB/550

MAX JAMMER: Concepts of Mass *in Classical and Modern Physics* TB/571

MAX JAMMER: Concepts of Space: *The History of Theories of Space in Physics. Foreword by Albert Einstein* TB/533

EDMUND WHITTAKER: History of the Theories of Aether and Electricity
Volume I: *The Classical Theories* TB/531
Volume II: *The Modern Theories* TB/532

G. J. WHITROW: The Structure and Evolution of the Universe: *An Introduction to Cosmology. Illus.* TB/504

A LETTER TO THE READER

Overseas, there is considerable belief that we are a country of extreme conservatism and that we cannot accommodate to social change.

Books about America in the hands of readers abroad can help change those ideas.

The U. S. Information Agency cannot, by itself, meet the vast need for books about the United States.

You can help.

Harper Torchbooks provides three packets of books on American history, economics, sociology, literature and politics to help meet the need.

To send a packet of Torchbooks [*] overseas, all you need do is send your check for $7 (which includes cost of shipping) to Harper & Row. The U. S. Information Agency will distribute the books to libraries, schools, and other centers all over the world.

I ask every American to support this program, part of a worldwide BOOKS USA campaign.

I ask you to share in the opportunity to help tell others about America.

EDWARD R. MURROW
Director,
U. S. Information Agency

[*retailing at $10.85 to $12.00]

PACKET I: *Twentieth Century America*
   Dulles/America's Rise to World Power, 1898-1954
   Cochran/The American Business System, 1900-1955
   Zabel, Editor/Literary Opinion in America (two volumes)
   Drucker/The New Society: *The Anatomy of Industrial Order*
   Fortune Editors/America in the Sixties: *The Economy and the Society*

PACKET II: *American History*
   Billington/The Far Western Frontier, 1830-1860
   Mowry/The Era of Theodore Roosevelt and the
      Birth of Modern America, 1900-1912
   Faulkner/Politics, Reform, and Expansion, 1890-1900
   Cochran & Miller/The Age of Enterprise: *A Social History of
      Industrial America*
   Tyler/Freedom's Ferment: *American Social History from the
      Revolution to the Civil War*

PACKET III: *American History*
   Hansen/The Atlantic Migration, 1607-1860
   Degler/Out of Our Past: *The Forces that Shaped Modern America*
   Probst, Editor/The Happy Republic: *A Reader in Tocqueville's America*
   Alden/The American Revolution, 1775-1783
   Wright/The Cultural Life of the American Colonies, 1607-1763

*Your gift will be acknowledged directly to you by the overseas recipient.
Simply fill out the coupon, detach and mail with your check or money order.*

HARPER & ROW, PUBLISHERS • BOOKS USA DEPT.
49 East 33rd Street, New York 16, N. Y.

Packet I ☐   Packet II ☐   Packet III ☐

Please send the BOOKS USA library packet(s) indicated above, in my name, to the area checked below. Enclosed is my remittance in the amount of _____ for _____ packet(s) at $7.00 each.

_____ Africa   _____ Latin America
_____ Far East   _____ Near East

Name_____

Address_____

_____

NOTE: *This offer expires December 31, 1966.*